PRINCIPLES OF FESTIVAL MANAGEMENT

Chris Newbold, Jennie Jordan,
Paul Kelly and Kristy Diaz

 Goodfellow Publishers Ltd

Published by Goodfellow Publishers Limited,
Woodeaton, Oxford, OX3 9TJ
http://www.goodfellowpublishers.com

British Library Cataloguing in Publication Data: a catalogue record for this
title is available from the British Library.

Library of Congress Catalog Card Number: on file.

ISBN: 978-1-911396-82-6

 Design and typesetting by P.K. McBride, www.macbride.org.uk

Cover design by Cylinder

Printed by Baker & Taylor, www.baker-taylor.com

Contents

List of figures

About the authors

Chris Newbold is a freelance writer and producer, and part-time Lecturer in Arts and Festivals Management at De Montfort University Leicester. He has taught in higher education for over 30 years and has published widely on culture, media and research methods. Chris is one of the co-editors of *Focus on World Festivals* (2016), and *Focus on Festivals* (2015) and has produced two major media text books in *Approaches to Media* (1995) and *The Media Book* (2002). He is joint editor with Jennie Jordan of the *Discussion Papers in Arts and Festivals Management* series.

Jennie Jordan is Senior Lecturer Creative Industries, Leicester Castle Business School, and programme leader of the MSc Cultural Events Management at De Montfort University Leicester. Jennie has a significant track record as a consultant, having worked for the UK Government's Department of Cultural Media and Sport, national bodies such as Youth Music, Capacity Builders and Arts Council England, as well as local and national festivals. She is undertaking a PhD researching cultural festivals and has published on festivalisation, festival management and cultural policy. She co-edits the *Discussion Papers in Arts and Festivals Management* series with Chris Newbold. and is one of the co-editors of *Focus on Festivals* (2015) and *Focus on World Festivals* (2016).

Paul Kelly is a freelance festivals organiser and fundraiser. He spent seven years as Senior Lecturer and Course leader of the BA Hons Degree in Arts and Event Management at the Arts University Bournemouth. Prior to that he spent 15 years as Principal Arts Officer at Plymouth City Council where he devised, supported and staged a number of festivals including *Streets of the South West International Street Theatre Festival* (1994-2000), *Soundwaves Festival Fringe* (1995-8) *The Eclipse Festival*, Plymouth (1999) and *Plymouth's Queen's Jubilee Celebrations* (2002). He was Director of The Bluecoat Arts Centre, Liverpool (1987-9), worked for a Regional Arts Association and spent 10 years promoting jazz, mainly in the Midlands, also organising 30 national jazz tours and promoting concerts by Gil Evans, Clark Terry, Jan Garbarek, Carla Bley and Chet Baker amongst others. He is currently part of the team that stages the annual *Stompin' On the Quomps*, smooth jazz festival in Christchurch, Dorset, and in Bournemouth runs the *Westbourne Book Binge* and staged the *Parry 100 Festival* (2018). He co-authored the report on the benefits of contracting out local authority arts services for Arts Development UK (2010) and was editor of the organisation's *Arts at the Heart* magazine (2005-2011).

Kristy Diaz is a communications professional at Loughborough University and a freelance writer. She graduated from De Montfort University Leicester with a BA in Arts Management in 2008. Kristy is a former digital producer at Threshold Studios, where she led online communications, digital engagement projects, and marketing for *Frequency Festival of Digital Culture*, Lincoln. Kristy has been a passionate supporter of independent music for many years as a DJ and journalist, and is a regular contributor at *Track 7*. Her essay, *Why I'm No Longer A Punk Rock 'Cool Girl'*, was published in 404 Ink's bestseller, *Nasty Women*, in 2017.

About the contributors

Simon Brown spent 15 years as Senior Festivals and Events Officer in Leicester City Council directly managing and supporting on a variety of events. During this time he also spent a year in a strategic role as Cultural Programme Coordinator for the Local Authority. He has since joined ArtReach as Events and Special Projects Manager and recently taken up the role of Managing Director for the organisation. He is a part time lecturer at De Montfort University at Undergraduate and Postgraduate level, and has an MSc in Cultural Events Management.

Kevin Chambers is Course Leader in Festivals and Events at Solent University. He has a BA (Hons) in English and Politics from Manchester Metropolitan University and an MSc in Cultural Events Management from De Montfort University. He also has over 25 years' experience working as an event producer in both the cultural and corporate sectors.

Rosanna Dean is an experienced event operations manager and consultant across the music, sport, mental health and tourism industries. She is currently Events Manager at The Tank Museum Dorset. Her previous festival roles include, Head of Operations, *End of the Road Festival*, Artist Operations & Festival Hospitality Manager, *Larmer Tree Festival*, Artist Liaison Manager at *Groovin' The Moo Festival, Laneway Festival, Southbound Festival*, and *North West Festival* (Australia). She was also Headliner Liaison, *Vida Festival* (Spain) and Production Coordinator at the *Wychwood Festival*.

Richard Fletcher graduated from De Montfort University with a BA in Arts Management and later completed a MSc by research in Festival Impacts. He is interested in applying social science methods to arts audiences, cultural ecosystems and in the role of knowledge management in organisational cultures. He is an advocate for open-source methods, and is a member of the Alliance for Useful Evidence and the Open Data Institute. He has spoken at a number of national conferences for the British Arts Festivals Association, at a local level he has worked with support networks *Creative Leicestershire* and *Leicester Arts Festivals*. He has written in *Focus on Festivals* (2015), and for *Arts Professional* and *Festival Insights*.

Tony Graves is Associate Professor and Head of Subject for the Arts and Festivals Management, BA undergraduate degree at De Montfort University.

He has a background in the arts both as a performer and administrator. A former classical pianist, he was previously the Chief Executive of The Drum Arts Centre, Birmingham and a producer at Nottingham Playhouse. Tony has been involved in the delivery of strategic arts planning at a regional and national level with particular emphasis on cultural diversity. He is Director of the university's annual *Cultural eXchanges* festival, and has developed this into a major event over the past 16 years. Previous guests include Ken Loach, Jamal Edwards, Grayson Perry, Germaine Greer, Melvyn Bragg, Trevor Nelson, Bonnie Greer, Paris Lees, Meera Syal and Adrian Lester. He is a board member of Serendipity and amongst his publications are a report entitled '*Fear of the Artist*', produced in collaboration with Jude Kelly, former Artistic Director of the South Bank Centre, and funded by NESTA.

David Hill is Founding Director and Chair of ArtReach, which has a 20 year plus track record as a cultural consultant and creative producer. ArtReach works across the UK and internationally, delivering strands of its work with partners in 10 other European countries. David trained in Drama (Hull University) and worked in different parts of the theatre sector, as actor, director and manager, before establishing ArtReach in 1996. He has been Associate Director at Cheltenham Everyman, Artistic Director of Theatre Station Blyth and Marketing Director at Birmingham Hippodrome. Honorary positions have included being Vice Chair of Curve (Leicester), Chair of *Leicester Arts Festivals*, Chair of *Hat Fair* Winchester, and Vice Chair of Winchester Theatre Royal.

Samuel Javid is an executive producer at cultural development agency ArtReach, where he has specific responsibility for delivering its flagship event *Night of Festivals*. Prior to this he was a producer at Big Difference Company overseeing the project management and delivery of the annual *Leicester Comedy Festival*. In 2013 Samuel became the first Young Trustee of Curve theatre; he is currently a Trustee of Leicester Print Workshop and Leicester City of Sanctuary.

Oli Page is a producer for outdoor events and festivals at *ArtReach* and also co-ordinates volunteers for the *Leicester Arts Festivals* umbrella network. Oli has over 5 years of experience working in cultural and corporate events as a volunteer, contributor, programmer and producer.

Maddie Smart is an executive producer at *ArtReach*, a cultural development agency based in Leicester. Maddie has specific responsibility for *Journeys Festival International*, overseeing the development of the festival in Leicester, Manchester and Portsmouth. Prior to this, Maddie was a freelance creative producer, and has also worked for Curve theatre, New Art Exchange, Artichoke Trust and Big Difference Company.

Introduction

by Chris Newbold

Principles of Festival Management was conceived and designed to be a single-source for the knowledge and practical skills needed in successful festival production. It takes a multi-disciplinary approach to understanding festivals and festival organisations and engages with the principles, key concepts and debates in contemporary festival management. Festivals are complex, social and commercial events, so mixed economy models, social entrepreneurship and stakeholder networks are highlighted as are the symbolic roles festivals play in communities. *Principles of Festival Management* aims to provide a step-by-step guide to all aspects of festivals production from inception through operation to evaluation. The discussions in each chapter are illustrated with a wide range of examples, case studies and actual festival management experiences drawn from contemporary festival managers. The advice provided is supported by templates, models, illustrations and exemplars of the materials needed to manage a festival. There is also direction to further reading, other sources of information and contacts.

Festivals are unique environments in which to enjoy cultural events and experiences; each is different from the next, yet there are features that distinguish the festive from the everyday and festivals from other forms of cultural production and events. Immersive and spectacular environments, celebratory arts and performance, and fewer distinctions in status between artists, audiences and participants, have been the hallmarks of festivals. That they are often time-specific, culture-specific and place-specific events has been the traditional expectations of festivals and why they are uniquely appreciated, eagerly anticipated and growing in number.

The word festival is said to derive from the Latin *festa* meaning feasting, joy and revelry, it is also said to come from *feriae*, meaning time off for honouring the gods. A festival is thus something that is different to or outside of the norm, and is a cultural celebration of some kind, usually of a defined or limited duration. They are exciting, creative, expressive, emotional, educative and often challenging. They are the moments when people and places become most animated, most alive, when they express and display their deepest held values, relationships and hopes. To put it another way, festivals are something special to look forward to, a peak in an otherwise routine world. Falassi calls them a 'time out of time' and sees them as ever-changing and evolving, however he says that:

> "With all its modifications, festival has retained its primary importance in all cultures, for the human social animal still does not have a more significant way to feel in tune with his world than to partake in the

special reality of the festival, and celebrate life in its 'time out of time'"
(1987: 7).

Other authors such as Van Gennep (1961) and Turner (1969) discussed how
special events or rituals have the capacity to deliver liminal experiences,
whilst Roy (2005) pointed to festivals' suspension of 'normal time' being
related to the 'play element in culture'. The desire to celebrate, to break away
from the everyday, is arguably part of human DNA. But how we celebrate
changes from culture to culture and time to time (Ehrenreich, 2007).

Religious festivals remain important to the various faiths they serve; *Eid*,
Diwali, *Passover*, the *Summer Solstice*, *Chinese New Year*, etc. are important
markers in the religious year, but they are also community festivals and are
increasingly becoming open to wider audiences, and promoted as tourist
attractions. Globalisation has meant that many traditional cultural festivals
have been adopted far beyond their areas of origin, so *Holi*, *Carnival*, *Dia de
los Muertos* are familiar festival themes to many around the world. The South
Asian *mela* is seen to have travelled the globe with Asian diaspora, with the
key to its success being its ability to adapt to the host culture whilst still maintaining its core values (Kaushal and Newbold, 2015). It is arguable that in at
least some parts of the world as life has become more secularised, we still
want and need to celebrate, but now we do it differently. Arts and cultural
festivals have grown in significance, just as some religious festivals like the
Christian *Harvest Festival* have declined in importance and visibility. Arts,
performance and culture form a key part of many religious festivals, especially through music, song and dance. However, secular arts festivals seem to
be in the ascendant in terms of numbers and profile, there has been a proliferation of biennials that add festivity through competition, and street art, or
graffiti festivals, use the making of the work as a form of performance. Music
festivals have also mushroomed and grabbed many of the headlines, as the
music business itself has had to change its business model due to technological developments. The number of specialist festivals have also grown; these
tend to focus on a particular artform or genre, although some may even focus
on a particular artist. The list of specialisms is extensive. In music alone, the
specialisms can include folk festivals, jazz festivals, blues festivals, opera fes-
tivals, early music festivals, baroque music festivals, contemporary music fes-
tivals. Then there are film festivals, fashion weeks, book and literature festi-
vals, dance festivals, street theatre festivals, poetry festivals and even history
festivals. Festivals don't have to be restricted to the arts and culture. There are
myriad flower festivals, village festivals, festivals of ideas and even festivals
of shopping. The other significant growth area has been food festivals, which
may not be artistic, but they are without a doubt cultural. Clearly, there is
now a much wider variety of festivals in existence than ever before, providing a diversity of festival content and festival experiences.

Elsewhere (Newbold et al., 2015; Newbold and Jordan, 2016) we identified the contemporary process of festivalisation, whereby cultural products as well as a wide variety of events were using the festival form as their favoured mode of delivery. The five key dimensions of festivalisation were identified by Jordan (2016b: 6) as:

♦ **Festivity**: a time and space for celebration and play that is distinct from everyday life.

♦ **Experimentation**: opportunities for audiences, producers and artists to try out new personas or artistic approaches.

♦ **Spectacularisation**: highly visual or sensual, surprising and often large-scale art works and performances.

♦ **Theming**: a method for establishing an intelligible identity for disparate activities.

♦ **Participation**: experiences that are immersive or co-created by audiences.

Festivalisation is a response to and a cause of new audience expectations that pose challenges and offer different opportunities to those facing venue managers and touring companies. Creating celebratory social spaces, often in sites not usually used for cultural activities, working collaboratively with communities, volunteers and opening up parts of the production process means thinking and working creatively not just in the festival design, but as innovative social and cultural entrepreneurs (Jordan, 2016a).

Understanding the process of festivalisation with its concern for the delivery of arts and culture provides important markers for festival managers in assessing the 'festivity' of their events. It also speaks to a desire and belief that festivals can deliver a whole range of social, cultural and economic benefits, this has particularly drawn in, as we shall see, all tiers of government wanting to encourage, support and promote festivals. However, this involvement does not always prove as helpful as you might think; some years ago, an English local authority decided it wanted to become a 'city of festivals'. After a few years of various festival activities, it approached this by linking all the festivals into a *Summer Festival* that lasted three months. Another city combined a number of individual festivals into one *City Festival* that took place over a 10-day period, making it difficult to notice the special parts of each. This first approach flattened the peaks, and the second killed the differentiation between the individual festivals. It *is* possible to have too much of a good thing.

There is no doubt that festival provision is firmly established on the agenda of all sections of society – it is important in a myriad of ways:

♦ Promoting artistic innovation and vitality

♦ Providing liminal and liminoid experiences

- ◆ Experiencing – it can be transformative and educational with moments of challenge and ambiguity
- ◆ Enhancing, reputedly, local cohesion, citizenship, *Pride*, sense of identity and recognition of place
- ◆ Sustaining and developing to tourism development and city/regional marketing
- ◆ Enhancing the quality of urban life, celebrating cultural diversity
- ◆ Encouraging intercultural dialogue and intercultural competence
- ◆ Providing a source of entertainment, pleasure and experience
- ◆ Providing, reputedly, positive impacts – culturally, politically, socially, economically and environmentally
- ◆ Providing significant permanent, temporary and casual employment and work for suppliers and contractors

Clearly there can be seen to be a largely positive environment for festival provision, and as such the need for good festival management has never been higher. Long et al. observed:

> "Alongside the growth in the number of festivals, there has also been a general increase in the degree of professionalism in the occupations that are linked with festival planning, management, organisation and operations reflecting their social, political and, importantly, their economic roles" (2004: 2)

Festivals have been with us since ancient times, yet the shift from religious and symbolic events to iconic cornerstones of popular commercial culture has been comparatively recent and mostly post-1945. The growth of what we now know and think of as festivals is the product of a changing social and economic environment in which artists and creative people have had enough time and resources to create new artistic work, and audiences have had enough leisure and desire to view the work and enough disposable income to purchase it or access to it.

The route to today's plethora of festivals, especially music festivals, has been anything but straightforward and has been marked by a period of distinct historic social divisions between the 'established arts' and 'counterculture'. Ironically, there are signs in recent years that these opposing strands are now starting to merge. Traditional arts festivals like *Brighton, Edinburgh, Bath* and *Cheltenham* started on a diet of classical arts, with orchestras, opera and recitals. Yet in 2017, the long-established *Bath International Festival* promoted the former Led Zeppelin singer Robert Plant, 50 years after Led Zeppelin played the nascent *Bath Blues Festival*. Others like *The Brighton Festival* have brought in guest artistic directors who have broadened the artistic programme.

Some would argue that it was the very growth of counterculture in the 1960s and 1970s that created the festival culture we enjoy today. In Britain, the origins can be traced to an annual jazz festival at Beaulieu, Hampshire, a *National Jazz and Blues Festival* founded in 1964 which used a number of venues in South East England before winding up in Reading where it became the *Reading Festival*, and a large but short-lived rock festival on The Isle of Wight that ran from 1968 to 1970, attracted international artists like Bob Dylan and Miles Davis and an estimated audience in 1970 of 600,000. All of these initiatives pre-dated the iconic *Glastonbury Festival* and also the celebrated American *Woodstock Festival* (1969). They have also been well documented in films like *A Message to Lov'*, *Woodstock* and the BBC's *Festivals Britannia* documentary (Lerner, 2005; Wadleigh, 1970; Bridger, 2010).

Whilst all of the above created cultural landmarks, celebrated to this day, they also flagged up significant problems in managing the popularity of this new-emerging culture and significant tensions between the enthusiasm of youthful enterprise and establishment values and practices. These were challenges not just of scale and logistics but also of values. The 1970 *Isle of Wight Festival* led to the passing of an Act of Parliament preventing overnight open-air gatherings of more than 5,000 people on the island without a special licence from the council. It took 32 years, until 2002, for someone to find a way of satisfying the Act's requirements and bring a large-scale festival back to the Isle of Wight.

This one instance is symptomatic of a running battle that took place through the 1970s and 80s between authority in the shape of local councils and the police and countercultural festival organisers and the artists they booked. Many of these had a very different concept of society, one that ran counter to the political values of the time which through the 1980s focused on defining success increasingly through financial success and monetary value.

The Public Order Act of 1986, which regulated public gatherings of anything more than 20 people, was a game-changer. It required festival organisers to obtain police consent for their events. That meant that if they were to survive, festivals had to professionalise themselves. That process of professionalisation also involved financialisation. If you had to meet more demands to get a licence to stage your event, you had to find a way of paying for the extra costs incurred. This all took some time to develop. It wasn't until the early 2000s that the issues of managing the large audience numbers that this new breed of rock festivals had created were fully addressed.

The new millennium also heralded technological change that had a huge impact on music festivals. The digitisation of music and resultant file-sharing meant that established music revenues from physical sales declined dramatically, which led to musicians reverting to live performance as a primary means of earnings. The increased availability of live bands was part of the reason for the growth in music-fuelled festivals.

That in part explains the incredible increase in the number of festivals over the last 20 years. But music is just one part of the equation. The breadth of festival offerings also increased with a growth of book and literature festivals, street theatre festivals and many other types. All of these have had to contend with changing times and legislation. As the ambitions and scale of festivals have grown, so have the risks. In an increasingly crowded market that has led to one or two festivals failing. Others, after an honourable period of spectacular growth, have decided to quit the market altogether. *Secret Garden Party*, one of the first boutique music festivals started in 2004 with an audience of just 500 (Square Mile, 2017). It ended up attracting around 26,000 people when it finished in 2017.

In 2016, the *Financial Times* reported in 2015, "more than a thousand festival events took place across Britain, a figure that has doubled over the past decade". In 2015, they continued "UK Music, the industry campaigning organisation, calculated that 3.5m people attended a festival, with the market estimated to be worth £2bn to the economy" (McNulty, 2017).

McNulty also asked whether the festivals market had reached saturation point and noted "a marked rise in the number of city-based and one-day events and a decline in traditional camping weekends" (ibid). She also reported "the growing dominance of multinational promoters such as Live Nation (*Reading, Latitude* and this year a majority stake in the *Isle of Wight*) and AEG (Hyde Park's *British Summertime*)" (ibid). Smith (2013) drew attention to the increasing number of festivals in urban parks, and to the tension this causes as cash-strapped local authorities attempt to balance the needs of local residents and with their need to find new income streams. These issues of growth in attendance and number of festivals, increasing legislation, professionalisation, possible saturation and corporatisation mean festival promotion is much more complex than in past times and festivals management needs a much more carefully considered and rigorous approach.

This book is a result of that growth and the need in the industry for a clear and precise set of principles guiding festival producers, would-be managers and students in all related subjects. As previously stated, this book is about the principles of festival management; it provides a single port of call for developing and running a festival; it covers all aspects of festivals management and discusses the key central issues and contemporary debates such as the use of volunteering, sponsorship and the impact and use of digital technology in festival management.

The chapters are organised such that readers begins in Chapter 1 with an understanding of their roles as leaders and managers, particularly in the face of the unique challenge's festival management provides. Here the importance of having values and a vision are emphasised alongside the importance of having a solid organisational structure behind you.

The second chapter builds on your enthusiasms and ideas, pointing out the importance of having a clear vision and rationale, and knowing what is involved and the possibilities of festival design and programming. It looks at the processes and practicalities of festival design, and the details of good programming. Chapters 3 and 4 then have the daunting task of discussing how you find the money to start and run your festival (funding and investment); and how to manage your money once you've got some (budgeting). Following on from this, Chapter 5 starts by helping you understand the factors involved in producing a good festival, looking at several project management planning processes and all aspects of planning and logistics.

Chapter 6 then takes a moment to stand back and examine festivals and the law, looking at legislation affecting festivals and ensuring that you understand the types of licences you may need and where to get them. It also considers other areas such as copyright, insurance and drawing up contracts. Further chapters will also ensure that you have a grounding in your basic legal responsibilities, whether that be staffing, health and safety, or wherever necessary.

In Festival Operations (Chapter 7) we assume that you now have a viable plan, that you have the licenses and insurance you need and that you are now ready to put that into operation pre-festival and on-the-day. This chapter then looks at the processes and key operational documentation such as the event management and operations plans you will need. It also looks at health and safety and risk management. Two other key operational areas are discussed here: logistics and communications, and the chapter emphasises that operations management requires a great deal of planning and attention to detail.

In Chapter 8 it is the management of people that is recognised as being crucial to the success of your festival, thus it provides you with an overview of the principles of human resources management as it relates to festivals. Designing an organisational structure and job roles is discussed alongside team working, motivation and development needs. Motivations are also central to Chapter 9, but rather than workers, the focus is on audience members' motivations. Why would someone decide to attend your festival? Marketing's strategic role within your festival organisation is discussed and an overview of the principles of festival marketing provided. The chapter also helps you to understand and apply marketing tools such as segmentation and targeting, branding, customer relationship management, the marketing mix and marketing research.

Chapter 10 argues research is at the heart of good festival management and is essential to the development and success of festivals. It relates the key methodologies that are available to festival managers, and discusses their advantages and disadvantages. Practical advice is given on designing questions, and all aspects of research are explained from sampling, piloting, and data analysis to triangulation. The increasing importance of evaluation is emphasised both within the festival organisation and from without.

The final chapter examines managing festivals in a digital world and is designed to help festival managers make the most of developments in digital technology. First, by helping them understand the key developments and theories surrounding digital media, second by giving them insights into how it can be most effectively used, and third by looking at the opportunities it presents and how to manage the potential pitfalls. One of the largest areas the digital world has impacted on in festivals is marketing, particularly social media marketing, this chapter provides a much-needed guide to working in these areas. It also deals with digital public relations and communication. Finally, it recognises the contribution that digital technology is making to festival content and creativity itself.

Of course, these eleven chapters can also serve you well as stand-alone points for reference, advice and help. The authors of this book believe festivals are an important part of the fabric of modern society, and that festival management whenever or wherever you find it is rewarding and fulfilling. We hope that this book provides its readers with a set of guiding principles that helps them not only to develop and manage successful festivals of their own, but also enjoy and appreciate the work of other festival managers around the world.

References

Bridger, S. (2010) *Festival Britannia,* http://www.bbc.co.uk/blogs/bbcmusic/2010/12/festivals_britannia.html, London, BBC

Ehrenreich, B. (2007) *Dancing in the Streets: A history of collective joy.* New York: Metropolitan.

Falassi, A. (ed.) (1987) *Time out of Time.* Albuquerque: University of New Mexico Press.

Jordan, J. (2016a) Festivalisation of cultural production: experimentation, spectacularisation and immersion. *Journal of Cultural Management and Policy,* **1** (6), pp. 44-55.

Jordan, J. (2016b) The festivalisation of contemporary life. In: Newbold, C. and Jordan, J. (eds.) *Focus on World Festivals: Contemporary case studies and perspectives.* Oxford: Goodfellow.

Kaushal, R., and Newbold, C. (2015) Mela in the UK: A 'travelled and habituated' festival. In C. Newbold, et al. (eds.) *Focus on Festivals: Contemporary European case studies and perspectives.* Oxford: Goodfellow.

Lerner, M. (2005) *Message to Love* [DVD] Isle of Wight: Sanctuary

Long, P., Robinson, M. and Picard, D. (2004) Festivals and tourism: Links and developments. In P. Long and M. Robinson (eds.) *Festivals and Tourism: Marketing, Management and Evaluation*. Gateshead: Athenaeum Press

McNulty, B. (2017) Has the UK's festival scene reached saturation point? *Financial Times* www.ft.com/content/622d56e2-157f-11e7-b0c1-37e417ee6c76 [Accessed 2 November 2018]

Newbold, C., Maughan, C., Jordan, J. and Bianchini, F. (eds.) (2015) *Focus on Festivals: Contemporary European case studies and perspectives*. Oxford: Goodfellow.

Newbold, C. and Jordan, J. (eds.) (2016) *Focus on World Festivals: Contemporary case studies and perspectives*. Oxford: Goodfellow.

Roy, C. (2005) *Traditional Festivals: A multicultural encyclopaedia*. Santa Barbara: ABC-CLIO.

Smith, A., 2014. 'Borrowing' public space to stage major events: the Greenwich Park controversy. *Urban Studies*, **51**(2), pp.247-263

Square Mile (2017) *A Brief History of UK Music Festivals* https://squaremile.com/features/history-of-uk-music-festivals/ [Accessed on 2 November 2018]

Turner, V. W. (1969) *The Ritual Process: Structure and anti-structure*. Chicago: Aldine.

Van Gennep, A. (1961) *The Rites of Passage*. Chicago: University of Chicago Press.

Wadleigh, M. (1970) *Woodstock* [DVD] Woodstock, USA, Warner Home Video

Acknowledgements

A book such as this is the result of a great many conversations, questions and experiences with a great many different people both inside and outside the festival world. We thank them all for their time, advice and patience. A special thanks to Kim Hart who worked for the British Arts and Science Festivals Association (BAFA) for her thoughts at the early stage of this book's production. As teachers, our greatest sounding boards are our colleagues and students and we would like to thank all of them, past and present, from DMU's BA Hons Arts and Festivals Management and MSc Cultural Events Management courses and Arts University Bournemouth's BA Hons Arts and Event Management. Their enthusiasm, ideas and questions inspired us to want to write this book.

Thanks to all at ArtReach for their enthusiasm and contributions to this book, indeed, thank you to all our expert contributors for sharing their industry experiences. A special thanks to Rosanna Dean for reading and making some useful additions to the Festival Operations chapter and Simon Brown for his reading of the Budget and Law chapters.

Thank you again to all at Goodfellow publishers for their continuing support of our ongoing work on festivals.

1 Festival Leadership, Structures and Roles

by Jennie Jordan

After reading this chapter you should:

■ Be aware of the difference between leadership and management

■ Understand different leadership types and characteristics

■ Understand management structures and roles within festivals production

■ Be familiar with the concepts of cultural and social goods

■ Be able to categorise your festival's social, cultural and economic purposes

■ Appreciate the role of leadership and its unique challenges in festival production

■ Understand the relationship between values, vision and organisational structure.

Introduction

Running or working for a festival, you will find that you have to deal with issues related to structure and staff roles almost on a daily basis. These management issues will sit alongside leadership questions about your festival's purpose, values, governance and ethos. In this chapter, you will be introduced to leadership models and different management structures and roles within festival production. The chapter will emphasise the role of leadership in the cultural sector, including artistic and creative vision. It will introduce the concept of organisational culture and discuss the relationship between structure, culture and values. It will also discuss and illustrate the key roles in festival management and delivery.

So, what does the term 'leadership' mean and how does it differ from the term 'manager' which is also often used to describe people in authority? Titles have over the years changed, so what were once 'managing directors' at the top of companies are now 'chief executives. So, are leaders and managers or directors and chief executives the same role but by a different name? The answer is that it very much depends on the individual and the organisation. But in general terms leaders and managers are now thought of in different terms, both in terms of skills and roles.

Leadership and management

Modern management skills emerged in the late eighteenth and nineteenth centurys with the foundation and rapid expansion of factories in order to utilise the first generation of technological development for profit and public benefit. This is commonly known as the Industrial Revolution. Both management theory and theories of leadership emanate from this time, although they weren't fully formulated until industrial manufacturing was refined in the twentieth century. At that point management theory became a discipline through studies by people like FW Taylor, Abraham Maslow, Peter Senge, Peter Drucker and John Adair. These and others turned management studies into an academic discipline.

Historically, managers have often been thought of as people who sit in offices and spend their time in meetings. American management scientist Tom Peters (2015), showed a very different style of management and coined the phrase 'managing by walking about'. In this the managers engaged in all aspects of a company's operation by getting out onto the factory floor and talking to the staff. On the one hand, this is less relevant to a small festival than large industrial concern, but it is nevertheless a very good principle to remember. If you are working for a festival in a junior role, how often do you see the festival director(s)? They may not need to know the detail of what you do, but an occasional bit of recognition can be very good for staff morale.

Management of and leadership in the arts and culture, including festivals, has taken a more functional approach, often built around one of artistic vision, marketing or finance, and the focal point has shifted over the years, often from the creative to the financial, and structures and team roles have changed accordingly. For example, the development of the music industry in the 1960s and 1970s was led by a number of music-loving 'mavericks' who set up their own record labels to record the artists they loved and challenge an industry long-dominated by companies like EMI and Decca. People like Gerry Bron (Bronze), Chris Wright (Chrysalis), Tony Stratton-Smith (Charisma), Richard Branson (Virgin Records) and most notably Chris Blackwell (Island Records) had no formal management training but had a passion for music. These were music industry leaders of their time, finding bands, signing, developing and releasing them. Chris Blackwell at Island signed and developed the careers of first Bob Marley and then U2 amongst others. Behind these music leaders were a series of label managers who engaged in the detail, trying to keep pace with their bosses' artistic ideas and turn their visions into production schedules and product releases.

In the arts, people like Thelma Holt and Peter Hall played a similar leadership role in theatre and Dame Marie Rambert in dance. Sir Nicholas Serota, now Chair of Arts Council England, spent over forty years, first at the Museum of Modern Art, Oxford, then at London's Whitechapel Gallery and finally at The Tate Gallery championing and growing the interest in and opportunities for the visual arts, and has clearly been a leader in that sector.

In terms of music festivals, everyone talks about Michael Eavis, founder of *Glastonbury* as a leader in the field. But in the late 1990s and early 2000s *Glastonbury* ran into serious security and health and safety issues and came close to being closed down. So, in 2002 Eavis brought in the highly experienced festival producer Melvyn Benn, who became *Glastonbury*'s licensee and remained so for 10 years. Benn's companies, the Mean Fiddler group and then Festival Republic, also developed *Latitude* and *Benicassim* in Spain as well as running London's '*Fleadh*' and gaining outdoor dance licenses for *Tribal Gathering*, *Creamfields* and *Homelands*. He has also run the *Reading* and *Leeds Festivals* since 1989 and a number of others. It is the less prominent Benn who has been a clear leader in developing music festivals in Britain. Others less prominent but equally influential in this field include Jo Vidler, who co-founded the first of the 'boutique festivals', *Secret Garden Party*, before leaving to set up *Wilderness* and running festivals in Mexico and Thailand.

Just being a good manager is not enough. The above examples are of people who all had or developed management competencies. But more importantly they all had creative visions which helped change artistic outcomes in their fields. The way they did this and the relationship between leadership and management varied according to their sector. But overall the distinction between leadership and management can be reduced to a short, but generally true aphorism neatly put by the management theorist Peter Drucker, "management is doing things right, leadership is doing the right things" (Drucker, 2000).

Leadership entails creating a vision from an analysis of what the future could look like, but based on a set of values rather than rules. That is the starting point. Management is the discipline of producing practical systems and processes from that vision and creating outcomes that work in financial and product terms. Management is about efficiency and organisation to produce products, services or experiences the public want, can afford and enjoy. Leadership, particularly the kind of entrepreneurial leadership involved in setting up a new festival, is about seeing opportunities others haven't and persuading people it's a good idea.

Industry example: Don't lose sight of your vision

Whilst I could write for hours on operational tips for festivals and events in general, I feel this book has that covered and for me the most important thing of all is your festival's ethos and how this fits in the market.

The festival industry is ever-evolving. Gone are the days when headliners ruled the ticket sale success. Nowadays the secret to victory is a strong focus on the full customer experience, not just who is heading up the bill.

In 2017, Festival Insights (https://www.festivalinsights.com/2017/07/uk-festival-market-report-2017/), respected festival market researchers, found that 50% of ticket buyers took advantage of an early bird offer. The important thing to note is that at the point early bird offers are publicised, many festivals haven't actually announced and perhaps don't even know their full line-ups. Reinforcing this finding, the same survey showed that only 19% of buyers bought tickets after the headliners had been announced. Glastonbury sells out in 30 minutes before any headline acts are known! So, what is driving the majority of customers to part with their cash earlier on?

Having worked on many festivals across the Australia, Spain and the UK over the past few years, I have seen a lot of small festivals start up but simultaneously many of the larger ones close down. The most successful ones that come to mind though aren't the ones who have the biggest line-ups or the ones that have the huge sponsorship deals (and probably have a reasonable sum of money behind them to avoid the threat of bankruptcy). They're the ones who have been run independently and haven't lost of sight of what they envisioned at the very beginning. It's common practice to set out your business Vision, Mission and Values in any industry, but festivals aren't just business, they are life events that form personal and long-lasting memories. At *End of the Road Festival* (NME multi-time winning Best UK Small Festival) we would receive emails from customers telling us what a big part of their life the festival had become. Some had met their partner at the festival, got engaged there or even conceived their child there, and were now looking to return as a family. These returning customers and advocates of your brand were likely captured at year one, two and three and are the ones you need to consistently think of during your forward planning process. Keep them in mind and ask yourself if they will still come if you made that change you are considering? If it's a potential no, you may have veered away from your core vision and values and may wish to reconsider.

Although I mention above that headliners aren't necessarily the key any more, it's important to acknowledge that each promoter will have their dream line-up in mind. But line-ups depend on many factors; who's touring that year? Do they fit in your budget? Have they played locally recently and therefore how will this affect your ticket sales? Can you logistically meet their production requirements? What promoters are bidding against you and will they commit exclusively to your festival? Are you even a festival they want to play? Maybe you can get through all of the above hurdles, and even if not for your first choice, your second or third will hopefully pull through, but what else do you have on offer to entice the market when you're not having the strongest of programming years?

In today's climate, we see big international music institutions buying up the smaller festivals on a path to dominate a large percentage of the industry. In many cases, they will succeed. Managing artists and festivals simultaneously makes work extremely easy from a programming perspective, especially having the power to put exclusive offers on your own artists in order to ensure that no independently run festivals you compete with are bidding against you. On paper, it's the business plan of the century. But in many cases, the festival companies that swallow up others have actually found a loss in sales, leading to closure. So, what's going wrong? Whilst I have no hard statistics to prove this, in my experience it is that these promoters have a primary focus on programming the biggest acts, as on paper these will generate the best ticket sales, however, they are expensive and not necessarily fitting with the overall experience generated for previously loyal festival goers. So not only does this provide internal challenges in relation to budgeting, but external challenges on trying to maintain that pre-existing customer base.

My guess is that you have picked up this book because you want to start a festival and have identified a strong gap in the market. If so, good. But are you passionate about it enough to ensure financial deals don't steer you away from the vision in which you started this project? If you answered yes, my suggestion would be that you're about to start on the right path to success, but it won't be easy.

Starting and managing a festival isn't just work, it's a lifestyle choice. It's not a one-weekend event, it's a 365 day project that will challenge you emotionally, financially and intellectually, but if done right, it will introduce you to and allow you to surround yourself with many like-minded people who will support you throughout it all.

So, my advice in a nutshell? Discover your vision and stick to it. As not only will your life change, but you'll be creating the driving force behind special memories for those loyal customers too.

Rosanna Dean is Events Manager at The Tank Museum Dorset

It is possible to do something competently, but still fail to meet people's needs and aspirations. Arts marketeer Gerri Morris described how, in the late 1980s, British theatres became focused on subscription marketing, facilitated by computerised mailing lists. This, she said, had a significant effect on the audience, "laundering our mailing lists and jettisoning anyone who hadn't exhibited sufficient loyalty", it also had, she continued, a debilitating effect on the artistic programming in theatres leading to a safety-led revenue focused model "…where artistic directors completely gave up on their vision and just made assumptions of what the audience would respond to – bankable hits, pot boilers, cash cows, money spinners – and it always seemed to be Noel Coward" (Morris, 2004: 6-8).

Theatre audiences started to grow again in the 1990s, Morris explains, when artistic directors were encouraged to re-connect with a social vision, treat their audiences as people rather than marketing statistics and engage with them. For Morris, artists and artistic directors were successful when they used their expertise and followed their values – then audiences were willing to follow them.

Leadership theory has gone through a number of phases. Theorists in the 1900s believed leaders were born not made. Researchers in the 1930s tried to find lists of personality traits common to all leaders. This was refuted in the 1960s when contingency theory became the trend – this argued effective leadership styles depended on the specific situation. And then from the 1970s and into the 1980s, transformational leadership theory was in vogue. This argued leaders were inspirational agents of change.

All of this might seem rather academic if you are contemplating developing a festival and are at the early stages of planning. Yet you will find it useful to reflect on your role in staging the event – are you a leader or a follower? – and the style you are going to bring to your interactions with others. Do you have a rigid vision on which you will not compromise? Or will the shape and detail of your festival be determined in a more collective way?

Whatever your festival vision and regardless of how it is determined, there will become points where judgements will have to be made and decisions taken. Some of those may not lend themselves to a collective process. Some may have to be made swiftly with little or no time for lengthy discussion. Who makes these may be a result of the legal structure of your festival. How they are made is also an issue of judgement and leadership style.

Before we come onto issues of management structure and roles. We need to expand a bit more on leadership in practice as festival leaders, in common with all leaders in the arts and cultural sector, have a wide and quite complex set of relationships. On the one hand they have to ensure the vision they have established is delivered. That is very much an inward facing role. It is about ensuring that others involved in the festival's initiative understand the mission and fulfill their roles to deliver it. In addition, the festival leader is quite probably going to be the event's public face, representing the festival to a wide range of interest groups and stakeholders. That is very much an outward facing role. Got a problem on your doorstep? A local resident or several who don't like something they think is about to be done to them? Much as you might want to delegate, most people are not fully happy unless they've had a chance to 'talk to the person in charge'.

The British arts leader and manager Helen Marriage described leadership in the form of six c's: challenge, certainty, communication, charm, consultation and confidence. (Marriage, 2008). Whilst leadership theorist Jo Owen identified the key behaviours expected of a leader at the top of an organisation as being:

- ◆ Ability to motivate others
- ◆ Vision
- ◆ Honesty and integrity
- ◆ Decisiveness and
- ◆ Ability to handle crises

(Owen, 2005: xv)

Marriage and Owen usefully and succinctly outline leadership processes and competencies. We now need to think about these in our own festival situation, and place them into some cultural context.

Cultural and social goods

In thinking about festival leadership and management, it is important to note that festivals are cultural and social goods. This matters because it states that they have a meaning for festival-goers and wider society beyond the price of the tickets, so are likely to have a wider range of stakeholders than organisations in other industries. So festival producers have to be aware of how significant the various elements of their festival, such as the artistic programme, levels of production, ability to participate and so on, are to the wide range of groups, stakeholder, they affect. Managing this complex ecology to produce a festival demands internal and external leadership.

The terms *cultural goods* and *social goods* are economic concepts. Cultural goods are products and services you buy because they have a symbolic meaning for you. It might be a haircut which identifies you as a member of a subculture, or participation in an annual ritual that bonds you with friends or family. Cultural goods have an emotional resonance and symbolic meaning. Festivals are cultural goods because they bring communities together to share cultural memories and reinforce communal identities.

Festivals are social goods because they are intangible experiences rather than products, so one person 'consuming' the 'good' does not reduce the amount of experience available to someone else. Social goods are usually paid for by 'pooled financing', such as taxation, or shared labour. One final characteristic of social goods is the beneficiaries – the festival-goers – may not be the people who paid for the 'goods'. A festival designed to boost a city's image may benefit restaurants and hotel owners, but be paid for by local taxpayers, the Arts Council or a variety of sponsors. Star TV supports Leicester's Mela which is primarily of benefit to local residents. Many festivals (but not all) are supported by a mix of public and private finance, some are free to attend, and most have an element of voluntary work, so fit these definitions.

This matters because as producers of cultural and social goods, festival leaders and managers operate in a complex environment, juggling artistic judgments, and social and community demands, at the same time as finding ways to balance the budget or make a profit. So festival leadership combines managing creative individuals, with a need to balance the books; and when the organisation is publicly funded, civic responsibilities add layers of complexity (Hewison and Holden, 2011). Festivals can have long and short terms effects on localities. They can change the image of a town or area as part of local placemaking or marketing initiatives. *Festivals of Light* such as those in Durham or Amsterdam extend the city's tourist season by attracting huge numbers of tourists who spend money in hotels and restaurants. This makes them popular with leisure businesses. But they also close roads and the crowds make life difficult for local workers and residents who have to fight their way through traffic and visitors to go about their everyday life. So, in addition to the pragmatic aspects of relationships with artists, stall holders, venues, suppliers and audiences explored in later chapters of this book, festivals have a responsibility to reflect the wishes of their funders, understand the needs of local residents, who may or may not like the festival, and to remember they are seen as articulating or symbolising their cities or communities. Jen Snowball's (2016) evaluation of positive and negative social effects of an arts festival in South Africa is a good place to start in thinking about the range of people a festival should consider.

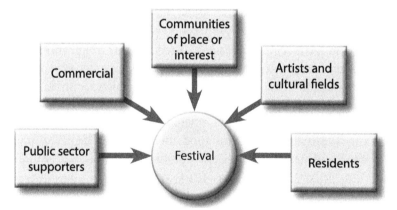

Figure 1.1: The complex governance ecology of festivals

This intricate web of interests is the festival's ecology and, because of the cultural significance of festivals, it is wider than the list of suppliers and customers included in most management textbooks' list of stakeholders. As public organisations they have social responsibilities so their 'governance', the processes of deciding and overseeing strategies and organisational policies often goes beyond board members to include funders, sponsors, workers and volunteers, artists and residents. One of the consequences of this is that festivals need leaders who are able to manage this complex set of relationships while producing a festival that will live up to their expectations and minimise concerns.

Values and organisational culture

The *Business Dictionary* defines values as:

> Important and lasting beliefs or ideals shared by the members of a culture about what is good or bad and desirable or undesirable. Values have major influence on a person's behaviour and attitude and serve as broad guidelines in all situations.

> The monetary worth of something in areas such as accounting, economics, marketing or mathematics (Business Dictionary, 2018).

In this section we are concerned with the first of these, although that is not to say the second is not important. Without an understanding of monetary worth your festival will likely not make it past its first edition. However, the question of what something is worth in the cultural sector is usually reliant on shared beliefs about whether something is good or bad. Why would you pay more for one headline act than another? This is a question of taste. Where did your taste come from? One point of view is taste is socially constructed – we learn to like and approve of what our friends and family like and approve of. So, whether or not we eat certain foods or wear particular clothes marks us out as members of a particular group.

Beneath these visible factors there are also shared understandings in a social group about what is or isn't acceptable behaviour or standards. Teams and organisations are social groups and develop tacit as well as written rules-in-action, such as knowing what sort of clothing is acceptable at work, whether it's normal to phone or email or message colleagues, or who buys the milk. This is known as organisational culture, and it guides all of the decisions groups members make. It is generally not noticable, but if you are part of a strong culture it is clear when something 'feels wrong'.

Organisational cultures can be good or bad, positive or negative, inclusive and democratic or highly regulated and directive. Group leaders set and enforce group culture in the way they themselves behave in the work place. If a leader shows concern for the welfare of staff members or volunteers, it sends a message this is something we should all consider important. If the leader spends hours poring over sales figures, it is clear that's a core value.

Culture is also expressed in the way festival organisations are structured. Leaders need to be aware of the decisions they take about these structures and whether they reflect the type of culture they want the organisation to have. So, a community festival is likely to have open opportunities for participation at various points. Local people might be on the board or steering committee or there might be a stage for local bands or dance groups run by a youth group or school. By contrast, commercial music festivals actually charge people to volunteer, because their values are centred on how best to make a profit for shareholders. Similarly, the topics on meeting agendas and included in board reports send messages about what matters most. Does the board pay more attention to the finances, the artistic programme or who the audiences are? How does this reflect your organisation's vision and mission (see Chapter 2)?

Industry example: The importance of community involvement in the success of festivals

'Community' is a word I use a lot. Community arts, community leaders, community cohesion, community networks, community activity, community setting, community participation, thriving communities, vulnerable communities, community-led... I recently considered implementing a swear-jar type system in the office, but I have realised that if I only use the word when I really mean it, I might be able to save it.

There is a real risk of 'community' becoming another buzzword that Arts and Cultural professionals drift towards before thinking what it means. Like 'diverse'. Funders, local authorises, central government, and to a large extent, our peers, tasked the sector with being more diverse – and not without good reason, but overuse of the word has somewhat detached it from its meaning. We explored new diverse projects, new ways of working, different recruitment and procurement practices; now we plan diverse, we think diverse. We are diverse. And we keep saying so. We say so until the word becomes a pre-fix to all other action: diverse meeting, diverse partnership, diverse attendance, diverse programming, diverse talent, diverse-led... (consider another swear-jar system?). Overuse of a word can numb the meaning behind it; we stop talking about the reasons behind 'X' and just focus on 'X'. I don't want this for 'community'.

Festival managers are increasingly encouraged to think about 'the community' and how to involve them in the design and delivery of projects. Funders, local authorises, central government and our peers have once again tasked the sector to think differently. We need to make sure our actions are different, not just our words.

I'm going to put on a community festival, I've chosen some artists from the community and I want the community to attend. I put an advert on a community Facebook page, I dropped some flyers off at a local community centre.... why aren't the community here?!

There is no one-size-fits-all methodology to community involvement in festivals, but by developing a sincere and integrated approach, you are more likely to involve the community in a meaningful, and ultimately successful, way.

Night of Festivals (www.nightoffestivals.com) is a free access multi-artform outdoor festival. It celebrates the values of freedom and democracy through great art. Since its inception in 2010 there have been 17 editions of the festival. It's been to Nottingham, Leicester, Lincoln, London, Hounslow, Barking and Boston (Lincolnshire). It has been used to 'Welcome the World' as part of the London Cultural Olympiad programme in 2012; it celebrated the bicentenary of Latin American Independence in 2010; and in 2016 it helped Leicester mark the 70th anniversary of Pakistan and Indian Independence. Its themes and content vary year-to-year, as does its location. To keep each festival relevant and well attended, it needs to be embedded. They key to this is community involvement, in both planning and delivery.

Figure 1.2: *Night of Festivals* Sagar Ladies (photo Aimee Valinski)

There are many good and effective ways to do this, but as a foundation I recommend the following:

Advisory groups

Form a group made up of key project partners and members of the community. It's important that any community members in attendance are seen to be on an equal footing with professional organisations. This demonstrates to the group that community input is as important as professional input. Take and distribute minutes and actions so community members can see they are being listened to.

Advance activity

Build in resources for advance activity form the beginning. This provides an opportunity to make relationships with local groups and people. Importantly, it can also give you a local platform to start exploring and discussing the festival's themes. For *Night of Festivals*

London 2018 ArtReach set-up a series of artist led workshops in partnership with a local housing association. Each workshop was aimed at an existing group: an over 50+ Arts class, a family 'Sunday-funday', and an under 25's youth group. The artist facilitated a discussion on the theme of 'welcome' and what this concept meant to different people. The groups then made placards depicting messages of 'welcome' and brought them to the *Night of Festivals* site over the weekend. As a result, ArtReach had an additional 150 local people on site who were in engaged in the festival's themes, could talk to others about its themes, and ultimately had a deeper engagement with the work.

Schools workshops

Schools receive a lot of approaches from arts organisations, but are often under-resourced to fully engage. It helps to find a named contact – maybe the Art or Music teacher; they'll see the value in what you're offering and can often lobby internally for wider engagement with your project. The product or outcome of the workshops should have a dedicated space within the festival site or programme; e.g., if an artist has spent time with students creating flags and banners depicting the festivals themes then display them at the event.

Performance or exhibition opportunities

Artists live everywhere. Wherever your festival is taking place there will be local people who have creative skills they want to use to enhance your event. Let them. If you're worried about quality or a mismatch of programmed activity then think of an interesting way to frame the community contribution. For example, if a local felt maker wants to get involved in your Spoken Word and Activism festival, they could lead or support on-site workshops where attendees use felting technique to add to a participatory installation, or you could commission them to make felt signage for your venues, or you could ask them to re-decorate the green room. Be creative.

Involving the community in your festival won't always have immediately measurable outcomes. It won't always set you ahead of the competition, make you financially sustainable or win over that one stubborn councillor. But if you do it properly, and sincerely, it can provide you with a few money-can't-buy outcomes.

It gives you a better understanding of people and place; through face-to-face discussions, formal and informal meetings and regular coffee and cake catch-ups you can start to understand what really makes a place tick. What local people do and don't want, what's been tried before, and what excites them about the future.

It can encourage ownership and buy-in of brand: people better understand the purpose of a festival, what its themes are and why; why you make the decisions you make and the intended impact on audiences.

It provides producers and programmes with the knowledge they need to curate, commission and programme relevant content; knowing the artforms and themes people enjoy is key – even if the purpose is then to challenge them.

It offers insights and advice on how to get the message out; from suggestions of local newsletters and online publications to drinks and networking at a local event.

And if you really work it, you'll have a guaranteed and enthusiastic audience who know what you are, what you stand for, and want all you've got to give!

Samual Javid, Executive Producer Artreach.

Vision and values

Because of their complexity, most festivals find it easiest to lead through strong cultures. Strong cultures are those where everyone in the group or organisation shares an understanding of why they are producing the event. This is known as a vision. You will see vision and mission statements in annual reports and on websites.

Debating point:
Look at the stated vision of a festival organisation you think is effective and one you think is poorly conceived. Think about what works well for the good one and why the poor one fails and how you would improve it. Incorporate these into your own mission statement.

Emotional intelligence

How do you know what these values are that you need to articulate and model? Self-knowledge is key here, but can be very difficult. It requires emotional intelligence. Emotional intelligence is:

> the ability to perceive emotions, to access and generate emotions so as to assist thought [...] to reflectively regulate emotions so as to promote emotional and intellectual growth (Mayer and Salovey, 1997: 10).

According to Mayer and Salovey, emotional intelligence had five components: self-awareness; the ability to self-regulate in terms of mood; internal motivation – the desire to work above and beyond money and status; being able to understand and empathise with others' emotional reactions; and social skills, including building rapport, finding common ground and sustaining relationships.

Although the best leaders score highly on all of these, that does not mean they were necessarily born with those skills. Emotional intelligence, like any other sort, improves with awareness, reflection and practice.

One tool used in psychology to help you identify where your emotional intelligence is strong and where you might need to work harder is called the Johari Window. This model argues that we all have areas of our personalities that we are honest about, things we try to hide from the world, and things we are not aware of.

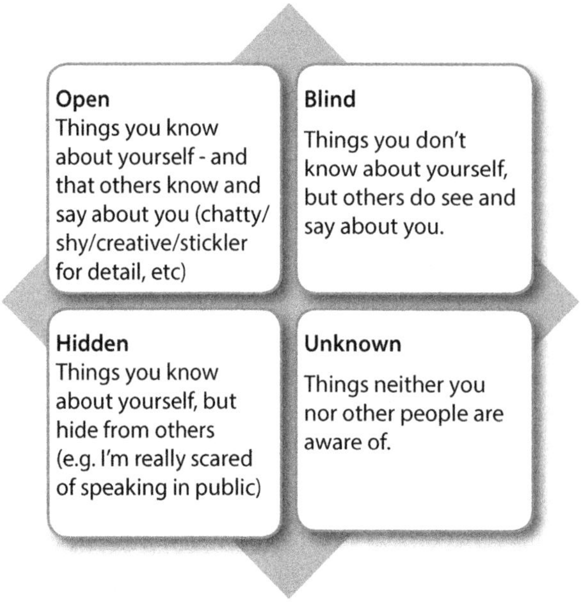

Open
Things you know about yourself - and that others know and say about you (chatty/shy/creative/stickler for detail, etc)

Blind
Things you don't know about yourself, but others do see and say about you.

Hidden
Things you know about yourself, but hide from others (e.g. I'm really scared of speaking in public)

Unknown
Things neither you nor other people are aware of.

Figure 1.3: Johari Window

Self-awareness is the first stage in emotional intelligence, which means being honest with yourself about your strengths and weaknesses, likes and dislikes, and the things you are secretly ash amed of. The Johari Window process suggests asking our friends and family for honest feedback via a questionnaire. Some organisations use a process called 360° appraisal where line managers are given feedback by the people they manage as well as from their supervisors. This can be problematic in small teams where it is clear who probably said what, but can also be very powerful.

People from an arts or performance practice background may be able to apply evaluation and feedback techniques learned during their training, but if you haven't had an arts training, one of the most common techniques leaders use is to keep a reflective journal of some sort. Writing seems to be a very effective way or organising your thoughts and means you can come back to a problem at a later date, or see patterns in the way you react.

Other methods for sensitising yourself to your own emotions and those of others include looking for role models – someone you admire and want to emulate (or, alternatively, someone you never want to be like!), finding a mentor or coach or joining an action learning set.

Mentors and coaches

Mentors are people in the same field as you who have more experience they are willing to share. Generally, they are not your boss, as it is important you feel confident opening up about problems and weaknesses. Mentors are a neutral guide who can advise and open doors. The relationship is focused on the mentee's career development. In some ways this relationship is like one you may have with a tutor or supervisor at university – except the mentor will not be marking your dissertation. Many experienced leaders enjoy sharing their experience and supporting new people coming through and will be flattered to be asked, so go ahead and send that email.

Coaches are not necessarily experts in your field, so they don't give advice. But they are expert in asking the right questions to help you reflect on problems you are facing and helping to learn to overcome them. A coach might be a line manager or someone outside the organisation you arrange to see independently – it's up to you.

Action learning sets are small groups of 5-7 people, usually peers at a similar career stage, who commit to meeting regularly for a set period of up to 18 months. The set focuses on a work problem presented by each of the members in turn. The presenter is then questioned by the others to uncover underlying assumptions and perceptions that might be contributing to the problem. Group members share any relevant knowledge or experience. The aim is to generate different insights that lead to new understanding and actions. The actions are then tried out and the outcomes fed back and reflected on at later sessions.

However, you choose to do it, improving your self-awareness and emotional intelligence is not a one off, but an on-going process. At the heart of it are clear personal values you can use as a guide for making decisions. Does this 'feel' right? This is also true for organisations. If your festival has a strong set of shared values, everyone from the director to your volunteers and audiences will know whether choices and actions fit, and your festival's brand image will be strong and consistent. We will return to the connection between values, design and brand in the next chapter.

Leadership style

There are various ways to think about leadership. One of the best known is Lewin's et al.'s model which distinguished three leadership styles: authoritarian, democratic and laissez-faire.

Democratic leaders consult with their team members, and may delegate decisions. This style allows teams to use and develop their expertise, but can be problematic in the heat of the festival as calling meetings and ensuring agreement is a slow process.

Laissez-faire is a French term which translates as 'leave them to get on with it'. Laissez faire leadership can be a very effective style if the people being led are clear about the organisation's vision and values, and have the expertise to do the job. Here it is true delegation and demonstrates faith in the team, which can be motivating. However, in complex situations like festivals there are always going to be some staff or volunteers who are new, or inexperienced and need more guidance. At this point, laissez-faire can look like abandonment of managerial responsibility.

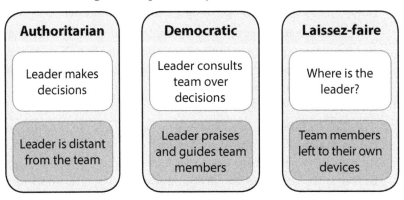

Figure 1.4: Leadership styles (adapted from Lewin et al. 1939)

This model was created in 1939 for a more formal society based around manufacturing, so it is worth asking if it is still appropriate. Workers in creative and cultural sectors are to a large extent highly educated. One survey found 78 per cent of creative media workers had degrees with more than a quarter having post-graduate qualifications (Creative Skillset, 2014) and almost half were freelancers (Creative Skillset, 2016). If someone works for themselves, or has expertise you rely on, they are unlikely to be willing to just do what you tell them. This, and the fact there are too many jobs to be done at the same time for one person to be able to oversee everything, helps to explain why *authoritarian* leaders are rare in the festivals sector. However, they are not unheard of. One festival director insists on approving every item of expenditure from the contract with the headline act to the bill for toilet paper. The benefit of this kind of attention to detail is very little tends to go wrong at his festivals. The disadvantage for people working for him is they are always second-guessing what he will want and often feel frustrated and demotivated by what they perceive as a lack of trust in their ability to do the job. Richard Branson keeps on top of expenditure in a slightly different way; he signs all the bills but only once a month. That way he keeps in touch with the detail but without undermining his staff.

Other ideas of leadership have questioned whether leaders have just one style they apply in all situations, or if good leaders are able to use different approaches depending on the task or the people being led. One of the best models for thinking about which style to use is *Tell-Sell-Test-Consult-Co-create*. This model identifies five methods and explains the pros and cons, where and when each can be used to best effect.

Tell

Leader makes the decisions and gives orders.

Good for emergency situations or when team members are inexperienced or lack knowledge of the situation.

Can be demotivating, as team members have no chance to influence decisions.

Can be reassuring for inexperienced team members or in times of uncertainty.

Sell

Leader makes the decisions and tries to persuade team members it is the best way.

Good for inexperienced teams as starts to give information about the underlying rationale. Builds emotional 'buy in' to shared values.

No room for team members to share their expertise or influence the decision.

Test

Leader has an idea or a plan and invites feedback, or offers alternatives for comment.

Good in situations where there is team with medium skill and experience and as an introduction to strategic decision-making processes.

Can be used by the lader to 'test' how well the fetival's values are understood within the team.

The plan might be improved through wider staff input. Staff feel motivated as their ideas influence decisions.

Consult

Leader presents the problem faced and asks the team for suggestions about how to solve it. The leader makes the final decision.

Consultation is appropriate where team members are experts in their field, but may lack knowledge of the organisational factors, or if the decision is high risk so needs a senior person to take responsibility. It is an opportunity to share and develop shared values.

The benefits of consultation are it broadens the range of expertise and ideas from team members so solutions are likely to be better. Team members are more likely to support the solution if their ideas are included.

Consultation takes time, however, and if ideas are not taken up for reasons that are not explained, it can look like a 'paper exercise' designed to placate workers.

Co-create

Leader defines scope and boundaries of a problem and delegates responsibility to the team, who then come up with, present and implement the solution.

Effective when the team is skilled and knowledgeable and the leader trusts the strength of shared values to inform team members' understanding of the implications of their decision for the organisation.

Motivating for skilled workers who feel valued.

Can be risky if the leader over-estimates the competence of the team.

Figure 1.5: Stages of staff involvement in decision-making (adapted from: Senge, 2014)

Festivals are projects that go through different phases (see Operations Management for project planning and management) and include highly skilled artists, technicians, stage managers and so on, as well as community volunteers who have never done anything like this before, so it is conceivable all of these stages would be evident over the course of a festival's year. The core team would co-create the festival's design (see Chapter 2). They might consult with funders, artists, staging contractors and so on to check the viability of their ideas. They might produce a couple of plans to take to possible investors, their board or perhaps stakeholders such as the emergency services. Then they might sell their idea to residents and friends' groups, or potential volunteers. Finally, during the festival itself, the leaders might be highly directive as time is of the essence.

Staffing structures and key roles in festival management

Unless you are able to raise a large sum of money – or have a house you are willing to re-mortgage or even sell (as Simon Taffe, founder of *The End of The Road Festival* did), you will probably be starting very small and you might be the only person running the festival. So, the issue of a festival staffing structures might be a dim and distant dream. If on the other hand you become a festival employee, then a staff structure is what you will walk into. To be effective in your new job you will need to get to know both the organisational structure you are working in and also people's roles within that as fast as you can.

Some of this, you will find, is about defined responsibility and some about style. One student on work placement with a leading festivals management and events company had to obtain the car registration numbers of all the bands appearing on a stage they were managing at *Glastonbury*, a mundane but important security task. But she also happened to be working alongside the organisation's mercurial director. She found herself undertaking the informal but important role of figuring out all the initiatives he was dreaming up ('what was going on in his head') and feeding the information back to other staff so that they had a sense of where the company was going and what might be on the horizon.

Festival management structures are usually functionally based. They will have sections or departments based around artistic/creative, finance, marketing, production, fundraising (usually called 'development'), box office and front of house. In some cases, marketing may also manage the box office function. If the festival takes place indoors in a fully-equipped venue then the festival organisation may not have a production department as that will be handled mostly by the venue. If it's on a green field site then it could have a large production team, though some or all of that may be outsourced. Indeed, most festival organisations have a very small core team which is enhanced significantly in the run-up to the event by freelancers, external companies working to a brief or a contract, and by volunteers.

Front of house is a theatre term and covers both setting up the venue so it is ready for the public and liaising with them. In terms of green field festivals it will probably be called 'site management' and could cover a wide range spanning volunteers, stewarding, ticket management, camping, environmental services such as toilet cleaning, and also security.

Inevitably each festival will have its own preferred management structure and operational methods. A management structure is merely a means to success. If you are a start-up festival with only two or three people involved, then you will probably be meeting at least weekly and in the final stages daily to ensure that everything that needs to be done has been or is being done and that 'the right things get to the right place at the right time'. In fact, if you are a small festival you and your team may almost be joined at the hip.

As festivals grow and more and more staff get involved, then some form of management structure will be needed to ensure that important things get discussed and communicated and people's time is well used. For example, *Boomtown* started with 3 staff in 2009 and has now grown to employing 40 full time staff and a festival crew of over 12,000.

If you are responsible for managing volunteers and stewards at a green field site festival, you don't really need to be involved in a discussion about stage rigging, PA, lighting and pyrotechnics. However, if you have a responsibility for health and safety or artist liaison, you might need to either be at the meetings or know about the outcomes.

Company structures are often perceived as hierarchies and there is truth in that. The higher up the ladder you are, the more you will earn, but the more responsibility you will also have. There is a management saying that no one person should have more than six people reporting to them. In people management terms that is the most you can manage if you are going to give your staff proper time, attention and support. So, management structures get introduced to ensure good communication between staff, between different sections of your event and to ensure that no one person is trying to do too much and putting the whole venture at risk.

Summary

This chapter has shown festival managers have to be aware of a wide variety of stakeholders because festivals are public and cultural goods, which have impacts on the communities and places where they take place, even if residents don't attend. Festival leaders have to have acute emotional intelligence so navigate the complex web of relationships needed to produce a festival – from artists and technicians, to venues and local authorities, from residents to audiences.

Emotional intelligence had five components: self-awareness; the ability to self-regulate in terms of mood; internal motivation; empathy; and social skills. Self-awareness is the first of these and is particularly important for leaders as without it, the messages you send out are likely to be mixed. So, the chapter introduced techniques from leadership training that can help you to think about the values that underpin your own motivation and that of the festival.

Strong, clear and widely shared values lead to resilient organisations with agreed and inspiring visions. Shared values mean everyone involved has the same idea about what is right and what is wrong, so decisions are in tune with each other. Workers in festivals with such organisational cultures trust each other and leaders are, therefore, more comfortable delegating.

References

Business Dictionary (2018) *Values*. Available at: www.businessdictionary.com/definition/values.html#ixzz2gjsgNDyL [Accessed 8 Sep. 2018-09-10].

Creative Skillset (2016) *2015 Employment Survey Creative Media Industries*. http://creativeskillset.org/assets/0001/0465/Creative_Skillset_Creative_Media_Workforce_Survey_2014.pdf.

Creative Skillset (2014) *Creative Media Workforce Survey 2014*. http://creativeskillset.org/assets/0001/0465/Creative_Skillset_Creative_Media_Workforce_Survey_2014.pdf.

Drucker, P. (2000) *The Essential Drucker: The Best 60 Years of Peter Drucker's Essential Writings on Management*. New York: Harper Business.

Hewison, R. and Holden, J. (2011) *The Cultural Leadership Handbook: How to Run a Creative Organisation*. Farnham, UK: Gower Publishing Ltd.

Lewin, K., Lippitt, R. and White, R. K. (1939) Patterns of aggressive behaviour in experimentally created 'social climates'. *Journal of Social Psychology*, **10** (2), 269-299.

Mayer, J. and Salovey, P. (1997) What is emotional intelligence? In Sluyter, D., and Salovey., P. (eds.) *Emotional Development and Emotional Intelligence: Implications for educators*. New York: Basic Books, pp. 3-31.

Marriage, H. (2008) Conference Speech, London.

Morris, G. (2004) Keynote address to Arts Marketing Association, Belfast, July.

Owen, J. (2005) *How to Lead*. Harlow: Pearson Education Ltd.

Peters, T. and Waterman, R. H. (2015) *In Search of Excellence: Lessons from America's Best-Run Companies*. London: Profile Books.

Senge, P. M. (2014) *The Fifth Discipline Fieldbook: strategies and tools for building a learning organization*. Crown Business.

Snowball, J. D. (2016) Valuing Arts Festivals: a case study of the South African National Arts Festival. In: Newbold, C., and Jordan, J. (eds.) *Focus on World Festivals: Contemporary case studies and perspectives*. Oxford: Goodfellow Publishers, pp. 164-175.

2 Festival Design and Programming

by Paul Kelly and Jennie Jordan

After reading this chapter you should:

- Understand what is involved in designing a festival

- Recognise the importance of having a clear vision and rationale for your festival

- Know the possibilities in festival design available to you

- Understand the importance of designing experiences into your festival

- Gain an insight into the relationship between branding and festival design

- Understand the key aspects of festival programming

Introduction

In this chapter we set out the principles, the possibilities, the processes and the practicalities of designing your festival. We start from the principle that festival design is first and foremost the artistic creation of the event, mentally and physically. That is, first the festival is conceived in the designers' mind: it is imagined, reflected on and desired. Second, the designer works through the possibilities and practicalities of what they want to do, including the key area of programming, before moving on to the process of festival production. As we shall see the increasing necessity of designing a good festival 'experience' is all important. There is, however, no shirking the many physical and practical considerations, such as venue size, utilities, and duration, all of which have to be considered at this design stage. This chapter assumes you are starting from scratch, because that ensures we cover all of the bases. If you are designing or redesigning a festival that already exists, the main difference is that you will need to know what your audiences and other stakeholders value about the festival's current design so you don't alienate them.

This chapter defines what festival design includes and stresses the importance of being clear on why you want to produce a festival. It looks at the central factors that sustain a festival. What is the festival's rationale? What is its vision? What makes for a good programme? You may already have a clear idea of what you want to do and why, in which case this chapter will be a good means of testing it. Alternately you may know you want to stage a festival but may not be clear on the theme or rationale. This chapter will help you focus on that.

Finally, festivals are a combination of vision and detail. It is often easiest to start with the details such as logo design or decor, but don't let that distract you from the core questions of why you want to undertake this difficult, tiring and risky project, and who you are producing it for. The chapter starts with the vision and rationale as this will inform the all-important detail that will follow. You don't build a house without first laying the foundations. Festival design can involve a wide range of rationales and motivations. These can include personal motivators including beliefs and philosophy, aesthetic and artistic rationale, place and spatial issues and of course finances. We will examine all of them in this chapter.

The principles

Why 'design'?

The term design can be interpreted in a micro and a macro way. The micro application is the physical, graphical or digital look and feel of the outcome; its aesthetic qualities, and those are of course important. In building terms, the design is the iconic aspect of the construction. Visual design is what is most memorable about places like Sydney Opera House, the Eden Project in Cornwall and the Pyramid Stage at *Glastonbury*.

In contrast, the macro way of planning a festival starts not with the detail of aesthetic design, but with your festival's overall rationale. What is the purpose of your festival? This is a crucially important aspect of design. How will it function? Does your proposal work to achieve what you set out to do, your purpose? A building that looks beautiful, but doesn't meet the functional requirements of the people who use it will be deemed a failure. The same is true of your festival.

Sometimes the function of a festival is extremely clear. A key part of the mantra of *Burning Man* in America's Nevada Desert, alongside 'no spectators', is 'leave no trace'. *Burning Man* attracts thousands of people to a pristine *Wilderness* where it creates a memorable nine-days of 'immersive environmental theatre' in which all sorts of extraordinary human-made activities take place (see Bowditch, 2016). It then departs leaving no trace. That is festival design in action: the form, a sustainable participatory festival, follows the function, to create and celebrate a community of environmentally concerned activists. Much as aesthetics form an important part of it, *Burning Man* is about much more than just aesthetics. It is the mix of location, activity, experience and a concern for the environment.

Festival design incorporates a number of aspects such as festival function, festival objectives, festival mission. All of those are applicable. But assume for a moment that you are starting with a blank sheet of paper. Things like function, objectives and missions are inanimate until you define, coordinate and produce them. Festival design is a conscious and focused activity that synthesises and energises the component parts into a coherent whole; and you, the festival instigator, are the festival designer.

Design can be a big and rather intimidating word. But your initial festival design can be quite modest. When Michael Eavis started the *Pilton Pop, Blues & Folk Festival* in 1970 he wanted to put on good music and support his family farm. What he ended up designing (or creating) became a world-famous festival, *Glastonbury*. There was certainly a form of festival design when he started but it is doubtful he envisaged then just how it was to grow. But if you do want to start big or dream big don't let anything prevent you.

Why?

It's worth pausing here to introduce an important and memorable concept that will help you with both your budget and other aspects of the festival. We call it 'Kipling', after Rudyard Kipling, the one that wrote *The Jungle Book* and *The Just So Stories*. One of those Just So Stories, 'The Elephant's Child' (1902) contains the following short poem:

> "I keep six honest serving-men
> (They taught me all I knew);
> Their names are What and Why and When
> And How and Where and Who." (Kipling, 2007)

Memorise those six honest serving men, for in your festival planning they will serve you well and are the basis for all festival design. *Who, what, when, where* and *how* are relatively easy to define and apply. *Why* is harder, but festivals that can't answer this question have something missing: they are less attractive and less memorable.

Why is at the heart of your event or activity. It's not just about the event. It's about you and your commitment and beliefs. If you don't believe in the event then why should others? If you cannot define why you are investing hours of time and energy in planning and delivering it or what makes your festival important and distinctive, then why should others get enthusiastic about it?

The why is not just important for devising and planning festivals, it's important to all businesses. As author and organisational consultant Sinek (2009) argues, the biggest problem facing most companies is customer loyalty. Most companies try and retain customers through some form of manipulation which could include price incentives, special promotions or even fear

– 'what would you miss if you didn't take up our special offer?' This ends up leading customers to look for the next special offer. Arts organisations have often been guilty of this as Hill et al. (2012) showed, discounting unsold tickets at the last minute led even loyal audiences who loved what they did to wait, knowing the price would come down. So, arts organisations had to keep creating more and more special offers and it ends up costing them large sums of money. Understanding why your festival is worth it, what makes it worthwhile, will give you the confidence in your offer and pricing.

So, what is it that makes the design of a festival so special that people will be willing to pay enough so you can cover your costs and even make a profit (if that's your aim)? New festivals are springing up all the time. No one can go to all of them, there just isn't time. Which ones do you pick? What are the factors that make one festival distinctive enough to attract attention in a crowded market? What is it offering that others aren't? Look at all those 'early bird' cheaper ticket offers if only you book early. Or those messages 'book now, selling fast'. These can work. But where are the early bird offers for *Glastonbury*? Have you noticed you can't get one for love nor money? And people go back year after year after year. Why? Because *Glastonbury* understands why it exists, and that's obvious in everything it does, from having special spaces for families, to giving money to Water Aid each year. Another example is *Buxton Opera Festival*, which produces rarely seen operas that are only performed at the festival. It has had the same vision since it started in 1979, and audiences book their hotel rooms in Buxton for the following year as they are checking out this year.

Festivals such as *Glastonbury* that avoided the temptation of manipulating customers through special offers have ended up as market leaders by inspiring people instead. *The Fringe* at the *Edinburgh Festival* started because some artists couldn't get selected for the main festival. So, they joined together and hired other spaces. *Edinburgh Fringe Festival* is now one of the biggest festivals in the world. It has kept its open access policy and inspired any number of other 'fringe' festivals. If you want to see the next big thing, the fringe of any festival is the best place to look.

In his argument, Sinek pointed out why explains why someone should buy your product or service. He used Apple as an example. Creative Labs produced an mp3 player nearly two years before Apple launched its iPod. The Creative Labs mp3 sold quite well. They described it as 'a 5GB mp3 player'. When Apple launched the iPod their message was '1,000 songs in your pocket'. Which one would you buy? The difference was that Creative Labs said WHAT their product was whereas Apple said WHY we needed it. With all the festivals out there appealing for interest, attention and ticket purchases, it's a lesson well worth paying attention to. One of the hardest parts of festival design is to think through not only who your audience is but

WHY should they want and need your festival. Why should they care? In some cases the answers are obvious. If not, there are things that can help you reach a compelling answer that are covered further on. But first, there is the question of authenticity.

Top commercial brands, including leading festivals, create an image based on an authentic set of values that run throughout the organisation and they work hard to protect it. Think of Apple, Harley-Davidson, Virgin and Burberry as leading examples. These values act like a touchstone, so everyone working for the company knows when they take a decision if it is the right thing to do. In festival design this goes from booking acts (is this band or theatre company the right 'fit'?), to deciding on whether or not to allow plastic bottles on site, or choosing to have purely vegan catering. This would be perfect for some festivals, and completely wrong for others. Companies – and festivals – appear authentic where all the decisions and actions that result 'feel right'.

All of these factors have a bearing on festival design. What makes it distinctive? Who is it for? What are its core values? Why should your customers care? How do you express that as a brand? And most crucially how do you act in a way that expresses your brand values? Does your entire team, however big or small, behave in a similar way?

Debating point:

Try asking three questions that will get to the heart of your why:

- What do you want people to say about your festival in five years' time?

- What is unthinkable (who wouldn't you book, for example)?

- What would you be most proud of having achieved?

Successful festival organisers we asked talked about the international artists they have persuaded to star in their festivals; or the surprising places they have put on shows; or the fact that they have managed to run events that appeal as much to teenagers as family audiences; or that they got 500 people to watch a piece of contemporary dance, or that their festival staged 60 or 600 events… and when we asked other people who knew the festival as audiences, or funders, they talked about similar things. Why? Because the festivals' image and actions were aligned. They knew why they were booking those artists, or producing a site-specific work in an abandoned building, so could explain it to their audiences. But if you don't know WHY you do WHAT you do, how will anyone else?

Getting to why

What motivates people working in the creative sector? After all creative managers labour for hours, days and weeks on end to create all kinds of distinctive events – some of them festivals. Those events often require quite similar management skills to ensure they are properly planned and effectively run. You might run a community arts festival for local families in a neighbourhood park, or a comedy festival in your town's bars and pubs, or a film festival, or a food festival in the city centre square. The purpose and style of those events will all be quite distinctly different because events are the product of human labour and ingenuity, and they reflect the values of the people who design them. So, what motivates festival managers is a really important factor in the nature of the festival. It is also a key issue in understanding 'why'. There are essentially three different motivators or 'drivers' that lead people to spend hours planning, creating and delivering events.

Aesthetics

The key driver here is the artistic outcome. The costs involved are either of no importance, or secondary. The main objective is to produce the best piece of artistic/creative work possible regardless of anything else. As public funding for arts has declined across Europe, festival producers have found they have to consider business factors more and more. The rise in festival numbers has also created more competition for grants, so investment income is harder to secure, whether it be public sector grants or private sector investment or sponsorship, so a purely aesthetic rationale has become harder to sustain.

That does not mean if your motivation is to promote an art form you love you should either give up now, or sacrifice artistic quality, rather that you will have to be more creative in how you book and package your events, or how you raise money for them. *Buxton Opera Festival*'s Friends raise enough money each year for the festival to produce an extra opera. *Rock in Rio*'s sponsors pay for and run distinctive areas on its site.

Social change

The second driver is entirely different. It is the desire in its broadest terms to contribute to social change. With this driver the quality of the artistic/creative content is less important and sometimes of no consequence. It is the impact that the work creates that is important and this is the key rationale for staging the festival or event. There is an old saying from the 1970s community arts sector that aptly sums this up; 'the process is more important than the product'. The social contribution or impact can cover a very wide span. It can be local; using a creative activity to raise awareness or money for a specific local cause. It can equally be global; seeking to create a festival or event that raises awareness of, for example, climate change, diversity or equality.

A *Pride* festival is a prime example of this. Such a festival has creative content, but the purpose of the event isn't about the quality of the creative content, which may or may not be excellent; it is about using that content to draw attention to or celebrate lesbian, gay, bisexual and transgender issues.

Money

The third motivating factor or driver is money. Ultimately the artistic or creative quality is less important. Nor are you staging the event to draw awareness to or celebrate a particular social issue. Instead at the end of the day the question is whether or not the festival has made a profit. You will only put in the effort and take the risk if there is the likelihood that you will make a meaningful profit, usually within three years. For-profit festivals are more common in the commercial parts of the creative industries such as music, film and gaming, and these industries can produce excellent cultural works. So, if you can put on a festival which entertains hundreds or thousands of people, makes enough to pay your bills and fulfils any additional purposes you have, then what's the harm in profit?

A mix of motivators?

Human nature is subtle, sophisticated, complex and conflicted. Inevitably people's motivations are a delicate balance between competing interests. Could what drives you be a mix of finance, social impact and aesthetics or just two of the three?

There are several important points to be considered here. First, what is the most important of these three that influences your thinking? If you had to choose one, which would it be? If you had to comp romise, where would you be willing to compromise and what issue would, for you, be something that you would not be willing to sacrifice? What is unthinkable? It is important to think about this and to get clarity on it as this is likely to be a key factor in how and why you design your festival.

Glastonbury, one of the world's largest, best known and most successful music festivals, features some of the world's leading musicians, an often-overlooked theatre and arts programme, children's activities and much more besides. It is financially successful and it also gives a portion of its profits to good causes like Oxfam, Greenpeace, Water Aid and, in 2014, 97 other community and charitable ventures. In that sense *Glastonbury* is socially driven and aesthetically driven. But could it be socially responsive if it wasn't financially successful?

It may be possible to mix two or more motivating factor in designing your event. But you need to be careful, as that can lead to confusion, or indeed to compromises that affect the focus and success of your event.

Experiences

Festivals are not tangible goods that you can pick up and take home, so what does design mean when your 'product' is an experience? Pine and Gilmore (1998; 1999) argued that increasing numbers of products and retailers are stealing ideas from the events and festivals sector to add value to their own products. Apple Stores stage events to draw people in to try the latest technology. A good example of the experience economy is the price you pay for a cup of coffee. The raw coffee bean costs about 2-3p a cup (at 2004 prices). Dry it, roast it and package it and sell it in a grocery and it's worth £2 - £3 a pack – equivalent to 15p – 20p a cup. Brew it for a customer and you might get £1.50 a cup if you are a kiosk or basic cafe. But, says Pine, "surround the brewing of that coffee with the ambience of a Starbucks, with the authentic theatre that goes inside of there and now, because of that authentic experience you can charge $2, $3, $4 or $5 for a cup of coffee" (Pine, 2004)

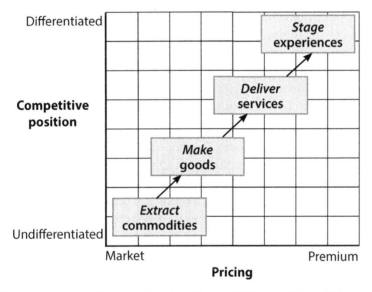

Figure 2.1: The progression of economic value, Pine and Gilmore (https://hbr.org/1998/07/welcome-to-the-experience-economy)

You can apply the same analysis to festivals. Put a competent band on a small stage in the middle of a field and you're not going to be able to charge the audience much if anything at all. The experience in that unadorned state will be slightly disappointing if not dismal. However, surround that field with security barriers, dress the site with flags and banners, create a beautifully decorated stage, add some street theatre, kid's activities, a high-quality PA system and lights and bring in catering stalls and bars and you are on the way to designing an experience that you might charge anything up to £100 per person or more for. Will the artists perform any better because of this?

Well, the music will probably still be the same as if they performed it on that 'raw-state' stage with none of the trimmings. But of course, 'the authentic theatre' of the fully fledged, multi-sensory festival will make the music and atmosphere feel so much better that the customer will be happier and think the ticket price was good value.

Today, festivals are a very visible and colourful component in the experience economy. Forget *Glastonbury* for a moment. That's an unusual hybrid surrounded by Arthurian legends and the symbolic Tor. A much more interesting development is the way that aspects of the traditional rock festival or commercial music festival, for example *Leeds, Reading,* or *Download* in the UK have been adapted and merged with a more longstanding arts festival tradition, such as Edinburgh. This newer hybrid merges commercial rock music and the arts. Examples include *Latitude, Wilderness, Kendal Calling, Boomtown,* and *Camp Bestival,* and the experience economy is at their core. Robinson (2016) discussed how these boutique festivals combine business savvy – it had become increasingly difficult for smaller festivals to book popular headline acts – with their core values. Audiences were encouraged to participate more by suggesting events and designing areas for the festival. At *Boomtown,* the costumes participants wear are as much a part of the show as anything the festival producers design. No one is a spectator, and the experience is deeper and more highly valued, and appears more authentic as a result.

What makes the design of a product or an event authentic? Do you have to be authentic to be successful or popular? One of the world's most popular and successful event experiences, Disneyland, is completely inauthentic (Gilmore and Pine, 2007). It is based on European fairytales and German-style castles, yet millions still flock there. The important issue in determining or creating authenticity is how you represent yourself to others. Disneyland knows it is a fantasy. It is genuine about presenting itself as that and is true to itself, and so is a 'fake real'. Contrast that with some of the dismal and fraudulent Christmas experiences that some unscrupulous operators create each year which attempt to offer snow and reindeers and sleighs and other Christmassy things. They are 'real fakes', they pretend to be something that they are patently not.

Disneyland is fine. We know it is a fantasy. People happily suspend their disbelief, buy, engage and revel in it. *Boomtown* follows the same example, albeit in a rather hipper fashion. It is a festival that has a running storyline through its succession of annual festivals and a series of impressive theatrical sets with stages embedded in some. *Boomtown's* design has made rock music a theatrical, participatory experience, just like 'Mamma Mia' has done on stage and in the cinema.

In event sponsorship, this is known as 'activating a relationship' (Anderton, 2011). It works where festival audiences are given additional experiences by sponsors, such as drinks or free gifts, and live music, but only when audiences can see how the sponsor fits with the festival's ethos. A Southern US-style bar selling Southern Comfort and playing live music at *Latitude* or *Womad*? Yes. At a family-orientated event with lots of small children? Probably not. Where it works seamlessly, audiences start to feel the same about the brand's product as they do about the festival, and each augments the other.

The possibilities

So far, this chapter has introduced some theory that will help you shape your thinking and approaches to designing your festival. It has yet to address the problem of coming up with an idea for a festival, or a new strand to an existing festival. As we have seen in the introduction to the book there are festivals available to meet all tastes and interests, most of them annual events ranging from between one day and three weeks, it's clearly a crowded market and one eager to capture our attention, money and diminishing time. So how do you find a way in? Where are the gaps and the market opportunities? Because to make a festival work and be sustainable you have to appeal to more than just friends and family.

Distilling this information

You may be reading this with a clear idea of what you want to do and a rationale that has been burning through your veins. Equally when it comes to defining and planning your event, you may be staring helplessly at a blank piece of paper trying to think of an idea that hasn't been tried before. But there are actually few truly original ideas, so if you feel you haven't got an original idea, don't worry. After all, *Reading* and *Leeds* are not original ideas, they just do what other festivals do, but they do it well. Trying to think of a unique festival idea may not be the best approach. Observing and talking can be very productive - go to as many different types of festival as you can, talk to audiences, participants and organisers, get to know as much about festivals as you can. It's surprising how much expertise you can gain this way.

Your enthusiasms

Festival production is hard and time-consuming, so it's important that your idea is something that grabs you, that you are genuinely interested in and committed to. What are your passions and enthusiasms? If it's textiles or 15th century German choral music, can you find a way of developing a festival around them? But don't forget the WHY. The idea has to appeal to you, to the people you may work with, AND to a potential audience.

Market trends

What's happening in the world? Key into the news, go online and search 'festivals' and 'festival news', watch and listen to arts programmes, buy music or arts magazines, engage with the various festival management organisations. Try to identify trends and new ideas. Are there things happening elsewhere that can be translated into your 'patch'. 'Elsewhere' could include other parts of the UK or abroad. Indeed, bringing a cultural festival from another culture to the UK has proved very successful for the organisers of melas, and *Dia de los Muertos* celebrations seem to be gaining support, too.

Industry example: Journeys Festival International

Journeys Festival International (JFI) is an annual festival that takes place in Leicester, Manchester and Portsmouth. It showcases and celebrates the work of artists from the refugee and asylum seeker community, and shares their stories through art events, performances, film screenings and workshops. The festival programme is made up of two core components: grassroots participatory events embedded within the Refugee and Asylum Seeker community; and internationally renowned touring artworks and original commissions. This results in a vibrant mix of music, street theatre, film, visual art and installations, family activities, discussions and workshops.

Exploring the experiences of refugees and asylum seekers through artistic events is a much broader topic than it might appear on the surface. It enables us to look at the impact of migration and forced migration on society, stimulating discussion about statelessness and the wider political context that causes people to seek asylum. It challenges our understanding of what home is, what it means to feel at home and to build a new life. It exposes the root causes of why people have had to make these journeys, including conflict, corruption, war, unstable governments. It highlights how people are treated once they have resettled, as well as celebrating the positives of an increasingly diverse society and highlighting what we can learn from one another. The festival's focus enables us to create *Cultural eXchanges* that broaden our knowledge of the world outside of our immediate surroundings and promote integration and more welcoming societies.

This results in a festival programme that is a mixture of celebratory, uplifting events alongside hard-hitting and more controversial work. The multi-facetted nature of this kind of programme creates a unique challenge for us as festival curators and managers. One of the most complex issues we deal with is the appropriateness of content for different audiences. We have to tailor events to our different stakeholders and clearly communicate these to the public. Sharing work that demonstrates the harsh realities that refugees and asylum seekers experience can have a big impact on audiences and be a very effective tool to raise awareness of the injustice and exploitation that takes place in their everyday lives like *This Is Who I Am* by Ice and Fire Theatre Company and *The Invisibles' Journey* that we presented with Secour Catholique in 2018. However, these artworks can be upsetting and disturbing and therefore may not be appropriate for refugees and asylum seekers to experience themselves. Sometimes the stories and experiences that are shared are too close to their own, which they may not have come to terms with or been able to process. We have a responsibility to safeguard our audience and participants. We should not put them in a situation which might retraumatise them or expose them to content which is upsetting. But we also appreciate that this explicit content is powerful and compelling for audiences who have little or no personal experience of what it is like to be a refugee, and therefore has value within the festival programme. It helps them to understand the context and prompts them to ask "what can I do to change this". This is a vital role that the arts can play in creating social change and improving the lives of others. Examples of artworks that we have programmed that fit within this strand of work include: *Burning Doors* by Belarus Free Theatre (2016), *#JeSuis* by Aakash Odedra Company (2017) and screening Ai Weiwei's 2017 documentary *Human Flow*.

It can be difficult to for us to maximise the potential of JFI because our commissioning ethos is open and non-prescriptive. We don't highlight who within the programme is a refugee and who isn't. Many artists do not want to be identified and will be listed as anonymous or under a pseudonym. First and foremost, we work with people and artists who tell important and compelling stories or believe in celebrating each other's culture through artistic events. Some artists tell their stories through their work, others don't directly engage with the subject matter. The definition of refugee and asylum seeker is broad; each person has their own unique circumstance and story. We choose not to define people by their legal status and do not force anyone to share anything that they do not want to.

Curating and creating opportunities for the refugee and asylum seeker community, who come from around the world, are made up of many ages, religions, languages and cultures, with broad interests, means that our work is sometimes more focused on community integration, play, entertainment and bringing people together to take part in an activity regardless of their background, cultural heritage, religion or immigration status.

This identifies three strands of work within the festival:

1 Work that explores the refugee experience from an outsider's perspective, raising awareness and exposing the realities of their lives

2 Work that is created by professional refugee and asylum seeker artists. Some of this may reflect their experiences while others will not explicitly explore this topic

3 Participatory projects, including creating work that will be presented within the festival, for the refugee and asylum seeker community

Our aim is for these to be integrated so that we can have high quality artworks and performances in the same event as opportunities to learn how to plant herbs or make traditional Syrian coffee from local refugees and asylum seekers, creating safe spaces where conversations can happen and people can come together. It is this combination of community-led participatory activity alongside professional artworks, and the wide range of partnerships that define the programme, that makes JFI such an exciting and unique festival to manage.

Maddie Smart is an Executive Producer at ArtReach

It was done so badly

Have you been to a festival or an event where you've been disappointed by the content or the organisation? Was it a good idea but it just lacked a touch of magic? Do you have the ideas or the capability to do something similar but better? We live in a Trustpilot era. With so much quality around to choose from the public can voice their opinions online, and often do. So, what are they saying? Are their comments justified? Can you create a festival that gives them what they want?

A lack of provision

Although festivals can be planned from a distance, it's not sensible to do that for start-up events, and certainly not if you don't have lots of experience. We are assuming you are going to be staging your festival within a 30 mile/one-hour drive time of where you live. So, what's happening in the town, area or region? Is there a gap or opportunity either in terms of number of festivals or a particular type of festival? If there are already festivals happening, what time of year are they, and is anything missing? Are there other times of year when there are gaps when people might be looking for things to do?

Themes and anniversaries

As mentioned above, themes are a good way of tying together different events in a festival. The births and deaths of famous people or anniversaries of significant historical events can inspire ideas for commissions or productions. Themes are another idea. You could create a theme from an anniversary. For example, something like the 100th anniversary of women getting the vote 1918-2018 offered programming opportunities to both reflect this and address equality issues.

Taking over an established festival

At the extreme end of things and for those with a bit of experience under your belt, you might not need to come up with a festival idea at all. You may find there's an existing festival that needs new blood. It could be failing in some way, in which case look at any and all of the available data with considerable care. It could be that the people running it have decided they want to pass it on to a new team who can take it on and keep it running. Some of these situations might be advertised. In other cases, you'll have to pick up such opportunities from the bush telegraph. So, keep your ears to the ground.

Alternatively, you could approach an existing festival with an idea for a new strand to sit alongside their main programming. *Kendal Calling* in Cumbria is a greenfield music festival that has an area called Lost Eden, an area showcasing installation and light art works. *Buxton Festival* launched a literary strand in 2000 to sit alongside the operas it produces. Festivals should never stand still, they should evolve and change over time, it's an essential part of their appeal and survival.

Considerations in designing your festival

In this book and elsewhere we have talked about the festivalisation of contemporary life and have discussed the possibility of there being a festival aesthetic (Jordan, 2015, Newbold and Jordan, 2016). As well as being fascinating debates for those interested in or studying festivals, they also provide a range of useful considerations for festival designers. The key to much of the debate is that festivals are seen to create a time and space distinct from everyday life. Festival designers achieve this 'special reality' in a number of ways, through creating immersive and sensory experiences, through theming, participation, and creating an atmosphere of experimentation, but also as we shall see later in this chapter with our industry case study of Arcadia, through spectacularisation. Clearly then, these areas provoke a number of questions that festivals designers can consider:

- ♦ Is the festival providing an immersive environment and experiences?
- ♦ Can the festival be seen to be multi-sensory, not only sight and sound, but also smell and taste?
- ♦ Does the festival and its associated activities create an intelligible identity or unifying theme?
- ♦ Does the festival provide means by which the audience can participate and engage with activities as co-producers?
- ♦ Will the festival provide participants with unusual, extraordinary and experimental experiences?
- ♦ Does the festival contain elements of the spectacular? – large scale, bright and colourful décor, loud music and ambient sounds, hi-tech, pyrotechnics, eye-catching and impressive art works and performances?

These are all features then that distinguish festivals from everyday life and other cultural events and experiences, and thus are important considerations that the festival designer could take account of. Not all of the above are essential. You need to select the ones that fit your brand and values

Length and timing

The length of your festival is quite likely to be determined by your artform. Most big commercial music festivals seem to run for a long weekend – three or four days. In contrast, multi-artform arts festivals tend to run for a week or two and occasionally longer. Book and literature festivals vary in length from a weekend to a whole week or even two. Cultural festivals such as Holi, Chinese New Year (Spring Festival), or Dia de los Muertos tend to take place on a specified or traditional day. Most other festivals are designed to take place during holiday periods, and if outdoors, when the designer feels there is the possibility of good weather.

Place

The next chapter on planning and logistics will look at some of the detailed issues about your festival site. But it is worth saying here that the nature of your venue or site will have a significant impact on your festival's design. Maguire called this place animation, he said, "the relationship between people and place is given particular poignancy through festival and cultural engagements" (2016: 53).

In thinking about your festival site or place, we have found it useful to draw on landscape design theory, particularly Girot's (1999) Four Trace Concepts theory. Here Girot identified four stages of a designer's developing relationship with a place: landing, grounding, finding and founding.

♦ **Landing** is when you first arrive at a place, it is impressionistic, it's about feeling, trying to understand a place on an emotional as well as practical basis.

♦ **Grounding** happens on subsequent visits, researching the place's history, as this might have an influence on the type of event, or aspects of your festival design, rooting a festival in a place is key. For example, Leicester's *Riverside Festival* is rooted in the city's relationship to the river Soar.

♦ The **finding** stage is about discovery, noticing significant features in the site that can then become part of your festival design. It might be an object, a feature of the landscape or simply an evocative feeling, clearly the name *Glastonbury* is evocative of the place's legendary connections.

♦ The final phase, **founding**, is where all the previous phases come together to create something new, transforming the site, and extending its existence and significance over time, which is what festivals do for a place in many ways.

Where the festival is going to take place will constrain its capacity, how loud you can be, and what sort of art works will be suitable. It might also make a significant dent in your budget. Whether you are using one or more indoor venues or a 'green field' site or indeed an inner city 'brown field' site, there are a great many practical questions to be addressed. Is the site, venue or venues serviced in terms of light, power and water? Do they have stages or focal points for performers or exhibitors or areas where stages or similar can be created? How will audiences get to and find the venue? How will artists get to and find the venue? Is the access relatively easy or quite difficult and what impact will this have? Is there parking for artists and audiences nearby? Is there storage space in the venue for equipment?

Case study

One festival staged a concert in an a delightful old 19th century theatre in a major city. The concert required a grand piano and we were able to hire a good quality Steinway piano relatively cheaply from the local Arts Association. The piano was delivered in a large removals lorry. The only way of getting the piano into the theatre and onto the stage was through the theatre's dock doors (used for getting scenery in) and these dock doors backed onto a narrow one-way street in quite a busy part of town. In order to get the piano into the theatre, the furniture van had to block the entire street so that its tailgate could reach the dock doors and the piano could be moved into the theatre. At one point there was a gap of a couple of feet between the van's tailgate and the theatre with the £35,000 grand piano balanced rather delicately between the two and impatient motorists backed up and waiting for the job to be finished. It was not a comfortable moment.

If it's an indoor venue how does it look and feel? Is it drab with sticky carpets? Or is it plush and nicely decorated? What are its acoustic like? If you are putting on music, the acoustics can be very important. Large empty venues and churches can have very 'bright' acoustics with a sound delay of several seconds. It's fine for classical music and much acoustic music. But if you put on a group with lots of amplification and especially drums, the sound can end up being a muddy mess that even the best sound engineer will struggle to rectify.

If the venue is full of soft furnishings (and clothed people add to the soft furnishings) then the sound can be very 'dry'. That can mean there's absolutely no reverberation and the sound is easy to hear. But no reverberation can make it quite hard for singers and brass and wind players (like saxophones) who have to work a lot harder, though electronic reverberation can compensate. If in doubt, find a friendly sound engineer and ask them to come and look at the venue and give you advice. If they have an in-house sound and lighting team they may have lots of experience and useful advice.

Just as important as sound design is the lighting. What is the primary lighting? Is it dimm-able? Is the lighting zoned so the lights on the audience section can be dimmed and the stage lighting left up? Is there an in-house lighting rig or fixing points where lights can be fixed? Neon strip lights can completely kill the atmosphere in a room. The lighting aspect of festivals, especially small ones, is often overlooked. If you are staging a music event and it's the sort of event where the artists need to be able to read music or lyrics the last thing you want is a stage where it's too dim for them to see. Good lighting is not just important for the artists. It can create atmosphere and transform an event producing a magical experience for the audience.

If you are booking a theatre for your festival, then there ought to be an in-house lighting rig. The venue ought to have competent people on-site who know its capabilities. Talk to them about what you want and what they can do. Give them a brief if need be.

If you are working outdoors, and in the evening, or at night, you will need a lighting rig to ensure the artists can be seen. But there's also another factor to consider. What time is sunset and where does the sun set in relation to the stage? Sunset can be a wonderful natural contribution to outdoor events. Think about what you are programming at sunset. You can really create something magical. But sunset, and the direction the stage faces, can also be a hazard for artists. At one outdoor festival on a warm August day where the stage faced west, the artists were facing into the sun which slowly dropped during the course of the afternoon and the stage was uncomfortably hot as a result.

The outdoor venues you create can also contribute to the look and feel. For 27 years The Swanage Jazz Festival operated on a lovely site overlooking the bay. It used two large plain white marquees, each holding around 500 people. A new festival director decided to use colourful Circus Big Tops instead. Each had the same 500 capacity but brought a completely different look and more colourful feel to the festival.

Site dressing

Drab venues can always be decorated according to the nature of the event and again lighting can help. But also, simple things like balloons, old parachutes, large swathes of cloth can make a huge difference to the look and feel and can be quite inexpensive.

> **Debating point:**
> A group of university students produced an event around the theme of food waste. They used a community centre housed in a deconsecrated 19th century church. The venue was not unattractive, but it had a very high ceiling (the classic V roof) and lacked intimacy. The students used large bolts of cloth running from a balcony on one side to fixings on pillars on the other side and created an attractive multi-coloured false canopy ceiling. It transformed the venue and created the desired sense of intimacy.

If you intend staging an outdoor festival, then there are things that can be easily done to create atmosphere on a greenfield site. If your event is likely to attract families with children, then why not create a children's play area? You ought to able to contract this out to a third-party supplier and earn revenue from this. But make sure they have all the necessary insurances and have sufficient staff to install and supervise the equipment. The combination of high winds and inflatables have led to injuries and even fatalities.

Many outdoor sites are dressed with flags, bunting and banners to create a really attractive visual look and feel, even if they are becoming a little ubiquitous now, they can be hired or bought outright. Or, for community events, work with local groups and schools to get them to make banners for you. You can provide the materials, and perhaps get an artist to visit the groups if you have the budget. Not only will you have unique decorations, the groups will all want to come and see their banners on display, guaranteeing an audience!

Signage is important both on and off site, the two key design issues are clarity and positioning. People need to know how to get there and then how to navigate around the site, they need to be warned of dangers, and private areas need to be indicated. Signage can be part of the branding and can also create atmosphere if done in a more crafted way.

Site dressing is particularly important for cultural festivals, using the colour red, hanging lanterns, paper cuttings and fire crackers are key to creating the feeling of Chinese New Year. The colour orange, skulls, marigolds and lots of candles create the atmosphere for Dia de los Muertos celebrations. To borrow a phrase from film, designing the right or appropriate 'mise-en-scene' is crucial to the success of your festival.

Technology

Technology is increasingly becoming not only an integral part of the site dressing but also a key element in festival design and programming. We shall talk more about the use of new technology in the final chapter of this book, but for the moment we can illustrate its contribution to festival design. Using lighting has always been part of music festivals, and search lights and lasers are now almost iconic for large music festivals such *Rock in Rio*. However, organisations like Artichoke have been using projection as a central feature of events, such as in their *Lumiere* project to illuminate the city of Durham. Along with the French company Royal de Luxe they have also used technology to create a giant mechanical Elephant for their 2006 The Sultan's Elephant project in London, and used their giant puppets for *Liverpool Giant Puppet Spectacular* (2014).

Figure 2.2: *Lumiere Durham* 2017 (photo Jennie Jordan)

Processes

You don't have to do this thinking and planning on your own and it's probably better if you don't. You are going to need a team to deliver your festival and if you come up with the ideas together you are all likely to be more committed.

Work out early on how you work best together, because people have different approaches to designing and planning. Some people like to talk about ideas endlessly before committing them to paper. Others like framing their thoughts on paper before discussing them. Some people like lots of words, some like diagrams. For some people the budget is the first thing to work on, so it's figures all the way. Some people will keep the conversations tight and private – don't tell anyone as the ideas might get stolen. Others will undertake surveys with the public or friends and family or share their ideas widely, as this will give valuable feedback and even things they hadn't thought of that will help shape their initial ideas.

If you think that sharing your ideas will result in something akin to theft, remember this. Coming up with ideas is quite easy; putting those ideas into practice and creating a festival is much harder. Not many people have the knowledge, commitment and staying power to take an idea to completion. Sharing your ideas to get feedback is not as risky as you might think and can have a lot of benefits through the ideas and suggestions it creates. This is *crowdsourcing* and commercial companies make surprising uses of collaboration to test and improve ideas and products (Tapscott and Williams, 2008).

Remember your stakeholders may well also want/require an input into the festival design process, and this may be artistic or practical. A council or local authority may have input to make vis-à-vis your site, road closures for parades or simply help via their events office. A local radio or TV station may have certain technical requirements. Any sponsorship deal will require the inclusion of their logo, or at least their banner on the main stage. At some stage you may also need to inform the Emergency Services (Police, Fire etc) who can also provide valuable experience, advice and support.

Branding and design

This is often one of the first things that many people think about when planning a festival. What's it going to look like? We've left it until now, not because it's not important, but because designing a good brand image on its own does not make a successful event.

The marketing chapter later in the book covers branding in more detail, but having a consistent design in the festival's brand image and site dressing, whether it's in a bar holding 150 people, a hall holding a thousand or more, a country park or an open field holding thousands, can add to the atmosphere, so it's important to think about how what your festival looks like and how its logo and communications fit with the rest of your design. If you are promoting an exclusive festival, a logo in neon yellow gives the wrong signals. On the other hand, it might be perfect for a dance music festival celebrating 30 years since the 1989 summer of love.

Your festival logo can say a lot about your event. It's worth investing a bit of time and money in this, but don't make the mistake of thinking a logo is the brand. Look at some of the best name brands on the high street. Are their logos beautiful, or even distinctive? Ford and Boots both have their names in similar oval shapes. They are recognisable because they have been around for a long time and have clear messages about what they do. Graphic designers can be really imaginative, but they can't turn a badly thought-out festival into a good one. They also need to be given a clear and tight brief. After all, time is money. Remember your brand ought to last a good few years, so whilst creating a logo and brand identity may seem to cost a lot, you are paying for five or ten years use upfront. Also check your brand with friends, family and random members of the public. What does your brand and logo mean to them? Is it clear and readable? Is the message they are receiving from your logo, the message or ethos you are intending to send?

Inevitably you will need a website, and social media presence, so start looking for a domain name and appropriate handles for whichever platforms you are going to focus on. As we will see later in the book, there are several companies online where you can buy domains quite cheaply. It may be your chosen name has already been taken, so be prepared to rethink, and if you can keep your domain name short, it will be easier for people to type and find. Keep the colours and messages consistent across your communications, and ideally with your site décor.

Programming

The artistic programme you put on, whether it be thrash metal or a series of book readings from new novels, is, of course, central to your festival design and at the heart of your 'why?' Programming is the art of balancing artistic vision with audience interest and costs, and the key tension is between playing safe in programming to maintain audiences or taking risks to develop new audiences. Obviously, the best festival programming will try to achieve both.

There are so many different permutations of artistic festivals that it is impossible here to give detailed commentary about programming for all these. But your festival will probably involve promoting a number of performances or creative activities for the public. The word 'programming' means deciding who you are going to book, and when and where you are going to present them. In the visual arts and museums the word 'curating' is more common.

Every good festival is likely to have peaks and troughs. That is not about quality but about the style and the range of programme. Three or four thrash metal bands back to back playing at 110% can be a little wearing for the audience (and the stage crew). Similarly, in a festival that covers a range of art-forms programming three Cajun bands on the trot is a little dull and misses an opportunity. Programming is a fascinating and very satisfying creative patchwork but inevitably you are sometimes going to have to disappoint some artists who want to perform. It's not that you don't like their work or that they are no good. They just don't quite fit your programme plan for that year. Let them down gently.

There are all sorts of different considerations and ways of programming. A good starting point is to decide what time your programme will start and what time it will end (often determined by licensing laws). Then work out how long each performance or activity will be and the amount of time you need to clear the performance space and set up for a new performance (this is really important). That will give you the number of performance slots you can host each day in each venue.

At music festivals running a succession of acts three models have been used very successfully.

- ◆ **Model 1:** A single stage was programmed with local acts who were given a 50 minute performance followed by a 20 minute turn round. It was hard work for the stage crew, but meant there was a reasonable continuity.

- ◆ **Model 2:** Two stages running side by side. Stage A was programmed with well-known bands, who were given 75 minute sets. Stage B had local acts with 45 minute sets. Stage B was set up and line checked whilst Stage A was performing and vice versa. The turnarounds between stages is literally 2 – 3 minutes and the audience gets a constant flow of acts.

- ◆ **Model 3:** If you have more space on site, you can run stages simultaneously. But when setting the times remember that audiences might want to see acts on different stages, so think carefully about crossover, as well as clashes between popular acts, and how long it takes to get from one side of the site to the other.

Generally, whether it's a book festival or a rock festival, your headline acts or biggest names are going to be the ones that are hardest to secure, so book them first and book them early. You can then design the rest of the programme around them. The headline act is often the one that goes on last. But not always and it doesn't have to be that way. You might want to consider the nature of their material. It's often best to finish with something rousing. If your best-known act is an acoustic folk musician they won't thank you for putting them on after a band that's just brought the house down. That's a matter of programming judgement and one of the best parts of the job when you get it right.

Programming local talent will often generate its own audience and many festivals now have a 'local stage' with purely local and amateur talent, sometimes drawn from schools and colleges, or performing arts groups. Clearly a quality threshold needs to be applied, but they can provide a good and cost-effective addition to the programme.

The essence of creative programming is finding out what is available, what the big themes, trends and issues of the day are in your chosen field, thinking about your audience; what they know and what you think they might like (or ought to know about) and also thinking about the nature of your venues. It's a fascinating jigsaw puzzle.

In *Focus on Festivals*, Australian artistic director Robyn Archer looked at the role of festivals in changing attitude to programming Aboriginal cultures and how both artistic directors and audiences are now enthusiastic for the theatre, dance, music writing and visual arts of Australia's first peoples. She explained the best artistic directors had a vision and were

"both quick to recognise the work which will please/provoke audiences and are also good at understanding the cultural significance of this work" (Archer, 2015: 233)

You will also benefit through thinking about the balance of your programme in relation to the nature of society. Does your programme include the best from a range of different voices? Those different voices might be determined by gender, ethnicity, disability and age. We would recommend avoiding a programme determined by quotas that reflect the above. But in this diverse age, a folk music programme or street theatre programme in which all the performers, to take one example, are male, is missing an opportunity – or several, and in this social media age, word soon spreads. We all want to see and support the best. But sometimes the best is hiding just under the radar. Good programmers seek out such talent and bring it to public attention.

Industry example: Programming *Cultural eXchanges* Festival

Cultural eXchanges started life in 2000 at De Montfort University. The brainchild of the then Dean, it was seen as a way to celebrate the Faculty of Humanities' move to the newly refurbished Clephan building and to enable the Faculty to engage with its wider community – a kind of 'town meets gown'.

This is an important theme as 18 years later, the ethos of connecting outwards is even stronger. However, in that first year the festival struggled for an identity. Nevertheless, it was decided that it should continue and was instated as an annual festival. I became director the following year and changed the name from Clephan Events Week to *Cultural eXchanges* Festival. I never imagined that 18 years later the festival would still be going strong and I would still be the director. I often ask myself how has that happened?

Well, perhaps one answer to that question is the way in which the festival is able to reinvent itself each year. Credit for this goes to a great degree to my academic colleagues, staff and public who contribute ideas to the programme. Their proposals are integral and ensure that the festival doesn't just reflect my own reference points as director. Another important element is the input of the student body on our Arts and Festivals Management degree course, who programme and produce the festival with me each year, which gives the festival its energy and identity and helps ensure its currency.

This diaphanous approach to programming is not without its difficulties. Empowering the students in particular, who are on an enormous learning curve, whilst also ensuring that the festival stays true to its ethos, particularly around cultural diversity, is possibly the biggest challenge as director. More often than not the student team, who may not themselves come from culturally diverse backgrounds, do manage to embrace the full concept of *Cultural eXchanges*, and the significance of the fact that it takes place in a culturally diverse city such as Leicester.

Over the years I've had to learn when and how to intervene in a manner that gives the students ownership of the festival, even if not all their ideas can come to fruition. As part of this I hope that the students gain an understanding of the curatorial process, in particular how to represent the needs of differing demographics and subjects to achieve a balanced programme.

The challenge can take many forms, not necessarily all related to programming. For example, choosing the festival image to appear on the various promotional channels such as brochures and posters can be extremely fraught. Each year we have to consider how we can convey the concept of *Cultural eXchanges* through a particular design or photo in a way that is challenging but doesn't exclude.

To my mind the festival is hopefully communicating an important, albeit understated, message. That cultural diversity in terms of race, disability, gender, sexuality or however we may interpret it, isn't something that we pursue for its worthiness. It isn't a tick box exercise. And it isn't an afterthought. Diversity is central to our thinking and each programme tries to be a reflection of this. That is the non-negotiable within the festival. And that is perhaps where the most valuable learning takes place for the students – developing an understanding that for the most part when they go out and work in arts organisations of whatever identity they will need to reflect the aesthetics and focus of that organisation and reflect that in their thinking and ideas.

So, guests such as Benjamin Zephaniah, Meera Syal, Jamal Edwards, Nitin Sawhney, Paris Lees, Roly, Josette Simon, Carol Ann Duffy, Grayson Perry and Ben Okri all create the vibrancy and diversity that we hope to achieve within the festival. And of course, as director I myself am learning each year from the students as they make me aware of the changing agendas, issues and thoughts that reflect the world as they see it.

So, what have I learnt in the 18 years of running the festival? That the atmosphere generated is what makes a festival, the sense of being part of a communal celebration. That events you don't necessarily expect to be successful can often have the most impact, and visa-versa - a headline name is no guarantee of a full house. And that ultimately, it's about keeping your nerve and judging the timing of things so that you build momentum in your planning and reflect that in the rhythm of the festival.

Of course, experience plays a part. Trusting your instincts is crucial. The diaphanous approach I've described enables the programme to be fresh and create a collective sense of ownership which is so important. However, it also needs intelligent design so a key aspect of being festival director is the ability to keep an overview, knowing where you are trying to take the festival as a whole so that individual decisions are made with the complete picture in mind.

Last but not least I've learnt the importance of having a party, especially at the end. You might be exhausted but it's essential to acknowledge the team that has worked to bring it together and what better way to celebrate the fact that you've experienced something timeless. Then take at least a weekend off to recover before planning the next!

Tony Graves, Director of Cultural eXchanges.

Summary

Festival designers should approach festival design with a clear sense of why they are doing this, what they want to achieve, as well as what is practicable. The WHY is important here as we have seen: "why should people want and need your festival?" This is an important question to ask yourself and the answers can be most revealing in helping you in your design. This chapter has also offered some advice on generating ideas for your festival. Knowing what is going on in the festival world is crucial, and especially your local 'patch'. We have highlighted the importance of designing your festival as an experience, and creating a time and place that is distinct from everyday life. We have focused on the key areas of consideration in design, as well as looking at site dressing, the use of technology in festival design and the importance of designing a good brand image.

The final section of the chapter devoted to programming gave advice on what kinds of talent to book and in what order to present them, a central piece of advice was to start with the performance time available and allocate 'slots' accordingly. Programming a range of representative talent is important in your festival design as we have seen, using local talent can pay dividends in many areas, and being aware of cultural trends and movements is key. The essence of good programming, as with good festival design, clearly develops as you research and understand your chosen field.

References

Anderton, (2011) Music festival sponsorship: between commerce and carnival. *Arts Marketing: An International Journal*, **1** (2), 145-158.

Archer, R. (2015) A View from Australia. In Newbold, C., Maughan, C., Jordan. J., and Bianchini, F., *Focus on Festivals: Contemporary European case studies and perspectives*. Oxford: Goodfellow.

Bowditch, R. (2016) Republic of the Imagination. In Newbold, C. and Jordan, J., *Focus on World Festivals: Contemporary case studies and perspectives*. Oxford: Goodfellow.

Gilmore, J. H., and Pine J.B. (2007) *Authenticity: What Consumers Really Want*. Harvard: Harvard Business Review Press.

Girot, C. (1999) Four Trace Concepts in Landscape Architecture. In Corner. J., (ed.) *Recovering Landscapes: Essays in contemporary landscape architecture*. New York: Princeton Architectural Press.

Hill, E., O'Sullivan, T. and O' Sullivan, C. (2012) *Creative Arts Marketing*. London:Routledge.

Jordan, J. (2015) Festivalisation of Cultural Production, ENCACT, ed. In, *The Ecology of Culture: Community Engagement, Co-creation, Cross Fertilization*, Conference Proceedings of the 6th Annual ENCACT Research Session, 21-23 October 2015, ENCACT, 244-255.

Kipling, R. (2007) The Elephant's Child in *The Just So Stories*. London: Walker Books

Maguire, M. (2016) Animating Places: A new festival phenomenon? In: Newbold, C. and Jordan, J., *Focus on World Festivals: Contemporary case studies and perspectives*. Oxford: Goodfellow.

Newbold, C., and Jordan, J. (2016) *Focus on World Festivals: Contemporary case studies and perspectives*. Oxford: Goodfellow.

Pine, J. B. (2004) What Consumers Want. Available from: https://www.ted.com/talks/joseph_pine_on_what_consumers_want?language=en [Accessed 3 September 2018]

Pine, J. B., and Gilmore, J. H. (1998) Welcome to the Experience Economy, in *Harvard Business Review*, July-August, 97-105.

Pine, J. B., and Gilmore, J. H. (1999) *The Experience Economy*. Boston, MA: Harvard Business School Press.

Robinson, R. (2016) *Music Festivals and the Politics of Participation*, Routledge.

Sinek, S. (2011) *Start With Why: How great leaders inspire everyone to take action*. London: Penguin.

Tapscott, D., and Williams, A. (2008) *Wikinomics: How mass collaboration changes everything*. London: Atlantic Books.

3 Funding Your Festival

by Paul Kelly

After reading this chapter you should:

- Understand potential sources of funding

- Understand different motives of different fund givers and investors

- Understand the basics of strategic fundraising

- Understand where to find potential funders

Introduction

Every organisation needs money to get going, and this includes non-profit ventures. The reasons why they need it may vary, as may the sources. To get a venture off the ground it generally needs 'start-up funding', whether it be borrowing £50 off your auntie to pay for the costs of printing some flyers, or maybe setting up a limited company, or borrowing £250,000 from a bank or financial institution to open several shops and an office. Whichever it is, you will have costs. So, unless you have a large sum of cash lying idle, you will need to find a way of raising money to get things started.

Another reason for needing cash is if you know your venture, be it a new festival or a community arts venture, will not generate enough box office or other earned income to cover its costs, meaning you will be making a loss from the outset. In this case, if your project meets a well-articulated social need you will be able to make a case for start-up funding and money to cover its running costs. How you make the funding approach very much depends on your festival's ethos and its legal structure. We covered the first of these in Chapter 2 and the legal issues are covered in more detail in Chapter 6. This chapter will give you the framework that ties together your festival objectives, its legal structure and the potential funding sources as well as some of the techniques you will need for raising that all-important cash.

This chapter focuses mainly on fund-raising for not-for-profit or social enterprise festivals. The principles of persuading donors or bodies like an Arts Council are not that different from those of persuading commercial

investors, other than that the return you would promise commercial investors would be financial rather than social or artistic objectives. The chapter
starts by looking at those differences.

What is funding?

You need money but the first thing you actually need to know is about language. If you have a profit-making ethos then the word you use isn't 'funding', it's 'investment'. You need investment to get started and you will need
further investment to grow. What banks, social entrepreneurs and venture
capitalists want to see and be assured of is *return on investment* – ROI. They
invest in ventures that they see have the potential to be both financially successful and to grow – the word 'scalable' is often used. That means can you
turn a cottage industry with two or three people and a bright idea, into a
business manufacturing thousands of units or attracting thousands of people.

If you are a non-profit venture, or a charity, then you talk about 'funding'.
It's money that doesn't come back, at least not as money. Your ROI is social or
creative and can be harder to articulate. The outcomes are, in the short term,
very visible – like smiling faces – but they are very difficult to measure in tangible and what is called 'longitudinal' terms, i.e. change over a period of time.

So, it's important to know what your business ethos and motivation are,
as these will affect how you will pitch your case, the tools and approach you
will need, who you will be pitching to and the language you need to use
to persuade them. And regardless of whether you are intending to become
a commercially-oriented festival with a turnover of millions or an arts or
socially-focused festival running on a few thousand, you are very likely to be
pitching to someone for your money.

Industry example: Funding festivals

Within festival organisations there are many budding great ideas and fantastic arts projects, exhibitions, workshops, performances that will transform lives, that will challenge,
that will create a spectacle lasting long in the memory. The reality for most cultural organisations however is that this activity cannot happen without financial support, and that
this becomes increasingly difficult with increased budget pressures on Local Authorities
and other funding agencies. A project may find funding to get it started, but how do these
become sustainable year on year? This is particularly an issue for festivals.

Unfortunately, there isn't a simple formula to solve this, however at ArtReach we have
gained some experience in achieving funding for various projects and helping others to
do so as well. Most arts organisations today are having to gain considerable experience in
fundraising and finding creative ways to continue to cover the costs of their activity.

Having worked within a local authority context previously I am very aware of the challenges in public funding for cultural organisations, and that for many Local Authorities tough budgeting decisions are having to be made. The other side of this however is that many forward-thinking councils recognise the immense value of arts, heritage and culture in contributing to the local economy both directly and indirectly, and that they are an essential part of the solution to declining budgets. This in particular can be seen through the use of city centre festivals as highly visible activity animating urban public spaces, and there are clearly opportunities for cultural organisations to contribute.

Night of Festivals was created by ArtReach in 2010 and has since seen 17 versions being presented in various cities and towns including London's South Bank, Leicester, and Hounslow. The festival is able to support the wider economic aims of local authorities through helping to attract visitors and promote inward investment. Though this may not always result in a financial council contribution to the festival, they may be able to offer in-kind support such as the free use of a public space, officer time in providing advice and contacts, and promotion through their online networks to help the events to happen. It's important to be realistic about the contributions a council can make, but where there is a financial contribution, even if only relatively small, it has been vital in levering considerably more in additional funding from other sources such as Arts Council England.

For many reasons it is important to develop strong partnerships in delivering our festivals: they add value to programming; they help in engaging local audiences; but are also important in strengthening funding bids and widening the type of funds that can be applied for. For some of the festivals we deliver it may be that a community or Higher Education partner is in a position to apply for a fund that we are not able to access, but may link with a project that will contribute activity to the festival. For example, it may be that an artist is able to apply for funding to develop new work and expand their practice, and the work is able to be showcased at the festival.

The importance of partnership working can be seen in one of the festivals ArtReach directly manages, *Journeys Festival International*, which showcases the work of exceptional artists from the refugee and asylum seeker community and explores refugee experiences through great art. There are many cultural and community partners across all three cities in which the festival is delivered (Leicester, Manchester, and Portsmouth). Though there is some short-term core funding for the festival, there is still a considerable amount of project fundraising each year in which ArtReach works with its partners in order to keep developing the festival and producing its high-quality programme.

There is also the potential of linking with other festivals or venues all contributing from their budgets to commission new work. This has been successfully done with Outdoor Arts through consortiums like Without Walls which brings together a number of festivals to maximise resources in enabling the creation of new work, and may well offer a potential route to support the sustainability of festivals in the future.

Another area that ArtReach has been able to use to develop the sustainability of the organisation is to utilise the skills and experience within the team to offer consultancy support in various different areas. Income brought in through this work is able to help off-set some of the costs of delivering ArtReach's creative projects.

Finally, it is vital to recognise the amount of time involved in fundraising for festivals and to allow for this. As well as the actual time for decisions to be made by funders there is much time required in developing the concept, ensuring that partners are on board, and that you are clear in responding to the criteria of funds or aims of an organisation. From the beginning there needs to be a clear and realistic timeline for achieving funding, with some contingency allowed if funding is not successful first time round.

Simon Brown is Managing Director of ArtReach (Trust) Ltd, encompassing ArtReach (Events) Ltd

Who does the fundraising?

Large organisations will often have a dedicated department with one or more people researching and writing bids. These days they are usually called 'development departments' with development officers, as they are trying to raise funds to 'develop the organisation'. In smaller organisations the development aspect may be a part of a marketing team. In very small festivals fundraising will probably be down to the chief executive or artistic director, or in fact anyone who shows any signs of having the time, skills and persistence to get the job done.

Where there are dedicated development/fundraising staff, they will probably do the legwork including research and bid writing. In instances where high level meetings are required either to pitch for funding at a senior level or to negotiate sponsorship deals, the festival's chief executive or artistic director, owner or founder will probably take over and negotiate the final terms.

Potential sources of festival funding and income

The *Complete Fundraising Handbook* (CFH) (2012) identifies eight main ways of raising money. Individual donors

♦ Community fundraising (often collection tins and buckets)
♦ Trusts and foundations
♦ The National Lottery
♦ Company giving
♦ Government funding
♦ The European Union
♦ Income generation, including 'earned income'

Other experts cite as many as 17 different ways, which also include:

♦ Business sponsorship (different from company giving)

♦ Bank loans

♦ Venture capital (including social entrepreneurs)

♦ Crowd funding

♦ Friends and family

♦ Self-financing

Case study

When the festival promoter Simon Taffe wanted to start *The End of The Road Festival*, he re-mortgaged his house in order to do so. The festival lost money for the first four years. However, the Festival grew, more than doubling in size over 12 years became profitable after its first four years (The Bottom Line (2018) BBC).

In all of the above your biggest source of festival income ought to be earned or box office income. You may also raise significant sums through selling concessions, for example for food or beer sales. The more earned income you can show, the more likely you are to attract investors and funders on board. But you need to be careful to project your numbers carefully, or you could be badly out of pocket.

Case study

In the mid-1990s, a large local authority in the South West of England hosted a rock and pop festival called the *Heineken Music Festival* that toured Britain from 1990 to 1995 in a large Big Top tent with free admission. Heineken stopped touring the festival and the following year the council decided to stage its own similar festival which it called *Soundwaves*. The council invested £60,000 of its budget in the festival which attracted up to 80,000 people over the weekend. It raised over £30,000 in concession income from food and drink providers.

Your event objectives, legal structure and funding sources

Whom you apply to for investment or funding very much depends on your legal structure and your ethos and objectives. If you have a commercial focus that will restrict the types of people you can approach. If you have a non-profit distributing constitution or status then you will be able to apply to a range of funders. Registered charities can apply to charitable foundations. You might think therefore you really ought to be a charity as it opens the door to much more potential funding. But you need to be careful you don't do what is known as 'ambulance chasing'; this is coming up with proposals just because there is money available for that type of project. Don't change your vision and mission (or objectives) just to get funding. It will not ring true and you are very likely to distort your festival objectives and credibility.

It is easiest to explain the relationship between your aims, legal structure and potential funding sources as follows:

Individual donors/philanthropists

At the high end of the spectrum there are 'high net worth' individuals willing to donate or bankroll cultural activities they care about with very substantial sums. These people can be very hard to find, but this may be applicable if you are a commercial festival and can find a high net worth individual (in commercial theatre they are known as 'angel investors' or 'angels') to invest in your company and enable you to ride out the difficult early years. Equally if you can find a philanthropist who likes a particular artform and you are featuring some or all of that, you may be able to secure a donation. In 2016, 88% of the UK population gave money to at least one good cause amounting to £10.3 billion. This source grew by nearly 20% in 2017 (Pharoah, et al., 2017: 2) Sadly, less than 2% went to arts and culture, so there this is work to be done persuading the public that arts and festivals are worthy of their support.

Another source of individual donations is through legacy funding. It is money that people leave to good causes in their will. It's not something you can plan for. You may well have no idea it is coming. But the sums can be large. In the UK, Routley, Sargeant and Day report, "the legacy marketplace is currently worth around £2.82 billion or 14% of charities' voluntary income. Here the average residuary legacy is worth £46,600 and the average pecuniary gift £3,300" (Routley, et al., 2018: 4).

Case studies

In the early 2000s an amateur theatre company in a city in South West England were able to buy and fit out their own rehearsal rooms. It was because one of their former members had left them over £100,000 in his will. (Ross, 2018)

In January 2018, Richard Cousins, the Chief Executive of Compass Services Group and four members of his close family sadly died in a seaplane crash in Australia. He left £41 million to Oxfam. He had been a regular supporter of Oxfam, donating around £30 a month. Oxfam staff had no inkling that a donation of that size was a possibility. (BBC, 2018).

Community fundraising

Community fundraising is giving at the other end of the spectrum. It is a very 'friends and family' approach and the way that many charities earn income, especially through small repeat donations. It can take a lot of effort for comparatively little return. You might also be able to collect on site, with collection tins and buckets. But you may need a licence for such collections.

Crowdfunding

This is a form of community fundraising driven by social media. It has a commercial dimension as it is used to raise start-up funds for new products. It also has a social dimension in raising money for non-profit projects. There are a number of web platforms designed to help you, such as Kickstarter or Patreon. You decide how much you want to raise and set up a funding page, where a short video explaining your project and its aims often helps. You then approach your friends, family and supporters to donate. You need to offer them something, preferably unique or exclusive, in return. If you have strong or extensive social networks, or the ability to connect with other online networks, this can be a very good way of raising start-up funding. To be most effective, you will need a communications plan behind it, as it is essentially a marketing campaign in itself. But you can also build awareness and interest in your festival this way too.

Most crowdfunding sites take a small percentage of the money you raise – usually 5% to 8%. In some cases, if you don't raise your funding target, you get nothing and the money is returned to the donors, so check the site's terms and conditions very carefully before launching your campaign.

In 2018, a jazz festival in South West England raised £20,000 from crowd funding, so it is definitely worth looking at. It is a lot of work though, so often better for specific campaigns and projects rather than regular or annual funding needs.

Trusts and foundations

There are around 4,500 trusts and foundations in England and Wales (Botting Herbst and Norton, 2012:135) and more abroad that support a wide range of good causes. All of these are charities, often with big capital sums invested from which they get an annual income, some or all of which they give in grants. They give around £4.1 billion a year (Pharoah et al., 2017:1). The top 300 foundations gave £2.9 billion in 2017 (ibid). You nearly always need to be a charity yourself to receive funding from trusts. Some of these trusts are large, well established and have very specific criteria and proper application forms. Others are smaller with less clear guidelines and just require a written proposal and a budget. The Directory of Social Change publishes several annual directories of trusts and foundations and runs a web-based version. Neither are particularly cheap, though they are very comprehensive. Your local library may subscribe to the directories or even the web service, and local Councils for Voluntary Service or Volunteer Bureau may subscribe, so members can access them that way.

The National Lottery

Contrary to many people's belief, the National Lottery does not give grants. The National Lottery, in all its many forms, is currently run by a commercial company, Camelot, which is required to give 25% of its revenue to four 'Lottery Distributors' often called the 'good causes'. These are:

- ♦ Arts Council England – which supports arts projects
- ♦ The Heritage Lottery – heritage projects
- ♦ Sport England – sports initiatives
- ♦ The Big Lottery – various social and community initiatives .

Arts Council England (ACE) has several funding schemes that you can apply to. The most relevant is the National Lottery Project Grants (NLPG) scheme. This has two levels of grants: under £15,000 and from £15,000 to £100,000. You will be expected to find at least 10% match funding and usually a lot more. The scheme has two main criteria: artistic quality and public engagement. Applications are made through an online form which is quite complex to complete. ACE supports a number of UK festivals, some through NLPG project funding and some through its National Portfolio Organisations (NPOs). These are larger arts bodies given four-year grants which cover the artistic programme, staffing and administration costs. The NPO bidding process is more complex, more demanding and highly competitive. It is possible to secure three-year funding from the Arts Council's National Lottery Project Grants, but this will not support full-time staffing costs. ACE has extensive advice available online. If you are considering starting a new festival and are thinking of applying to ACE, you should get advice from them direct or talk to someone who has made a bid to them. (Arts Council England, 2018)

The **Heritage Lottery** (HLF) may be willing to support festivals if they have a strong heritage aspect, which can be intangible, such as preservation of local cultural heritage in the form of traditions. Some buildings you might want to use for your festival could also benefit. HLF also has online advice and the application process is simpler than ACE's. You will need some match funding. It is likely that this source will be applicable to one-off festivals linked to a specific anniversary or site. (Heritage Lottery Fund, 2018)

The **Big Lottery** fund schemes have a community dimension and periodically these have included festivals that enhance the community. In 2017 it accounted for 11% of all British fund-giving (Pharoah et al., 2017:4) Their website shows the schemes they are running at the time. (Big Lottery, 2018)

Although the National Lottery is not officially public funding (that is, it's not tax monies given in grants by national or local government), it is treated in much the same way. The grant-makers expect to see benefit to or for the public, as this helps to justify the National Lottery as something different from private gambling concerns. It is important to remember this when applying.

Company giving

Some larger UK companies are concerned to demonstrate a relationship with the communities they operate in. This is known as corporate social responsibility (CSR). Their CSR initiatives include giving money and help in-kind (i.e. free goods, services or access, rather than direct cash) to activities that help the community. The purpose of such activity is to ensure the company has a reputation locally as a good citizen and a good employer. It is part of their company public relations (PR) strategy. Their support may be in the form of equipment or staff time. The Directory of Social Change publishes an annual directory listing company giving which may be worth a look if your festival has a strong community dimension and you have large companies in your area (Reynolds et al., 2017). Company giving amounts to £750 - £800 million a year (Botting Herbst and Norton, 2012:169)

Case study

A large city in South West England developed a community opera project in partnership with English National Opera, The Dolphin Opera with a libretto by Vikram Seth and music by Alec Roth. The local branch of Marks and Spencer seconded a middle manager to the project for 12 months to fundraise, develop and co-ordinate it, which was worth approximately £30,000 - £40,000 in salary and benefits.

This value of this time could also be used as match funding for other grants. Grant-makers like to see other institutions validating the organisations they support as it shows they are not dependent on one form of support.

Business sponsorship

The source of business sponsorship is the same as company giving, but the motive is entirely different. With sponsorship, companies are seeking a tangible return for their investment. This may be brand association and activation, hospitality opportunities for corporate entertaining, new customers, product placement or even staff training (Anderton, 2015). Business sponsorship can start as low as £100 or so. But it can also be substantial. *Rock in Rio*, a festival with editions across the world, is funded almost entirely by business sponsorship. Global brands run entire stages. Others work with the festival to distribute tickets to their customer base. One bank set up karaoke machines to look like cash points across the city. When customers sang the festival theme tune, the machines dispensed a pair of free tickets (Martin, 2016).

You will need to judge what your financial needs are, who your potential sponsors might be, and what your offer could be to them. This can be a highly competitive area. At the top end of the scale, large rock and pop festivals playing to big crowds can attract sponsors seeking to get their brand across to large numbers of people having a good time. At the other end of the scale, some professional services like solicitors, accountants, financial services companies may be interested in small sponsorships of festivals with a more traditional artistic theme which help them reach a new clientele. One estate agent in the East Midlands of England supported a local community festival in a neighbourhood park by advertising it on the boards placed outside the properties it was selling in the vicinity.

Bank loans

You will probably need to set up a business bank account, especially if you become or have a limited company. Your bank may give you an overdraft facility, but they may require some sort of security – such as your house. That means if you become insolvent, without the means to pay the debt from the business, the bank can force you to sell your house.

Without some form of guarantee, bank loans can be hard to obtain. The bank will almost certainly want to see a business plan for the next three years and income projections. Festivals probably don't fit their idea of a secure business with good growth prospects, unless you are well-established with business accounts going back a number of years, or a secure funding source, such as an Arts Council three-year grant.

Venture capital and social entrepreneurship

Venture capitalists are people who have built up a lot of surplus cash and are interested in making more. That's why they will consider investing in your business if you can show them good prospects that you will make them money. They may also give you valuable business advice and contacts. Festivals will probably be too small and not scalable enough to interest them, though one or two larger festivals, including *Love Supreme,* were able to re-finance through a form of venture capital once established.

Case study

Ingenious Media is a London-based cultural venture capital firm which invests in film, television and live entertainment. They have invested over £8 billion in the creative sector since their formation in 1998 and over £100 million in festivals including *Rewind, Love Supreme, SW4* and *Boardmasters* festivals. (Ingenious Media (2018)

Social entrepreneurs want a financial return on their investment but are more interested in the social outcomes than the scalability of business ventures. They sometimes work as consortia and it may be worth researching to see if there are any such consortia operating in your area. Social Enterprise UK is a good starting point (www.socialenterprise.org.uk/about-us). In other cases, the festival itself is a form of social enterprise. It operates as a for-profit organisation would, but rather than distributing profits to investors or shareholders, surpluses are either reinvested in the festival, or distributed to the nominated beneficiary communities. *Glastonbury* Festival donates a percentage of its profits to WaterAid, Oxfam and Greenpeace as well as a long list of local charities and community groups.

Both venture capitalists and social entrepreneurs will want to see your business plan and hear a short, sharp pitch of no more than a minute or two.

Friends and family and self-financing

If your start-up costs are quite modest, you may have parents or relatives who can help get you off the ground. But remember, you will want to be in a position where you can pay them back with interest as well as love, so treat them as a bank even if they don't ask for a business plan or a pitch – which they've probably heard over the months anyway. Perhaps a better way is to set up a crowdfunding initiative and get your relatives to contribute. Their donations may well encourage others and this means you also spread the load beyond your immediate family. A by-product of crowdfunding may be that it helps build a following at the same time.

Case study

Successful fundraising requires you to be fleet of foot, flexible and imaginative. In 2000, one of the authors raised £19,000 from PESCA, an obscure European fund, designed to give support to towns with fishing fleets that were transitioning to a new economy. The city in question was by the sea and had a fishing fleet and had experienced social and economic problems. The bulk of the grant was used to support a live outdoor performance by the BBC Concert Orchestra of Friday Night Is Music Night, a long-running popular Radio 2 show. The BBC paid the musicians and the PESCA funding went towards the infrastructure – principally a big outdoor stage and PA system. The PESCA grant needed some match funding in cash or kind, so the BBC quoted £50,000 as the cash cost of the BBC concert orchestra. The UK PESCA administrators were delighted as, for a £19,000 investment, the city benefited to the tune of £69,000. A significant social return for their investment.

Government funding and the European Union

The UK government does give grants, and grants to the voluntary sector amounted to £15 billion in 2017 (Pharoah et al., 2017:6). But those voluntary sector grants are for social or welfare schemes and other government grants are generally speaking for large scale commercial ventures. A number of organisations including the Directory of Social Change publish an annual Directory of Government funding schemes. The European Union (EU) also offers grants to cultural activities and their grants can be substantial. However, you usually need a partnership of three or more European countries to be eligible and the application process can be complex and lengthy. Some European funds are accessed directly from Brussels, others have been managed by UK regional offices. With Britain planning to leave Europe (at the time of writing) access to these funds is likely to end.

Fundraising psychology

It is very easy to approach fundraising as if you are holding out a begging bowl and are grateful for any crumbs you can get. Of course, you need to treat fund-givers with respect and courtesy, even if they turn you down time and again. But in many cases, the job of fund-givers is to give away money. So long as you do a professional job and give them what you have agreed, you are actually helping them do their job and meet their objectives.

Clearly, it's slightly different with individual donors, philanthropists and sponsors. But even here you should be able to give them unique opportunities, possibly including the chance to meet and talk to artists they have long admired or to meet and network with fellow business people in a conducive setting; thus do not undersell yourselves or the unique opportunities you can offer. What you are holding is not a begging bowl, but a gateway to a world that they may have longed to be part of. Your job is to find out the sort of offer or opportunity that will turn interest into commitment.

Case study

Bernard Ross, the UK fundraiser and Director of the National Arts Fundraising School, tells a wonderful story of a leading theatre in Glasgow which around 30 years ago was negotiating a major three-year sponsorship deal with a large Scottish bank. There had been a number of meetings and all was well on track for the conclusion of a deal. Just before the sponsorship agreement was due to be signed, the Marketing Manager of the bank decided to pay the theatre a personal visit so he could fully understand the nature of the organisation his bank was about to sponsor. It was just before Christmas and the theatre was performing Peter Pan. The Marketing Manager and the theatre's Head of Fundraising walked into the empty auditorium. The Marketing Manager looked at the stage and wistfully said 'You know I always wanted to fly.' Five minutes later he was in Peter Pan's harness and flying across the empty stage. The sponsorship deal was duly signed the next day.

Fundraising strategy

You should now know enough about the potential funding sources and the way they will relate to your unique festival proposition to be able to work up a fundraising or financing strategy. That strategy is important for two reasons. First, it will provide a focus so the limited time you have to research and pursue investment is spent profitably. Second, the funding prospects and amount you are seeking will feed into your budget, which we will come to in the next chapter. Your strategy needn't be lengthy – you could write it in a page of A4 or less. It should identify:

- ◆ The types of funding that you could secure,
- ◆ Some possible targets
- ◆ Amounts you are seeking to raise and
- ◆ The benefits to the sponsors/funders/investors.

Your strategy will be aided by some detailed research into funding schemes, potential local sponsors and trusts and foundations if relevant.

The funding pitch

In some cases you will be writing applications, in other cases you will need to prepare a pitch to send out or give verbally to possible funders. You need to keep the pitch short and succinct. Decision makers are likely to be busy people with little time to wade through large amounts of detail. If they like the initial proposal they may ask for more detail. Your pitch should be no longer than one page of A4. The opening paragraph, maybe four or five lines, should contain all the salient elements. The director of one large charitable trust fund that received thousands of applications said if he couldn't get the essence of the proposal from the first two lines of the bid, it would get rejected. That's an extreme case, but a useful message to bear in mind.

Driven by enthusiasm as you will be, it is very easy to pitch your festival in terms of features – what you will be doing – rather than in terms of benefits to the fund-giver. You need to think carefully about the benefits you can offer your potential funders. If they are trusts or bodies like an Arts Council, what they are seeking will probably be set out in guidance notes or aims and objectives. Remember, public funders and charitable foundations are not aiming to satisfy themselves, rather they want you to explain how your festival will improve the lives of the individuals and communities they support. Read their guidance carefully and use the phrases they use – with examples of how you will apply them – in your application. That is what they will be interested in.

If you are approaching business sponsors, are you offering them exclusive access or experiences, business hospitality and networking opportunities, branding opportunities (only really valid in the case of large audiences), staff development opportunities or something different? It can be hard to know what businesses are looking for without talking to them. The initial gatekeepers are often company marketing or corporate social responsibility (CSR) departments, so a call to them to try and elicit interest might be a useful first step and a meeting if you can get one, even better. People generally find it harder to ignore a personal or phone approach than an email, although they might ask you to send more details afterwards.

Another approach is to join your local Chamber of Commerce or Business Improvement District (your festival, after all, is a business) and go to their network meetings. Talk to businesses. It can be surprising what they tell you. There may be a burning issue or problem they have, which you might be able to help them with.

Case study

Many towns and cities now have Business Improvement Districts or BIDS. These raise subscriptions from local businesses and can also draw on other public and private funding streams. The resulting budget is used to make improvements to town and city centres and increase footfall and trade. These can include things like waste management, environmental improvements, town centre wardens and also events, including festivals. A recent festival funding approach to a town centre BID elicited that a key issue was increasing footfall and traffic to a hitherto affluent area of the town now suffering from shop closures. A bid for just under £3,000 was submitted and included the offer to list all the businesses in that part of town in the back of the A4 festival programme and offer low cost adverts at £25 for a quarter page as well as the usual BID logo on all literature. The festival included one concert with over 100 performers so those businesses were offered the opportunity to offer exclusive discounts and festival tickets as prizes or incentives. The funding bid was successful, and the festival delivered the proposal.

Persistence, visuals, statistics

Fundraising of whatever sort is not an exact science. You may feel you have the perfect bid. You may feel your proposal was warmly received. You may identify a funding prospect for whom you can provide the perfect solution. You may apply to Arts Council England and get a polite reply of, "not this time". You need to be prepared for rejections and setbacks. It happens to every fundraiser. You've just got to keep researching and keep bidding. Fundraising is a percentage game. The more you apply, the more chance you have of success. Persistence is everything – it's not you, it's them.

There are ways you can increase your chances though. A well designed and well written proposal gives funders confidence your final festival will be something they will want to be associated with. And a picture tells a thousand words. If your festival is up and running, make sure you get as many good quality photographs as you can. If you are attracting thousands of people then get a photograph that shows that – find someone with a drone and get an aerial shot if you can. If it's a smaller audience but they are engaged or happy, get photos of them and crop them if you have to. If you have star performers or well-known artists at your event, get photos of them in front of your festival logo. Tweet it out and post it on Instagram so sponsors know you can give them that kind of promotion, too. All of this adds to your visibility and credibility and creates a positive sense, which gives funders confidence. Similarly, if you have available statistics, audience numbers, website hits, social media likes or whatever it is that demonstrates engagement with the public, collate them and use them – an infographic is a popular way of presenting this data visually and creatively.

The ask

Writing pitches, bids or applications to people you have never met is easy. But meeting them in person and asking them to commit a sum of money is much, much harder and to some people almost impossible. Yet the ask is the crucial culmination to all that research and preparation. It is very easy to be in the room talking to the person who can give you that much needed sum and to fail to make the ask and close the deal. If you can identify someone with the sales skills to close such deals, whether a member of the team or a board member, delegate the ask to them – or get them to train you. That is far better than walking out from a warm encounter and failing to ask for the money. In addition, sometimes the opportunity won't come in a formal meeting. It may come in an informal encounter, at a business networking meeting, a drinks reception, or in a corridor somewhere. Be ready to make the pitch and make the ask. If you find it hard, practice with your staff or with friends. Remember you are not asking for money to line your own pockets; it's going to make an incredible festival that will benefit your local area, or art form, or children, or older people, or whoever you have decided to do it for.

Should you employ a consultant?

If you feel you lack the expertise or the time to raise the funds for your festival, you could consider employing a fundraising consultant. The advantages are that they will have a track record of success and considerable experience. The drawbacks are they will charge you. This might be a daily fee or a percentage of what they raise. They may come from outside your area and therefore lack local knowledge, or from outside the cultural sector and not really understand your offer. In the final assessment, the amount you are seeking may not justify the investment. Some consultants work on a 'no win, no fee' basis, but you have to be careful how much time they are willing and able to commit on that basis. Generally fundraising consultants are used for big schemes, often building related, seeking to raise large sums where a substantial consultancy fee can be justified as a relatively small percentage of the overall project budget.

Where to find more advice

Over the last 20 years, fundraising and development have become profession-alised roles and specialised roles. Professional support bodies have grown up to supervise and regulate the industry to ensure it is ethical as well as effective. These bodies include:

◆ The Institute of Fundraising – www.institute-of-fundraising.org.uk

◆ Arts Funding and Philanthropy – artsfundraising.org.uk/

◆ The Funding Network – www.thefundingnetwork.org.uk

◆ National Arts Fundraising School – nationalartsfundraisingschool.com

◆ Cause 4 – www.cause4.co.uk

Most of these offer valuable online guidance, some offer 1:1 or online train-ing, some offer certification as well as codes of practice.

Summary

You are going to need some funding from somewhere to get your festival off the ground, whether that comes from your own savings, your credit card, a grant, sponsorship, crowd funding or 'the Bank of Mum and Dad'. Each of these will require slightly different approaches and that will depend on the nature of your festival, your aspirations and the legal structure you have chosen. Even if you are up and running you will probably need funding or finance to grow and get to the next level.

To raise the money you need, you are going to have to pitch your project. That means people need to know about it and like your idea. Again, differ-ent funders have different aims, so you need to think carefully about who is likely to support it. It's very easy to be enthusiastic about your idea. But you may be more successful if you think about your potential funders or inves-tors. What are their motives, what might interest them and how can your festival help fulfil some of their aims? On the one hand those aims might be about brand awareness and profile, they may be about business hospitality, they may be bringing about social change in some way or about developing a particular artform. You can learn a lot from a bit of basic research and there is a great deal of information online. Read the words used by your potential funders. Does your festival align with them? And what can you offer them that is unique and distinctive? People offering you money whether it's a non-returnable grant or a commercial investment, are human. What makes them tick? What takes their fancy? What corporate objectives are they dedicated to achieve? How can you pitch your proposal in a way that helps them say yes? If you meet them, after doing the pitch, don't forget 'the ask'. It may be the only opportunity you get. Don't expect instant success. If you get turned down, it's probably not you, it's them. Though do think about any feedback they give you and use that to make your proposal even better.

References

Anderton, C. (2015) Branding, sponsorship and the music festival. In: McKay, G. (ed.) *The Pop Festival: History, music, media, culture*. London: Bloomsbury.

Arts Council England (2018) Funding, www.artscouncil.org.uk/funding [Accessed 29 October 2018]

BBC (2018) Businessman Richard Cousins 'leaves £41m' to Oxfam. www.bbc.co.uk/news/uk-45256241 [Accessed 29 October 2018]

Botting Herbst, N. and Norton, M. (2012) *The Complete Fundraising Handbook*. London: Directory of Social Change

Heritage Lottery Fund (2018) Looking for funding? https://www.hlf.org.uk/looking-funding [Accessed 29 October 2018]

Ingenious Media (2018) Our expertise Live Entertainment www.ingeniousmedia.co.uk/our-expertise/live-entertainment/ [Accessed 29 October 2018]

Martin, V. (2016) Rock in Rio: The Festival. In: Newbold, C. and Jordan, J. (eds.) *Focus on World Festivals: Contemporary case studies and perspectives*. Oxford: Goodfellow.

Pharoah, C., Walker, C. and Goddard, K. (2017) *Giving Trends 2017*. London: Association of Charitable Foundations. London: Directory of Social Change

Reynolds, J., Huyton, J. and Hobson, C. (2017) *The Guide to UK Company Giving* (11th ed.) 2017/18. London: Directory of Social Change

Ross B. (2018) National Arts Fundraising School [webinar] 18 September, The Management Centre webinar series

Routley, C., Sargeant, A., and Day, H. (2018) *Everything Research Can Tell Us About Legacy giving in 2018: A Literature Review*, Legacy Voice. http://legacyvoice.co.uk/wp-content/uploads/2018/05/Legacy-Voice-lit-review_full-report_03.pdf, [Accessed 15/10/2018]

The Big Lottery (2018) Funding, https://www.biglotteryfund.org.uk/funding [Accessed 29 October 2018]

The Bottom Line (2018). The Festival Business. BBC Radio 4. 26 July.

4 Creating Your Festival Budget

by Paul Kelly

After reading this part you should:

- Understand the principles of constructing a festival budget

- Understand how to scope cost estimates and assess best value

- How to format your budget so it is a working tool

- The importance of cashflow and how to construct one

- The basics of VAT

Introduction

The director of a company specialising in festival support services had just come back from a contract at London's Hyde Park, a big outdoor event, headlined by The Eurythmics, a fashionable band at the time. "What were they like?" an excited music enthusiast asked him. "I've no idea," came the droll reply, "I spent the whole evening unblocking the toilets" (Toby Short of Rock City Stage Crew, 1999).

To some, festival budgeting is a bit like that, it's a task that seems dull boring and repetitive, but it's also incredibly important. Doing endless budget projections – and they will keep changing – keeping a track of estimates and invoices, managing your cashflow and then counting the pennies at the end of the event is hardly glamorous. But if the finances get all blocked up or don't flow in the right way, the smell will be pretty unpleasant and, in extreme cases you might even have to sell all your worldly possessions to sort out the mess..

Good budgeting is crucial to the long-term success of your festival and also your peace of mind. It's not difficult, so long as you are careful and methodical. As your event grows, the financial numbers will obviously get bigger and some of the control issues get more complicated. But the principles remain the same. A growing festival will need to get the advice of an accountant, especially where tax matters are concerned. This chapter can only serve as an introduction; it aims to cover the following things:

- How to create your festival budget
- How to estimate costs
- How to control expenditure
- What a cashflow is and why it is important
- How to estimate ticket sales
- What VAT is and its potential impact on your finances
- What an audit is and why you might need one
- Taxation.

Even if you are not your festival's finance director, it is useful to understand how to budget so you can have a sensible conversation with the person who is, and so you don't get caught out unable to answer a question in meetings with your board or a potential investor.

Planning your budget

People who choose to work in festivals and other events are often driven by the enthusiasm for the subject or content be it a flower show, a drama festival or an electronic music festival, to take but three examples. A budget may not seem as creative or interesting as working with artists, but it plays a key role in translating the excitement of the idea into something deliverable. Your budget is a key part of the planning process. You will remember Kipling, who we introduced in the Festival Design chapter. His six honest men also apply to constructing your budget. For example, here are some sample questions you could use in a budget planning template:

Who is overall responsible for the budget planning and for approving expenditure? (it may not be the same person)

What are the likely costs and income going to be?

When will you have to pay people and when might the income come in?

Where are you going to find the money you need?

How on earth are we going to sell that many tickets?

Why are you paying so much for...?

Figure 4.1: Budget questions

What is a budget?

Put very simply, a budget is an estimated list of expenditure (costs) and receipts (income) with a 'bottom line' or 'out-turn' showing whether you have made a profit or a loss – or as people in the non-profit sector tend to describe it – a surplus or a deficit. Both your expenditure (costs) and your income (receipts) are likely to fall into specific categories. For example, costs might include:

♦ Artistic costs

♦ Venue costs

♦ Production costs including equipment hire

♦ Marketing and publicity costs.

Your income might include:

♦ Ticket/box office income

♦ Grants and sponsorships

♦ Income from 'concessions' (food/drink stalls etc)

♦ Merchandise (programme and T shirt sales)

It is worth giving these categories a bit of thought before starting to put your figures together as it will help you structure your budget. Think about all the different areas and aspects of your festival and then what the expenditure and income implications are. We have a sample budget template further on in this chapter that will help you. But if you do this without looking at the template it will get you into the right way of thinking.

Budget objectives

Our budget definition includes the word 'estimated'. You are estimating your income and expenditure. A budget is your best guess. As such, with your budget you are aiming to estimate costs and income to make sure they and you meet your objectives, whether this is to 'balance your budget' or 'break-even' or to make a healthy profit. Be clear on what your financial objectives are, make sure these dovetail with your overall objectives (your mission) and use your budget to help ensure you are meeting them.

Best guesses, estimates and research

When you start putting a budget together for a new festival, or a new strand of work, a lot of it will be guesswork. But don't leave it there. You need to turn guesses into actual figures. You may be lucky enough, if you have previous years' budgets to work from, to be able to look at actual costs and sales figures for your festival that will provide a guide. But even for festivals that have been going for many years, there are likely to be artistic choices that ask you to do something new and that requires some research. For example, if you need to hire a hall or a theatre, bring in lighting, hire chairs, a generator, portable loos or any one of the many things your festival might need, go and get some quotes and turn your guess into an actual figure. Two or three estimates of the same type will soon give you a feel and flavour for what is normal for that type of equipment. Suppliers are generally happy to talk new potential clients through the main issues they come across in their industry. A crane operator, for example, might point out you need to apply for a road closure you hadn't thought about, so this kind of research does more than give you figures – it helps with your operational planning, too.

But where and how?

First of all, do you have access to previous year's figures? If not, are there other similar events not too far away? If so, approach them and ask about the suppliers they use and roughly what you might expect to pay. Industry bodies such as the British Arts Festivals Association (BAFA), can put you in touch with local festivals, and provide information on specialist suppliers. Alternatively, you can use trade directories relevant to your area. Search on categories, for example staging. Contact the companies and ask for a quote.

Specification

Before you get your quote, though, you need to be able to specify what it is you want. Where this involves technical matters, the more detail you can go into the better. If you need 100 chairs for your event, should they be folding ones? Do they need to have arms? Should they have padded seating? Do the chairs need to be numbered? When should they be delivered and when can they be collected? All of that is fairly straightforward. But without that detail you may either not get the chairs you want or get a quote which does not relate to your specific needs.

It gets more challenging when technical equipment is required. Suppose you need to hire a PA system for your event. What's it for? A talk? A band? A musical? If so, what type of band or musical? Will the band/performers want foldback or monitors? (What is foldback?) How many microphones/channels will the PA mixer need? Will you need a separate monitor mix? How powerful a PA system will you need? Do you want sound clarity or volume or both? So, how big is the hall or the field? Will they provide a sound engineer or are you supplying that? Are you required to provide backline? (Backline includes amplifiers, drum kits and even musical instruments). Where and what is the power supply? How long have they got to set up the system? Can it be left overnight? Do you need a lighting rig or is there in-house lighting?

In many cases it's easiest to set up a meeting with the prospective supplier at the venue you will be using. You can talk through the requirements, discuss the various issues and they will get a clear understanding of the venue or location and any issues or challenges it creates. The more you get to know, in general terms, about staging, sound systems, lighting, marquees and the like, the better you will get at specifying and also at budgeting. Because you will have a growing knowledge of the technical equipment required to stage a successful event, what it costs, what you don't need and, vitally, what crucial piece of equipment might be missing from your technical list and budget.

This is true of all areas, even if you have in-house experts when you are budgeting you will at times have to negotiate with your marketing director or set designer about the budget available, and the more knowledge you demonstrate about what is needed in their area, the easier you will find those negotiations because you might be able to help them identify cost savings. For example, at one outdoor concert, the crucial missing piece of equipment turned out to be some clothes pegs to hold the music in place on music stands on what was a rather blustery day.

As you can see from the above, you may need to get quite a lot of detail ready before you can go and get quotes, and by doing that you are also ensuring you can compare like with like.

Researching suppliers

In putting your budget together, you will probably need to undertake research into different suppliers. A key component of those comparisons will be cost. But is the best price the only factor? What about reliability? Quality? Communication – can you easily reach the people if you need them? Remember, your festival is likely happening during other people's leisure time, so will they answer the phone on a Sunday afternoon? Sometimes it can boil down to who you like dealing with the most. When you are under pressure during the festival, this matters. Sometimes it can be worth paying a little extra for people who are a pleasure to work with.

Case study: Best value

A local authority was seeking to make budget savings and realised that by pooling purchasing services they could buy in bulk and save money. So, the council employed a procurement officer and undertook a best value exercise to specify the items that needed to be bought and identify the most cost-effective supplier. The festivals and events team at the council directly managed a number of events and was told that all the services purchased for these festivals had to be part of the new procurement service. The new system demanded that three comparative quotes were sourced on all supplies. The team leader could understand how this might apply to something like portable loos. But how, he asked were they going to compare a string quartet, a samba band and a street performer who juggles toy rabbits, to ensure best value for money? Or even three string quartets? Having asked the question, he was left free to programme the events (i.e. choose the artistic programme suppliers) without the need for competitive quotes.

This case study is a slightly long-winded way of saying that there are some things that you can get comparable quotes on and there are some things that you simply cannot compare in purely financial terms. A leading exception to the rule about getting comparable quotes is artists and creative suppliers. By and large they will have a price. It may be negotiable (see further on), but in all probability it won't be directly comparable. Everybody will have creative preferences, but objectively in this case comparing one artist to another is often a false comparison. So, make sure when getting estimates and quotes you can compare like with like.

Building your budget: Structure and format

To start your budgeting process you will need a clear festival plan, even if in outline. That should at the very least define how many events you are staging, in what type of venues, and the sort of technical equipment you might need to make it work. The more detail you have, the more accurate your first draft budget will be. With the above information you can start to devise and write your budget. This might seem scary or arduous. Actually, it shouldn't be and the more you do it, the quicker it gets.

An experienced festival producer can probably put an outline event budget together in as little as an hour, depending on the scale and the complexity of the event. That first draft might not tell you everything. But it will be a starting point and give the overall feel of the finances. It helps answer the question of whether the proposal or idea is viable. It also helps to identify where more work is needed, what you know and what you know you don't know, so where more research is needed.

That's all well and good, but how do you put all this together? There are several ways of constructing a festival budget. The two approaches focused on here are top down and bottom up.

Top-down budgeting

In top-down budgeting you put some headings together (see p. 71) and then put some estimated broad figures against them and see how they look. Are you facing a massive loss or a nice fat profit? Does your proposed event look viable?

If you are working as part of a team, top-down budgeting can be a useful first step for negotiating with 'heads of department' who will be responsible for spending the money and achieving their respective outcomes, if your organisation is large enough to have them. This approach gives you a tangible figure to focus on, but one that you are not so attached to that you are unwilling to be flexible. It can help you with fundraising as it gives a good target to aim for that hasn't involved you in lots of detailed, time-consuming work planning for an event you cannot afford.

Bottom-up budgeting

While top-down budgeting can be a good and quick starting point, ultimately you will also need a 'bottom-up' approach. That means doing detailed costings on every aspect of your festival – and if you have lots of events in lots of venues, then costings for each one of these. From this you may end up with a very big budget with lots of figures. But it also ought to be a very accurate one.

Spreadsheet software like Excel will help you to avoid arithmetical mistakes and make it easier to adjust your budget when you make changes – and you will be making lots of changes! If you don't know how to use a spreadsheet, there are lots of free online video courses on using Excel as well as paid for training courses. If you are part of a team and someone knows about spreadsheets, ask them to work on it with you. You will come to value the new skill you will acquire.

An important tip about budgets and spreadsheets

You will inevitably run through lots of budget variations and versions. It can sometimes be useful to be able to track the changes to these. To do this make sure you put the date and a version number in the spreadsheet file name. When you update the budget, don't just save it. Save it under a new name with the latest date and a new file version number. For example you might start with a budget called Cliveden Arts Festival budget v1 - 15 Oct 2019. You may then revise that in November. Save this version as say, Cliveden Arts Festival budget v1a - 12 Nov 2019. This means you always know precisely which budget version you are working from and which is the latest budget version and you can also track back to look at earlier versions if you need to.

As we said earlier, budgets are estimated lists of expenditure (costs) and receipts (income) with a 'bottom line' or 'out turn' showing whether you have made a profit or a loss. In putting your budget together it doesn't matter whether you start with income or expenditure, though if you start with income it tends to focus the mind on the fact that you will need some.

Budget formatting tip

Some people like to put income and expenditure side by side on the spreadsheet. Some put one above the other. That's a matter of personal preference. But if you put income and expenditure side by side in a spreadsheet, and you need to add extra lines for new budget categories, it will throw out the neat format you have. It is much better to have income and expenditure in one long column, with one above the other as in the example below.

Structuring your budget

Budgets can have masses of information and if you are not careful you can get lost in the detail, that's why it's important that you structure it. Excel allows you to have as many pages of information as you want and you can link these pages. If it's a big and complex event, it helps to have a simple opening budget page with totals and then more detailed workings, for example, marketing costs on separate spreadsheet pages That way you can clearly see the overview without being overwhelmed by too many numbers.

With each of the headings, income and expenditure you can add some general sub-headings and costs. Precisely what these will be will depend on the nature of your event, but here are some examples:

Income

    Ticket income (sometimes called earned income)

    Other sales (merchandise, programme or t-shirt sales)

    Grants

    Commercial sponsorship (or business sponsorship)

    Donations (could include crowdfunding, or that could be a separate category)

    Raffle(s)

    Concessions (fees from stall holders)

Total Income

Expenditure

    Artists costs

    Artist rider costs (see below)

    Booking costs (ticket agency fees (average 5 percent), credit card commissions)

    Venue hire

    Production costs (stage, sound, lights, décor, signage)

    Marketing and publicity

    Insurances and licences

    Staffing or organiser costs

    National Insurance (if you are employing permanent staff)

    Royalties and PRS

    Volunteer expenses (or similar)

    Contingency (see note below)

Total Expenditure

Here is a very simple spreadsheet example based on the above. We have added in a percentage column which Excel can calculate for you automatically, as this can be useful to see the proportion of costs in each category to the total.

Income		Percentage	Notes
Ticket income	£ 7,500	64%	500 x £15
Merchandise sales	£ 1,200	10%	100 x £12
Grants	£ 1,500	13%	
Business sponsorship	£ 500	4%	
Donations	£ 100	1%	
Raffle(s)	£ 750	6%	
Concessions	£ 100	1%	
Total Income	**£ 11,650**	**100%**	
Expenditure			
Artists costs	£ 2,500	24%	
Artist Rider costs	£ 250	2%	
Cost of Merchandise	£ 1,000	10%	
Ticket Booking costs	£ 375	4%	
Venue hire	£ 350	3%	at 5% of sales
Production costs	£ 750	7%	
Marketing and publicity	£ 2,500	24%	
Insurances and licences	£ 150	1%	
Staffing or organiser costs	£ 1,500	15%	
National Insurance	£ -	0%	
Royalties and PRS	£ 360	4%	at 4.8%
Volunteer expenses	£ 250	2%	
Contingency	£ 250	2%	
Total Expenditure	**£ 10,235**	**100%**	
Profit/Loss	**£ 1,415**		

Figure 4.2: Small festival budget

How much budget flexibility do you have in the above budget?

The budget shows a profit/surplus of £1,415. In addition, you have £250 in the budget as 'contingency'. So, you actually have £1,665 'budget flexibility' so long as you sell 500 tickets as projected. Your ticket prices are £15 so you could undersell by 111 tickets and still break even (you of course won't target to do this. You'll actually target to sell 111 more than you have budgeted for). But if you did undersell by 111, your ticket commission would also be lower, as would your PRS payment (music licenses), as both are income related.

In addition, you have budgeted 24% of you estimated expenditure on marketing. That's a good percentage. But when you do a detailed marketing budget, will you need all of that £2,500 or could you reduce the marketing budget without risking the ticket sales? What would 15% of your expenditure on marketing buy you?

Finally, who is getting the £1,500 organiser costs? Can you get by on less?

Your budget flexibility is based on a number of inter-relating factors. It is prudent to budget some areas generously, like marketing, and organiser costs, where savings can be made if needed. Some areas like equipment hire and artists costs are far harder or impossible to reduce once booked.

In the example above, we have covered just the basic budget headings. You might have quite a lot of sub-headings within some of those. For example, under marketing you could have posters and leaflets, social media marketing, photography and video production, press advertising, brochure/programme costs, website hosting and development, etc. You could organise all that detail on a separate marketing budget page in Excel, linked to a total marketing figure in your spreadsheet summary page.

Budgeting tip: Making your budget easy to read

You may well end up with a page covered in figures. If you can't read, understand and interpret those figures, you and your management team will be in potential difficulty. To make it easier to read, both for you and others, especially if you are using a spreadsheet:

■ Get rid of the pence. In the final analysis, nobody cares about 14p. The pence are detail you can do without; your budget is an estimate, not a set of end-of-year accounts. The spreadsheet can automatically round the figures up or down to the nearest pound and it makes it much easier to read.

■ If your numbers involve thousands, format the numbers to include a comma so that £1000 reads £1,000. Again, it makes it clearer and easier to read. Without the comma it can be easy to confuse £10000 and £1000. The result could be catastrophic.

■ Distinguish between subtotal and totals by putting subtotals in italics and totals in bold. It makes them easier to see. You could use colour, too, if that helps. Just be consistent.

Spreadsheets can format all this for you quickly and easily – and much more. They can also add up rows and columns of figures and give you totals. This means if you adjust one figure – and you will! – all the others will change. They can also calculate percentages quickly and easily, so you can see the proportion of money you are spending in a particular area. Again, these will auto-adjust when the numbers change.

A word of warning

If you use a spreadsheet for your budget and are getting it to automatically total rows or columns, and you have sub-totals in there, make doubly sure that your calculations are added up correctly. It is easy to add up a column of figures that include sub-totals and end up with an figure that is completely wrong. If it's on the expenditure side it might not be a disaster. But if you are double counting income, it could lead to a financial catastrophe.

So, apropos Kipling, there is a seventh honest serving man: do these figures look right? Check, check and check again!

Detailed budget issues

Artist and staffing costs

Artist costs may be negotiable at the middle and top end of the market. There are, however, industry standards in relation to minimums. In addition to the minimum wage, BECTU, Equity and the Musicians Union have negotiated minimum rates for their members that are widely used. (www.bectu.org.uk/home; www.equity.org.uk; www.musiciansunion.org.uk)

Estimating marketing costs

There are several areas of budgeting where there are no hard and fast rules, only judgement. For example, how much should you spend on marketing? This is a crucial area. It's what will ensure the public gets to hear about your event and hopefully buy tickets for it or just attend it, if it's free.

Specialist marketing people may suggest that you should spend a percentage of your total costs on marketing, with suggested proportions ranging from 12%– 25% of turnover (total costs). Let's take a 20% marketing ratio. Suppose before marketing costs you estimate your event will cost £10,000 to stage, then with a 20% marketing ratio you need to add £2,000 to that for marketing.

But what would that £2,000 buy you in terms of publicity and are you and your marketing team comfortable that you can sell enough tickets with that budget? Or is it more than you need? You can do an awful lot with a website and social media. You can also do a lot by buying into external services and agencies that will promote and sell tickets to your event such as Eventbrite or Ticketsource, for a percentage of the ticket price.

How much you decide to spend on marketing will depend on your marketing strategy and probably requires a detailed bottom-up budget (see Chapter 9 on Festival Marketing).

Contingency

Contingency in your expenditure is a tactic rather than a budget category. There will always be costs you can't predict. So, it is sensible to put in a contingency budget of whatever you think you can – 5% of total expenditure is a realistic figure, but you could consider more if this is your first festival, or a new area of work for a more established event, as there are more unknowns that you might not have accounted for. If unexpected costs come in, or if you have to adjust the budget because you get less in ticket income or grants, then your contingency budget provides a useful cushion. It's always the first item to be cut and if you don't need it, then it counts as surplus or profit.

Artist rider costs

A rider is a list of extras that form part of the contract that you the event organiser are required to supply and pay for. It is common in the live music industry – hence the inclusion in the budget template. Extras in the theatre tend to called *contras*. Either way, you need to check all contracts carefully for these costs prior to signing them.

If you are promoting local or emerging acts, the rider might range from light to non-existent. That said, a bit of light refreshment will always be appreciated by the artists or content providers and give you a good reputation in the industry.

Well established acts are likely to have riders that are specific and can be extensive and demanding. These can cover the specific supply of equipment to refreshments, meals, towels and overnight accommodation. Some rider requirements can be quite easy to provide, such as hotel accommodation.

In other instances, it is not clear that acts know what their rider specifies and don't seem to be terribly fussed if something isn't there, or don't need it on this occasion.

Riders

Some riders can be quite challenging. One festival promoter came across a rider that specified a particular type of amplifier that he had never heard of. He did some research and found that the company producing the amplifier seemed to based in America. The company had been bought by another company and the specified amplifier was no longer in production. So, he raised the importance of the specified amplifier with the agent, who didn't know much about it or the rationale. An alternative was negotiated with ease.

In conclusion, riders are costs that you need to allow for. But they can also be negotiated. If you have a contract with lots of riders items in it, and such contracts will probably come from agents, it's worth negotiating down to the minimum you can get away with; and then just ask the artists or content providers on the day, "is there anything I can get you?". If they feel looked after, their requests will probably be quite modest.

Estimating box office income

This is another big unknown that requires careful thought and judgement. Most festivals involve ticketing and box office income of some kind and level. You will need to budget for this and also track ticket sales to see if things are going to plan. If they are not, you might need to adjust your marketing and publicity.

Selling tickets for festivals involves a range of issues that are worth briefly outlining here as it will help you estimate your income. These issues include:

- The nature of the attraction you are selling tickets for
- How much in fees and expenses you are paying for it
- The nature of the audience you are hoping to attract
- The numbers you are hoping to attract
- The size of your venue
- Technical and other costs you might be having to bear to stage it
- What other promoters are charging for the same or similar attractions
- How people will buy the tickets
- What people in your target audience are willing to pay for tickets
- Whether an artist is a 'must-have' at your festival, so you are willing to risk a loss, or whether the festival must make you money.

There may well be other questions you will need ask, that will be specific to your festival and location. Ticket pricing and estimates will probably be very different for a talk by a children's author, a concert featuring a rising pop band or a demonstration by a celebrity chef.

The key issues in your budgeting estimates are:

- How much can/should you charge?
- How many people can your venue hold?
- How potentially popular is your offer?
- What are the costs of selling tickets?

Never budget on 100 % capacity, for two reasons. First, you will, inevitably, have to hold back some tickets for guests, VIPs, competition prizes, the press and the like – these are known as complimentary tickets or 'comps'.

Second, it is risky to budget on 100%. What happens if there is a major incident close to your venue and some of the audience who would have come, just can't get there? Or if there just happens to be the final episode of a gripping TV serial broadcast that night? What would the impact be from a major rain storm forecast for the day of your outdoor festival? Conventional wisdom is to budget at 70% capacity. So, if you are staging a festival that involves some sort of talk or performance and have a 300 capacity venue and decide to charge £15 a head and you budget at 70% that means you could expect an income of £3,150 (300 x 70% = 210 x £15 = £3,150).

But that assumes everyone pays full price. Are you going to offer any discounts for OAPs or children (assuming it's suitable)? Will you offer discounts for group purchases, or early bookings? Sometimes festivals go further and offer discounts to students and nurses or people on benefits. It all depends on your objectives, the nature of your festival and on the specific event within it. Take a look at any festival website and you will see the sort of matrix of options and prices on offer. But make it too complicated and you may actually put potential buyers off. Offers can be an incentive, but too many of them can be confusing.

Even if you sell all of your tickets at full face value price, you must budget for costs to be deducted. Ticket agency fees are usually charged back to the promoter, even if the agent adds extra ones of their own. Percentages will vary, but 5% is a reasonable average to use in your budget. VAT is a sales tax. It is charged on tickets but you will only have to pay this if your company is big enough to be VAT registered. The current VAT rate is 20% in the UK (see further on for more on VAT).

You might also have to take into account the deal you have done with any venues that might co-promote acts in your festival. Rather than charging you a hire fee, with you taking all of the ticket income, it is possible to negotiate deals known as guarantees and splits with some venues (see below). The purpose of these deals is to share the risk, and to encourage both promoter and venue to market the show.

Case study

A promoter learnt a very valuable lesson from a music festival for which they did the budgeting. They were cautious in estimating box office income estimating what they thought were relatively low-ticket numbers – as low as 35% – 40% of venue capacity. The ticket prices were reasonable. The tickets were mostly sold online. The ticket sales outlet was not the easiest to access and wasn't that supportive in spite of a healthy ticket commission. Some elderly people who might have attended may not have been comfortable with using the Internet and the publicity distribution was late and patchy.

All of this led to far poorer ticket sales than had been budgeted for. The other factor that probably had a major bearing was that too many events had been programmed. There was too much choice and more ticketed events than people had the disposable income for. The promoter had built some very large contingencies into the budget, so overall the event just broke even. But in terms of audience numbers and event atmosphere and in terms of financial effectiveness, the outcome was disappointing.

Venue deals

If some or all of your festival is taking place in professional theatres and concert halls, you are probably making use of the venues' marketing and ticketing services, as well as their stages and technical crews. They are benefiting from the additional marketing effort your festival provides and the pulling power of your festival to attract artists and shows. However, you may have to pay a contribution to their marketing costs. Their hire terms and conditions will specify this.

Hires

A hire is when a festival or event producer pays a fee to a venue and then receives all of the ticket income. Hires can include a menu of services, such as technical equipment and support, or sales and marketing. The minimum a hire might include is the venue being opened and closed and supplied with light and power.

Guarantees

A guarantee is a fee a venue will pay to the event producer for the show. A full guarantee would see the venue receive all of the sales income. It is common practice for venues and promoters to negotiate a deal that combines a guarantee with a split.

Splits

A split is a deal that literally splits the net ticket income between the promoter and the venue. Percentages vary, but are you could expect 70% to go to the promoter and 30% to the venue.

A guarantee against a split would ensure that the producer/agent receive the higher of the two amounts. Let's say your guarantee was £800 against a split (70-30 in your favour). Net ticket sales were £2,000. 70% of £2,000 = £1,400, so you would receive that. If net ticket income was only £1,000, 70% would be only £700, so you receive the guarantee of £800 instead.

Check your contract carefully to ensure you know what expenses will be deducted from the gross ticket sales as splits and guarantees are always based on net figures. Net means after VAT and any other taxes have been paid.

All of this applies to the 'bottom-up' method of budgeting. This method of budgeting ticket income is also really useful in setting out what you can afford to pay for your artist/production/attraction. If, say, you have a 500 capacity venue and you budget on 70% what's your maximum revenue? Well it all depends on how high you set the ticket price and what people are willing to pay.

If people think that an event is worth a ticket price of £30 then, in a 500 seat venue at 70% capacity you could gross just over £10,000 at 70% and £15,000 if you sell out and all tickets are at full price. So, if you are sure of that, if you can secure the act for say, £8,000, you are looking at a nice profit – or at least a surplus that can be used to cover other costs.

But what if you are not sure of an act's pulling power, but their agent is seeking a high fee? Well, one way of approaching this is to offer a lower guarantee against a percentage of the actual ticket sales. For example, if an agent is seeking £5,000 (or £500 come to that), and you feel that's a bit risky, you could offer them a guarantee of £3,500 (or £350) against 90% of the net Box Office takings. Then, so long as you are not registered for VAT (see later section on this), if your venue holds 500 and you charge £15 a ticket, you need to sell 234 tickets to meet the guarantee. If you sell 400 tickets at £15 then the artist will take £5,400 and you will make £600 surplus or profit. (400x £15 = £6,000 x 90% = £5,400). So, the agent/act will be better off and you won't be out of pocket. Net takings mean takings after costs and you may have other costs you will need to deduct to get from the gross (total takings) to the net. The above example has ignored this for the sake of simplicity.

There are lots of possible permutations here. Some of this will be affected by the nature of your locality, what other events are going on a month or so either side of your festival and just how much disposable income your audience really has and how much they want to see what you are putting on.

Budgeting box office income, indeed the whole process of budgeting, is a balancing act full of variables and nuances. Don't let that put you off! It can also be very creative and satisfying. Don't worry, get advice, do your research about what sells in your area and then just do it. The more you do, the more you will learn about your audience, your artists and indeed your suppliers, and the better you will get at it.

Box office variables and actuals

So, how do you turn all these variables into a sensible set of box office income projections that completes your draft budget? Well the answer is you just have to estimate your audience number for each event, multiply that by the ticket price, subtract any discounts you are offering and put the resulting figures in your income column.

So, for example a concert attracting 140 people (70% capacity) at £12 a head in a 200-capacity venue will give you income of £1,680. Allow 10% for concessions (that's 14 tickets) and you have a projected income of £1,512. To create your box office income estimate, you just have to do something like that for all the events you are promoting and total up the projected income. That's where using a spreadsheet helps, because you can do each event on a separate page and then create a total income figure on the summary page. You can link this so that if you change the detail, the total box office income figure in the summary automatically updates.

You will inevitably want to play around with the figures a bit. A spreadsheet also allows you also to run all sorts of 'what if' scenarios. For example, what if our audience numbers were 10% larger? What if we put the ticket prices up by 10%?

Once you are happy with your budget projections, have booked and contracted the programme, then you need to go out and publicise it and sell the tickets. But that's another story.

Cashflow

You should now have a good idea of what a festival budget is and how to put one together. You may also have heard of the term 'cashflow' and it is important to explain what this is, why it is different from a budget and why a cashflow can save you from disaster.

In accounting terms, the theatre business can be quite precarious. But quite a number of theatres have survived all manner of losses and accumulated deficits because they have very positive cashflows. When the acclaimed musical *Cats* played a large theatre in the South West of England, it was a hot ticket and sold out in a fairly short space of time. Looking at the ticket prices and knowing the theatre's capacity, it was possible to estimate that it took somewhere in the region of £1 million in ticket sales months before a cat ever set foot on its stage. If you want a ticket to a popular play or concert or festival, you are going to have to pay upfront and well ahead of the performance date. The venue or promoter will take all that cash and bank it, probably well before they have to pay for the costs of the production.

By buying tickets in advance, arts and culture enthusiasts bankroll many a venue, producer, and festival organiser. Whether they hang on to all that advance money depends very much on the costs and contracts they (and you will) have with the suppliers (the acts/artists, venues etc.).

But there will come a point where you, as event organiser, will have to pay suppliers, services and for the event content, artistic or otherwise. You ought to have the cash to do so having banked it all in advance, unless something else has intervened in the meantime requiring a substantial cash outlay. This should never happen, but it has been known to and it leads to companies becoming insolvent. They go out of business as a result and artists and audiences are the losers. So, cash management and cashflow are crucial.

A *budget* is a projection of where your income and costs will fall and what at the end of your festival you expect the outcome to be, i.e. how much profit or surplus you will make.

A *cashflow* is a projection of when income will arrive and when costs will be payable. Its purpose is to help you ensure you have enough money in the bank at critical times to meet your financial obligations. If cashflow is tight, which it often is in small festivals, you might be running your cashflow forecasts daily. But if you have planned carefully before you contract suppliers, you can build some wriggle room into your contracts. For example, if you have, say, 10 artists all requiring payment immediately after their performance but your box office receipts are with an online ticket seller and you won't get the money until 14 days after your festival, that could give you a serious cashflow problem – you don't have enough money in the bank to meet your obligations. Or you haven't adopted the right contractual terms.

Unless carefully projected and managed, a cashflow problem like that leads to loss of confidence amongst your suppliers or worse. Creditors – people to whom you owe money – could apply to have the festival wound up if they don't believe you will be able to pay them. A history of late payments because your cashflow management is poor makes this a possibility.

> **Case study**
>
> Managing your cashflow can mean making difficult decisions about who to pay first. One festival in Dorset paid all the leading artists on the performance day (or in a few cases partially in advance) as per their contract terms. The contract for all local artists specified payment within 28 days. That gave the festival manager time to call in all the box office receipts. Unfair on the local artists you may say. But it did mean they all got paid, which they wouldn't have done if the festival had gone bankrupt. It was the only way to make the cashflow work.

A cashflow format is like a budget, but stretched over 12 months, or possibly shorter for festivals, where it is the length of time you will receive income and make payments. The first column in the cashflow will be the estimated budget total. You will then have up to 12 further columns, one for each month. You take your total figure and divide this sum across the months when you expect to receive the income or make the payment. The monthly figures will show you how much cash you have or will need to keep your event running (see the cashflow example below).

A cashflow may not in itself solve any financial problems you may be facing. But it will tell you where and when they will be and allow you identify ways of meeting your needs and obligations. Suppose your festival is in October and your cashflow figures in September are negative, i.e. you have £2,000 less than you need. This forces you to ask some vital questions. Can you defer some payments? Can you bring forward payment of receipts – like box office income or grants if you are lucky enough to have some? If not is there anyone you know who can bankroll you (lend you money) to tide you over? Remember to find out how much interest will they charge!

Like a budget, a cashflow is a dynamic document, only more so. You will need to regularly update it. How often will depend on the size of your festival project. But expect to revise and update your cashflow monthly, and possibly more often.

VAT

VAT stands for 'Value Added Tax' and is a tax on transactions both for goods and services. The amount of VAT you pay is a set proportion of the transaction value . The VAT rate is currently 20%. The more transactions you do, the more VAT you pay. VAT is also a complicated tax as it levied on both income

My First Small Festival Cashflow

	Budget	Jan	Feb	Mar	Apr	May	Jun	Jul	Aug	Sep	Total
		Festival Month									
Opening Balance		1,000	1,000	1,000	1,600	3,100	4,225	4,400	2,665	2,665	
Income											
Ticket income	7,500		500	1,000	2,000	3,500	500				7,500
Merchandise sales	1,200						1,200				1,200
Grants	1,500					1,000		500			1,500
Business sponsorship	500					500					500
Donations	100			100							100
Raffle(s)	750						750				750
Concessions	100						100				100
Total Income	11,650	1,000	1,500	2,100	3,600	8,100	6,775	4,900	2,665	2,665	11,650
											-
Expenditure											-
Artists costs	2,500					1,000	1,500				2,500
Artist riders	250						250				250
Cost of Merchandise	1,000					1,000					1,000
Ticket booking	375							375			375
Venue hire	350					350					350
Production costs	750					375	375				750
Marketing and publicity	2,500		500	500	500	1,000					2,500
Insurances and licences	150					150					150
Staffing or organiser costs	1,500							1,500			1,500
National Insurance	-										-
Royalties & PRS	360							360			360
Volunteer expenses	250						250				250
Contingency	250										-
Total Expenditure	10,235	-	500	500	500	3,875	2,375	2,235	-	-	9,985
Closing Balance (Cash in bank)		1,000	1,000	1,600	3,100	4,225	4,400	2,665	2,665	2,665	1,665

Figure 4.3: Monthly cash flow

and expenditure. If you are VAT registered the amount you pay is the difference between the VAT on expenditure (inputs) and income (outputs).

The good news about VAT is that you are only obliged to register for VAT, charge it to your customers and pay it, if your turnover is above £85,000 (at the time of writing). This is the VAT threshold. The VAT threshold tends to go up year-on-year and is announced in the Government's annual budget, so check this threshold figure. You can register for VAT if your turnover is less than £85,000 and there may be good reasons to do this. You should take an accountant's advice on this.

There are five issues around VAT and your festival budget: supplier pricing; ticket income; sponsorships; cashflow and VAT exempt items

Supplier pricing

Many businesses are VAT registered. The prices they quote you can be without VAT. You need to check carefully whether their prices are net of VAT (without VAT) or gross (with VAT). If they are net of VAT, you may find yourself getting a bill for 20% more than you budgeted for. If in doubt, ask.

Ticket income

If you are VAT registered, your ticket income will be VAT-able. So, 20% of that income will be payable to the VAT-man (Her Majesty's Revenue and Customs or HMRC). That 20% can be offset against VAT on expenditure, so it may be less in real terms. But the expenditure figures in your budget will probably be gross (i.e. including VAT). If you are VAT registered you would therefore be prudent to deduct 20% income, and in your budget either show a reduced income figure or show the VAT element as a 20% cost in your expenditure column. If you do not do this your budget figures could be significantly wrong. For example, on ticket sales of £100,000, the full VAT liability is £16,666. If you do not account for this, your budget and financial results could be wrong by a large amount. You will be able to offset some of that VAT on income against the VAT on the expenditure side. But it is better to show the VAT on income as a cost even if the actual amount payable turns out to be less than shown, rather than omit it and find you have a significant budget gap. You should discuss this in more detail with an accountant if you think this will affect your festival. Grants are not subject to VAT so you will get the whole amount you are given. Sponsorship is VAT-able (see below).

If you are not based in the UK, check with your accountant, business advisor or tax office what taxes apply locally. Then remember to include such costs in your budget.

Sponsorships

If you manage to secure sponsorship and you are VAT registered, make sure the sponsorship agreement is for the agreed amount plus VAT. An agreement for £5,000 will actually give you only £4,166 (£5,000 less VAT at 20%). An agreement for £5,000 plus VAT will secure you the full amount.

Cashflow

If you are VAT registered you must budget in a quarterly VAT amount. This will be hard to estimate initially and for an annual festival will be quite different across the year. But you will have to pay it – falling out with the tax man is a very bad idea for a business – and it's an important cashflow item. It will be easier to calculate in years 2 and 3 when the trading pattern is clearer.

VAT exempt items

A number of items are VAT exempt and one or two have lower rates than the standard 20%. Printing posters and leaflets is VAT exempt. If your festival involves catering and you are providing it, you need to look carefully at the VAT on this. Most food is VAT-exempt but there are anomalies. Hot food sales are VAT-able – see 'Catering, takeaway food' (VAT Notice 709/1). Biscuits are VAT exempt but cakes are not. There is copious advice on this online.

Registered charities, non-profit organisations and VAT on tickets

If you are a non-profit body or a charity you may be exempt for VAT on festival admission charges if you can show that you exist for cultural benefit. This exemption also extends to museums, galleries, theatre shows and art exhibitions (Reza, 2018 and VAT notice 701/47). This is a complex and contested area, so you need to get advice from an expert accountant and consult HMRC. Mahmood Reza reported in April 2018:

> The scope of this exemption is currently being examined in relation to whether or not sales of admission tickets to films shown at the National Film Theatre and at various film festivals could fall within the exemption (Reza, 2018).

Annual accounts, auditors and taxation

At some point in the life of your festival, you will almost certainly have to produce a financial statement or set of accounts, possibly for the HMRC or for funders. You will also want to know how your festival did financially so you can plan for the next one. A well-structured and carefully put together budget will make the process of producing accounts much easier. You will be able to compare your actual figures against a good set of estimates. You will be able to see where the variances are and make adjustments in your plan for future years.

> **Tip**
> Your accounts, or if you contract this aspect out, the person doing them, may use dedicated accounting software. If so be careful to ensure that the account headings are a mirror image of your budget headings. If they aren't, you will either find it impossible to compare estimates and actuals, or have to spend a good deal of time trying to reconcile the budget and accounts. If the headings are the same, comparison will be quick and easy.

If you have to present accounts to the HMRC, or the Charity Commission if you are a charity, they will either need to be certified or audited and you will need an independent auditor to do this. If you are a small company, your accounts will only need to be certified. If you are a larger concern, your accounts will need auditing. The process is basically the same but an audit is more in-depth. An audit is a sampling of your financial records to ensure they are accurate. Your auditor will want to see the figures, bank statements, payment records, purchase orders and invoices and will check a sample of these so they can confirm your financial statements are accurate. You will have to pay for this and the costs can range from under £1,000 to several thousands, depending on the nature and scale of your festival.

If you are a commercial venture you will have to pay Corporation Tax of 19% of your profits. However, there are quite a number of allowances and ways that you can reduce your tax liability if you have one. This is where you need a qualified or chartered accountant to advise you. This accountant may also be your auditor. Corporation Tax is not a budget item. It depends on your profits. But if you expect to make a profit of, say £10,000, don't start making plans to spend that until you have, at least mentally, accounted for the tax you will have to pay.

Summary

Good budgeting is crucial to the success of your Festival. Start with some big numbers (top down) to get a feel for whether your proposal is viable or to set a target of how much income you expect or need to get from where. Once you have that and it looks viable then you need to do a lot of detailed 'bottom up' budget work. Make sure you know how to use a spreadsheet. It'll save you a lot of time in the long run. And structure your budget so it's easily readable. If you are bringing in external suppliers or contractors find two or three and get some comparable quotes. But remember that lowest cost is not always the best investment, quality and reliability can be just as important, if not more so. Also, not everything is financially comparable. Discussing the respective value of Taylor Swift and The Foo Fighters is safer as a fun office discussion than as a financial judgement.

Your budget will continually change during the run up to the event. Be prepared for it and build in some flexibility through a budget contingency category or another budget heading which you can trim if need be. Just as important as a good and accurate budget, is having enough cash in the bank at the right time so you can pay the bills when they arrive. A cashflow is an extended budget that will tell you that and identify if you are facing problems. Make sure you do a cashflow. At some point you will probably have to file accounts with the tax man or similar. You will also want to compare your budget with your actual results. Make sure your budget categories and accounts categories are one and the same. A lot of budgeting is quite simple. But there are technical complexities especially around VAT and Corporation Tax. Unless one of your team is an accountant, you will need expert advice at some point, so find a friendly accountant. If you are a non-profit body you may be able to get a fair bit of advice for very little or nothing. But expect to pay for an annual audit or certification of your accounts and budget for this. Finally, keep the paperwork of all your financial transactions; estimates, invoices, bank statements paying in slips, pay slips etc etc. Without proper records, the cost of producing and auditing your annual accounts will be much more than it should be.

References

HMRC VAT Notice 701/47 https://www.gov.uk/guidance/admission-charges-to-cultural-events-and-vat-notice-70147#qualifying-services

Reza, M. (2018) Making the best of VAT [online] Available at: https://www.artsprofessional.co.uk/magazine/article/making-best-vat [Accessed 29 October 2018]

Short, T. (1999) Conversation with the author, Plymouth (5th July 1999).

5 Planning, Logistics and Management

by Paul Kelly

After reading this chapter you should:

■ Have an insight into the factors involved in producing a good festival

■ Understand several project management planning processes

■ Understand how different venues affect planning requirements and the implications of using outdoor venues

■ Understand the interests and role of the emergency services in festival planning

■ Know what documents you will have to produce to ensure your festival is legal

■ Understand about artist contracts and riders

Introduction

The safe and efficient organisation of your festival is not just crucial to the artists who perform and the audiences who attend, it's crucial to your finances, your brand reputation and, ultimately, your career. Festivals are a chance for artists to show their inventiveness and brilliance and for audiences to be transported away from the daily humdrum of everyday life; to be entertained and inspired.

Those interactions between artist and audience can result in a range of outcomes from intellectually challenging, to entertaining and sometimes life-changing. But the perceived glamour that creative festivals inevitably suggest is built on the rather dull yet essential disciplines of planning and logistics. These days, given the increasing complexities of new technology and larger productions to bigger and bigger crowds, plus the creative desire to continually push boundaries and a growing concern for public welfare, planning and logistics have become ever more vital.

Benjamin Franklin famously said, "If you fail to plan, you are planning to fail". It is a saying widely adopted by the military, who are generally very good at planning. We would add to that, if you fail to plan, you will also heap stress on yourself and all your problems and challenges will probably arrive at the same time.

Successful festival operational planning should cover three main areas:

◆ Artist-related requirements

◆ Audience-related requirements

◆ Technical requirements

The nature and level of these requirements will very much depend on the type of festival you are staging and venue(s) you are operating in.

This chapter and Chapter 7 on operations contain the bedrock of festivals management. Get the festival planning right and even if your marketing doesn't produce the audience numbers you'd hoped for, even if your finances are awful or your creative content is disappointing, you will live to fight another day. But if you neglect planning and operations management, you put your reputation at risk with both artists and audiences, you may fail to secure future event licences and you may even, in some circumstances, put peoples' lives at risk.

There are three stages involved in taking your festival idea from conception to delivery:

◆ Plan

◆ Licence

◆ Manage

This chapter deals with the planning aspects. Chapter 6 covers the detail of licensing law and insurance and Chapter 7 looks at issues concerning operational management – that means what happens on the day, weekend or week of your festival and what you need to enable that. Your festival may take place in venues which are already fully licensed and insured, so you may not need to obtain these yourself. But you need to know what permissions are needed and what you need to do to comply with the law.

An essential reference point for festival planning, logistics and management is the *Event Safety Guide* (1999) also now known as *The Purple Book*. Produced by the Health and Safety Executive (HSE), a government agency in the UK, the *Event Safety Guide* has a health and safety focus. It does not cover the various types of planning processes you can use in developing your festival, but it does give you an invaluable introduction to the areas you need to consider: things like crowd management, barriers, special effects, provision for people with special needs – 33 topics in all. Some legislation and practice has changed since it was first published. The original 1999 edition is available for free online (HSE, 1999) but an updated version, *The Purple Book*, has been developed as an online resource by the Events Industry Forum, a consortium of 24 UK events industry trade bodies (Events Industry Forum, 2015). It is available for an online subscription fee.

Planning case study: The Millennium – New Year's Eve 1999

On 31 December 1999 towns and cities all over Britain staged events to celebrate the arrival of the new millennium. These were often led and organised by local councils. One large city council spent several months planning an outdoor event involving an open-air stage on an exposed site with live bands, films and, inevitably, fireworks hosted by a compère. A crowd of around 30,000 gathered and, in spite of deteriorating weather, all went smoothly until about five minutes to midnight when a seven-minute long film about community activities was re-screened to fill a gap in proceedings. Suddenly just as the sounds of Big Ben were about to be broadcast, the compère came on stage and announced "It's midnight!" and the fireworks went off. The night concluded with a Scottish piper playing Auld Lang Syne and the audience dispersed, some expressing disappointment. This resulted in criticism in the local press which blew over after a week or so. There was never any internal enquiry. The council had staged its millennium event. So why did such a pivotal evening ultimately feel so very disappointing? We believe so many people had got involved in the event from the council and external contractors, and there was so much discussion about special effects including lasers, fireworks, stages and bands, that the very purpose of the event had been overlooked. The purpose of the event was actually very simple; it was the countdown to midnight. For technical reasons which are too complex to go into here, that countdown never happened, leaving many of the 30,000 people feeling rather deflated rather than the elation they expected from the dawn of a new millennium.

Event planning is a complex process which can involve a lot of people and a lot of factors. But if there's one lesson from this it's this; in the course of the complexities, don't lose sight of the purpose of your event. The role of the planning is to support that.

What makes a festival successful?

There are two things that are crucial to the success and sustainability of your festival. First, that people attending are safe – and those people include audiences, artists, technicians, retailers and your staff. Second, and just as important, that you – the festival manager – are safe and happy. By safe, we mean that you can cope with the inevitable challenges, stresses and strains that live events and festivals inevitably involve.

Debating point:

You will probably either have a vision, expectation or experience of what a successful festival looks and feels like. That's worth writing down and being as specific as you can. Ask what are the things you need to do to make that vision a reality? What are the component parts of your vision? If you cannot think of any or more than two or three, don't worry, this chapter will be identifying plenty for you.

What makes a successful festival is obviously a very personal issue as artists and audiences will all have their own interpretation of this. For some it might be the nature of the ambience or site. For others it could be the way they were greeted or looked after. For audiences it might come down to the quality of the camping, if it is an outdoor festival, the length of queues at the bar, or even the quality of the toilets.

But there is one issue that is probably common to all artistic performances, whether indoor or outdoor, and one that can be applied to the visual arts as well. That issue is the nature of engagement between the artist and the audience. It's the nature of that engagement that makes live events, whether indoors or outdoors, truly memorable. It ought to be the same in every venue, every night. There are artists who have a reputation for giving 110 per cent every time. But human nature is complex and not that constant. Sometimes little things can get in the way to affect both artists and audiences and cause the level of engagement to slip to a pitch where it is just off the boil. But when that artist-audience relationship is right, magic can happen of a kind that is hard to describe and easy to feel.

As a festival manager you cannot possibly know or control all the small background distractions, fears or worries that are going on in the lives of your artists, let alone your audiences. However, there are things that are in your control that can affect the nature of a performance or exhibition and the relationship between artist and audience. These are the front of house and backstage operational mechanics. Regardless of the size of the team you might be managing, your job as festival operations manager is to ensure that you remove all the impediments that might detrimentally affect the artist's ability to perform at their best and all the impediments that might affect the audience's ability to enjoy the creative offering.

That means thinking about backstage facilities, catering for the artists, car parking and get-in arrangements, the quality of the sound and lighting that the artist rider requirements are met and that you are there for them when they need you, but not in the way when they don't. Similarly from an audience perspective, that they know where the car parking is, that the box office facilities are adequate, that the loos are clean and there are plenty of them, that they have somewhere to leave their coats (if it's an indoor performance) and can buy food or drink if they want without having to wait too long, that they are well-directed to their seats, that there's a programme to buy if they want it and that the performance starts on time. It's a festival manager's responsibility to make all of these work.

What is planning?

No matter how small or large your festival is, it will require planning. Planning is about you being in control. If you don't plan at all or plan insufficiently, you will find yourself running round, generally at the last minute, trying to keep multiple things from going wrong or fixing last minute problems. You will probably find yourself very stressed, if not exhausted, and in the course of this something will probably 'fall over', 'go pear shaped' or, in other words, go wrong. This will all be blamed on you and it will chiefly happen because you are not in control.

Planning is the amalgamation of your creative programme, your budget and your technical, crewing and operational requirements. It is about deciding what is happening where and when at your festival, and what you need to do to ensure that that it runs smoothly.

Putting a festival plan in place means you will be able to identify and fix potential problems before they happen. Control and planning are not exactly joyful words. Somehow, they have a restrictive ethos about them, they seem to fly in the face of what festivals appear to be about. But to enable that, organisers need to create a safe space, especially when thousands of people are present. That safe space is not an area or arena, it's an attitude to management – and planning is central to that attitude. Planning is neither dull nor difficult, it is can actually be very creative and satisfying and the process can be quite simple. Good planning requires a lot of background work but should be largely invisible. Most importantly it will give you, your team, and the people attending your event, confidence and peace of mind.

We recommend you will need three types of plan: the strategic business plan, the operational plan and the event management plan. The strategic business plan thinks about how your company will sustain itself and grow over the next three to five years. Here we are going to focus on the first of your operational plans, your internal plan for you and your team. This will feed into a formal external Event Management Plan (EMP) which will be required by licensing and safety people. We will cover the EMP in Chapter 7.

Your internal plan will start with an overview and then develop it in detail. Festival planning is a messy process which will inevitably go through a number of phases. You may benefit from having lots of big pieces of paper (A3 or flipchart is useful) and marker pens. Use that to draw what you are doing where and when, then list down all the things you are going to need to make that happen.

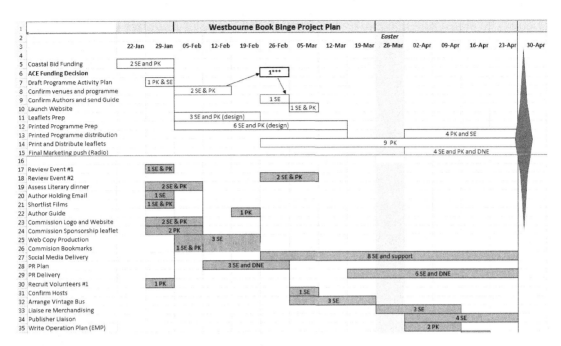

Figure 5.1: Westbourne Book Binge Project Plan

Your venues

The nature of your venues will of course have a significant impact on the extent and direction of your planning. There are lots of variables, but let's give you three quite typical venue models:

The fully serviced venue

This is typically a theatre, art centre, or concert hall. It will have a stage, audience seating and/or flat section for standing, sound and lighting, front of house area including a box office and probably a backstage area with dressing rooms. It will most likely have at least one bar and maybe even a restaurant and staff to run all of these. It will be supplied with power and water. It may be a producing venue that plans and stages its own productions. If so it will probably have a marketing department and regularly produce its own publicity, which will be useful to align your own publicity and marketing with to maximise reach. It will have all the necessary licences for alcohol and performance.

The receiving or occasional venue

This will be a hall of some kind. Or it may be a bar or a room in a bar or a restaurant or similar. Some of these are large and some quite small. It will probably have a stage or a performance space and may even have a backstage area and a dressing room or two. It may have some form of front of house area and it may have a box office facility or an area for one on the night. If it is not a designated bar it may have space for one. It may have seating. If it has sound and lighting it may be quite basic. It will have power and water. It may have a very small staff team. It may have the necessary licences for alcohol and performance (see Chapter 6), but it may not. It will probably have some of the services you need, but it's an occasional performance venue rather than a dedicated one.

The greenfield site

This will have nothing. It will probably be an open empty site in which you will have to build one or more event spaces and bring in all the necessary equipment. You may also have to supply power and water. It will have neither staff nor licences for alcohol or performance. It may be a park in a city or literally a field in the countryside. By contrast, the industry also talks about brownfield sites – these are usually in a city or town and may be city centres, market areas, car parks, pedestrianised roads, or even derelict areas of ground. It can include repurposed buildings such as empty warehouses or factories. They could have some facilities such as access to electricity, water and possibly nearby public toilets.

Now inevitably there are variants on these. But your first job as festival manager is to assess the venue or venues you are using and identify what each comes with and what will be needed to satisfy performer/exhibitor and audience requirements.

Venue tips: Access and facilities

A number of British venues in active use today were built in the 19th century and a few even earlier. Today we expect venues to be fully accessible to disabled people, with ramps and lifts front of house (FOH) and backstage. Standards of access and comfort were different in past times. Some venues have been almost rebuilt internally in the 20th century to bring them up to standard. But in some cases the architecture makes that difficult. If you are looking to use a venue, try and check it out from top to bottom. What is backstage access like? What are the dressing rooms like? How easy is it to get from the front of house to the backstage area if you need to? A very successful choral event was staged in a delightful Victorian venue. However, the dressing rooms were tiny and located up steep stairs and small corridors. In another old and much-loved theatre venue, the route from FOH to backstage was confusing and tortuous, making FOH to backstage liaison difficult.

You may have a number of venues you can choose from and thus be able to match a creative idea or act to a particular venue. And as you work with venues, year on year, you will get to know the quirks and foibles of each and how to manage those.

> **Case study: Portaloos**
> A music festival was staged in a large church. It had a capacity of 440 and had been used for concerts before. The organisers hoped the opening concert might attract an audience of 300 – 400. The church had only one toilet accessible to the public. It was felt essential to bring in three portaloos to be placed just outside the Church. The portaloos didn't have lighting and it would be dark by the time of the interval. That required an additional purchase of three battery powered lights and velcro to attach them inside the portaloos.

Project planning

Your plan is not just about what happens at your festival, it is also about all the things you need to do in the run up to the festival, which could take place over several months or more, so that everything is in place for the event itself. With a big festival, that could be thousands of separate tasks from contracting your artists to getting tickets printed and on sale, to recruiting security and hiring in fencing. All of these will have to be done by particular deadlines to ensure they are ready on time.

On smaller events it is possible to use a simple checklist for all of this. But large events with lots of staff working towards the same objective needs something rather more sophisticated. As festival manager you need to have an overview of the tasks you need to undertake to deliver the festival and to be able to ascertain quickly whether you are ahead of schedule, on track or lagging behind.

So, how do you plan? No matter how small or large your festival is, you will benefit from some sort of planning system. But at the heart of what you are doing lies a single principle. Festival and event planning is all about identifying what needs to be done and getting the right things to the right place at the right time and in the right order – and those 'things' include the artists and the audience.

A good starting point is the simple list; write everything that you need to do down in a long list. But you may end up with such a long list that it is hard to prioritise or see a sense or order or urgency in it. It might also look rather daunting. Some people think in linear ways and some people think more visually. If you are someone who thinks visually, then you will probably find a better way of starting the planning process is to 'mind-map' everything. You'll need a large sheet of paper for this and some marker pens. Try and classify all your thoughts into 'topic bubbles' or be even more creative (see diagram).

Figure 5.2: Doing Things Differently Mind Map. Courtesy of Paul Foreman, http://www.mindma-part.com/portfolio/paul-foreman/

This is also a good method if you are planning as a team. Stick your big piece of paper on a convenient wall and everyone can add to it, see what the overall result looks like and you can then discuss it.

Another useful method is to ask your team to write all the tasks they can think of on Post It notes and stick them on a blank wall. You then work with them to cluster these into common groupings and then further refine this by putting each grouping into a logical time-order. This is a more collaborative and entertaining way of putting together a project plan.

In Chapter 2 we talked about Kipling's 'six honest serving men' – who, what, when, where, why and how – they are also central to all good planning. List down all aspects of your event and then apply those six words. Not all may be relevant to every aspect, but many will be. For example, supposing you are staging a three-day festival on a greenfield site, think about:

◆ **How** will you get all the equipment on-site?

◆ **When** will it need to be there by?

◆ **Where** will the public, and maybe the artists, camp?

◆ **Who** will be arriving and when?

◆ **What** security will you need to ensure the site and the valuable equipment is secure?

♦ **What** are the implications of prolonged heavy rain prior to the event?

♦ **How** will you manage that?

Note that we have not used the 'why' word in the above sample list. We covered why in Chapter 2 and this chapter is focused on practicalities.

Business plans

We've referred to business plans elsewhere in this book. These are plans that you draw up to help you start and run your business. They serve two purposes:

1 They are an internal management tool in which you define your objectives and how you a re going to achieve them and also they help you monitor your progress.

2 Business plans have an external function to help you to:

♦ Raise finance

♦ Value a business for sale or purchase

♦ Find a partner or establish a strategic alliance

Most business plans project activities and finances for the three years ahead.

Your business plan is a pitch

Your plan is pitching to raise investment so you can start your business. You may not need start-up funding. But if you do, your plan will clearly state how much funding you need and show that you can service the debt, i.e. pay interest on the money you are borrowing.

You need to ensure your business plan has clearly identifiable goals and objectives (use Kipling). You also need to make sure you understand the needs of your target audience and tailor your plan accordingly.

External review and internal strengths and weaknesses

Many business plans will review the external environment the company is operating in, often using a PESTE analysis, this looks at the Political, Economic, Social, Technological and Environmental factors that may affect your business proposal. Many also look at the market and company by using a SWOT analysis which analyses Strengths, Weaknesses, Opportunities and Threats.

It is important also to find out about your competitors – you'll always have competitors. If there appear to be none, it could be because they've tried and failed.

Resources

Your business plan must consider what resources you need. These include:

♦ Physical – property and equipment

♦ Human – people

♦ Financial – start-up capital, working capital

♦ Intangible – brand image/ identity and the costs of establishing those

You may already have some resources such as money and equipment. In which case you need to identify and list these. Can you use them to lever in other resources or act as necessary security?

Market and finances

A significant part of your plan will involve estimating the potential size of your market and the sales revenues you are going to generate over the next three years. Experienced business analyst Phil Stone commented:

> "It never fails to amaze me how many entrepreneurs present forecasted figures that bear no resemblance to past performance, and can offer no real explanation as to how these can now be achieved" (2002: 38).

So, make sure your plan carries a credible explanation in an appendix of how you reached the figures in your budget and what your assumptions and calculations were. Whilst there are variations of style, format and length, a credible business plan will normally contain the following sections:

♦ Company/brand name

♦ Synopsis – a concise summary of your proposal and your key pitch – usually one page

♦ Your business background and history

♦ Background to your business or business idea with an outline of how/ why you got the idea

♦ Outline of your proposals

♦ What you need from your reader (investment, cash etc)

♦ The product or service you will be providing

♦ The operational process – how are you going to produce/deliver it

♦ Your market analysis – size, trends, segmentation, pricing, potential customers

♦ How much of this market you intend to capture and growth forecasts

♦ How you will grow the company and where you intend to be in three years' time

♦ A three-year budget and cashflow

The business plan style

Use clear plain language and avoid jargon. Explain what you mean/intend as clearly as you can. Use facts and figures. Show in appendices how you reached your figures or key financial assumptions.

Phil Stone comments:

"Many business plans that I have seen have not been very good, making no attempt to pre-empt any obvious questions that I would have [as a potential investor] and presenting lots of mainly irrelevant information. There was no clear strategy on how the goals and objectives would be achieved" (2002: 70)

There are plenty of books easily obtainable on writing business plans (Barrow et al., 2018; Evans, 2015; Genadinik 2015; Stone, 2002) as well as online tutorials and videos.

Project management and planning systems

Another term for planning is project management, which is a profession in itself. There is a considerable body of literature on project management and all sorts of techniques and systems associated with it – (Croft, 2013; Newton, 2016).

The Association for Project Management define the core components as follows:

1 Defining the reason why a project is necessary;
2 Capturing project requirements, specifying quality of the deliverables, estimating resources and timescales;
3 Preparing a business case to justify the investment;
4 Securing corporate agreement and funding;
5 Developing and implementing a management plan for the project;
6 Leading and motivating the project delivery team;
7 Managing the risks, issues and changes on the project;
8 Monitoring progress against plan;
9 Managing the project budget;
10 Maintaining communications with stakeholders and the project organisation;
11 Provider management;
12 Closing the project in a controlled fashion when appropriate

(https://www.apm.org.uk/resources/what-is-project-management/)

Kipling doesn't get a mention in the above but the Kipling principles are at the root of much project management. However, Kipling is not very good at dealing with multiple project management lines concurrently, which festivals often have – for example when you are running several venues simultaneously. There several other planning systems that are much better at this and that are worth looking at, including:

♦ Statement of Work

♦ The Ten Point Plan

♦ Gantt and PERT Charts

♦ Critical Path Analysis

It is useful at this point to make a distinction between planning systems and management systems. Planning systems are about what things need to be done to manage your festival. Management systems are about how you are going to manage all the activities. The simplest 'what' planning system is Kipling, though it also involves some management aspects (how and when?). We will now focus on two planning systems we have found helpful: the Statement of Work and the Ten Point Plan.

The Statement of Work

The Statement of Work is not dissimilar to a contract specification. It is a narrative description of the required work to be done by yourself or others. It resembles the operational plan used by managers who put together large festivals and events. It covers:

♦ Purpose of the project

♦ Project goals

♦ Scope of the project

♦ Deliverables – what you are specifically going to deliver by when

♦ Constraints – what might affect your ability to deliver the project

♦ Specifications and standards

♦ Reporting requirements

♦ Success criteria – how you will measure success

♦ Management guidelines

♦ Assumptions

A Statement of Work is a particularly useful tool when you are employing contractors/sub-contractors as it can specify requirements (which can include expectations, timeframes and specifications) very precisely.

The Ten Point Plan

The Ten Point Plan is better as an internal working document and also good for showing potential investors. It will also feed into your Event Management Plan. Your Plan will cover the following:

1 **General introduction**: Aims and objectives, stakeholders, sponsors – who are they?

2 **Parameters**: Specify the cost, time and quality criteria – what are they?

3 **Scope, boundaries and constraints**: This should describe what is and what is not to be done. (Known as the scope of a project)

4 **Event / project description**: Include event content, date, duration, site, programme.

5 **Resource needs**: Include all details of equipment needed to run the festival, e.g. lighting, staging, decorations, sound, programme, publicity.

6 **Responsibility and staff**: This should cover who has overall responsibility for the project, what staff you need to deliver it and what their roles will be.

7 **Assumptions**: What assumptions are you making about the project? e.g. amount of time available, who any partner organisations might be and your relationship with them, use of office and facilities, any weather-related issues.

8 **Monitoring**: How you are monitoring progress and deliverability? Are there critical points at which decisions will be made and, if so, when they are and what do they concern or effect? How will you know you are on schedule, within budget and achieving your objectives?

9 **Changes to the plan**: If changes have to be made, who will make those decisions, how will they be agreed, documented and communicated?

10 **Assessment criteria**: What criteria will you use to judge success? Success could cover a number of different areas including artist feedback, audience reaction, operational success, and agency or partner comments. The criteria could be quantitative, i.e. numbers of tickets sold, or qualitative, i.e. what was said in the media or by festival-goers on social media.

Both of the above systems – especially the Ten Point Plan – will set you targets. They will be really valuable reference documents to look back over if things don't go quite to plan (they seldom do!), but in themselves they won't help you keep track of day to day progress.

How you are going to manage?

At the simplest level an ongoing system of lists, updated daily, will help you monitor and keep track of progress and, if your festival is quite small, you might be able to get away with just lists. But if you are planning a large event, especially one using several different venues and a large number of staff, lists alone will probably not be enough. You need a more time-critical system.

Gantt

Professional project managers will invariably use a Gantt chart to set and track progress. Gantt charts take their name from the 19th Century American mechanical engineer and project manager, Henry Gantt. They list in table form the actions you need to take and when they need to be taken by. A Gantt chart will look something like this:

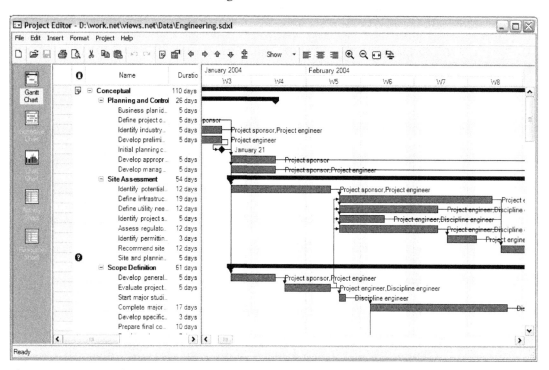

Figure 5.3: A Gantt chart

Gantt charts are really useful for several reasons. First, they offer a visual project view. Second, they offer a sequential timeline. Third, you can see from this where there may be particular pressure points; those are particular times when an awful lot of critical deadlines coincide. So, you can plan how to respond and where your resources need to be, or you can try and re-order things to reduce the pressure at critical points.

Gantt charts can be easily set up using an Excel spreadsheet. Alternatively, there are dedicated software systems on the market – some free to *Download*, and others like Microsoft Project which can cost several hundred pounds. The dedicated project management software programs will give you all sorts of clever features which will need some time to learn, so factor that in if you feel you need something more sophisticated than a spreadsheet.

PERT

There is no Mr PERT. The acronym PERT stands for Project Evaluation and Review Technique. It's a system developed by the American military when they built the first nuclear powered submarine. A PERT system is often used in large and complex projects. It incorporates uncertainty by making it possible to schedule a project while not knowing precisely the details and durations of all the activities. It is more of an event-oriented technique.

A PERT diagram will look something like this:

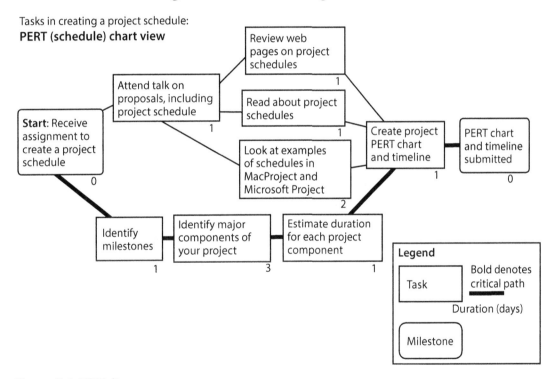

Figure 5.4: PERT diagram

You can develop a PERT diagram in a spreadsheet, and some management trainers like Chris Croft (https://www.youtube.com/watch?v=qkuUBcmmBpk) have developed simple and useful systems to give you a time-critical project management plan. Croft uses the 12 step Association of Project Managers system, which is worth investigating. (AfPM online)

CPA

This stands for 'Critical Path Analysis'. This is a time-critical method of planning. It focuses on what has to be done by when in order to deliver your project, in this case the festival you are organising.

Planning tip

One common failing in new festivals and new festival organisers is that they run out of time. There always seems to be a mad scramble in the final weeks to get everything in place, and this often affects one of the most vital things in the matrix – the publicity. Time and again we have seen publicity going out so late that it has very little impact.

How can you prevent this? What you need is clear dates and deadlines telling what has to be done by when. But those can be quite hard to determine when you are looking into the future. There is a very simple technique which can overcome this common failing.

Plan backwards

Most people when they plan take the day they are starting from and plan forwards. A better alternative is to establish the date of the event and plan backwards.

Supposing you are running your festival over a weekend. For sake of argument we'll say it is on the 11/12/13 July and that happens to be a weekend. So your set up completion date is 10 July. Everything has to be in place and ready by then for an 11 July start. How many weeks or months in advance do you need your publicity out in order to be able to sell your tickets? Let's say four months (it might be more, depending on how far in advance your target audiences tend to buy tickets). So, you need all your publicity ready by 10 March. How much of your programme will be in that first round of publicity? That's the date you have to have your key programme information including headliners, ticket prices, camping and infrastructure ready by – 10 March.

But is that right? Your publicity also needs to be devised, written, designed, printed and made available online, and how long will that take? Let's say four weeks. So, you actually need all the details that are going to go into your publicity by 10 February.

Now think of all the other things you need to do and use the same principle. You'll find it a lot easier to map the critical deadlines this way. And you'll also be surprised just how early you need to start in order to get everything in place in a timely way.

Planning backwards may not be Critical Path Analysis to the letter, but it exudes its spirit, and if you use this and Kipling you will be able to lay down the foundations of a solid event plan which will make your festival's operations and planning much smoother and a more manageable ride. Not all project management software will allow you to plan backwards, but they can offer you a big picture overview to ensure you have left enough time to complete all critical tasks.

Project management apps

There are now an increasing number of cloud-based apps like Asana, Zoho and Monday, devised to help you manage teams working on projects. These are like a cross between a spreadsheet and fully-blown project management software. They take the pain out of setting up a project management system but are also more tailored to your needs than a spreadsheet.

These apps can be free for small user groups but will charge a monthly subscription fee for larger user groups. Most allow you to trial a limited version to see if and how they work for you. Apart from looking prettier than a spreadsheet, one of their chief advantages is that they are often cloud based. So, as long as you have an internet connection, you and your staff can interface with it regardless of location. Many of these types of application make internal team communication easier, in particular, Trello – which focuses on task management – and Slack, which is real-time chat software that connects with other apps such as Dropbox, Google Drive, and Twitter and can be much faster than email, especially during busy periods. Bear in mind, however, that whichever tool (or combination of tools) you decide to use, there will be a setting up and 'bedding-in' period where everyone learns and adapts to the system. You also need to ensure the online systems you use are secure especially if you are dealing with commercially sensitive data. Getting the buy-in of the festival team to stick to the agreed system is crucial to making sure everything works effectively.

'Hard shell, soft content'

This chapter has covered the purposes and processes of planning, and several project planning systems. We have also highlighted how the nature of your festival sites and venues will have a bearing on the planning issues you will face. That, if you like, is the outer hard shell of festival planning. Within that is a softer human element that is equally critical. You are going to be dealing with many different people undertaking different roles and with different interests, all critical to the success of your festival. These include:

- Creative artists and their managers
- The audience
- External suppliers such as caterers
- External contractors – people working for you, but not employed by you, who might include lighting and PA technicians, stage builders and electricians or people decorating your stages
- Your team
- Volunteers

You need to factor all of these into your planning. That means you must think about the role they will be playing, when they will become involved, what information they will need from you, what information you will need from them, and when that information will be needed.

All of this is the soft content of your festival plan. Miss a bit of this, or get the dates or specifications wrong, or fall behind schedule and it can have a knock-on effect on one or more other items and possibly a large number of people.

Industry example: Volunteering

Volunteering is integral to the festival and events industry. People who choose to volunteer do so for a variety of reasons; whether it is for personal/professional gain or virtue-seeking. The crucial wording in this statement is that it is the volunteer's choice. They are the decision makers in most scenarios whether they commit the time and energy to undertake the desired tasks asked of them and to what extent they push themselves.

Volunteers may pursue personal gains such as the development of key skills, experience and confidence as well as networking opportunities and meeting new people. They may also look to give something back to an industry they have benefitted from or seek to make a difference in society and contribute to the development of others.

Multifaceted rationales also come into play for the festival organisers. In many cases, festival-producing organisations rely on volunteers as the financial implication in staffing is too large to adequately arrange. With less access to funding, tighter budgets and subsequent constraints in place, volunteers offer organisations a cheaper alternative to staffing. However, volunteers can also provide knowledge and expertise which may not be available in the organisation itself. Filling that gap in the short term may help the organisation identify areas where there is a lack of knowledge and expertise that will be beneficial in the long term. Utilising individuals in temporary roles can be a highly effective way to bring fresh new ideas into an organisation, which may well have become set in its ways.

My own experience is relevant here, in that wanting to enter the business I sought to take on as many voluntary positions as I could. It was during this time that I came into contact with ArtReach taking on voluntary roles such as Artist Liaison before I began to be employed on a freelance basis as a Stage Manager. Subsequently in May 2017 I was appointed as an Assistant Producer and as part of this role, I now recruit and co-ordinate volunteers for ArtReach events and the Leicester Arts Festivals umbrella network. My experience with volunteering has been an incredibly positive one and is proof that it can lead to undoubted success later down the line. This is not a guarantee and many could find voluntary roles go no further than a short-term interaction. However, volunteering can provide a platform to prove to a potential employer that you are worth investing time and effort in.

It is, of course, not a one-sided argument and examples of negative experiences can be found anywhere. A key issue with volunteering is a lack of a binding contract between the individual and the organisation. At this stage, formal contracts are not issued to volunteers. We have discussed the possibility of producing letters of agreement. However, the nature of volunteering means that people have the right not to commit especially if the circumstances dictate that they can't. This leads to a degree of assumed doubt towards commitment and uncertainty on both sides. In order to reduce this uncertainty, it is important to ensure that you are always looking towards the quality of volunteers as opposed to sheer quantity.

Although, it must be noted that success with volunteers often relies on further perks or incentives than simply a 'good experience'. Volunteers want to be made to feel like an important part of the team and must be given roles of real value, especially those who are of the quality that organisations want and will truly gain the most benefit from. If they are not, then it is highly likely that lethargic performances may follow.

Training is always given to volunteers and can vary depending on the situation or the event. For example, within *Journeys Festival International,* a significant aspect of the roles will be working with refugees or asylum seekers. Knowledge of the general situation on RAS communities, how to communicate effectively with people who have English as a second language and what questions audience members may ask about will be vital. For this year's festival, we ran a briefing session with our volunteers in partnership with the charity Asylum Matters. Asylum Matters were able to conduct exercises about the asylum process which was very helpful to the volunteers who had little to no experience of this.

In general, volunteers will need to be made aware of a number of things such as time-keeping, the location of events, the role they are expected to undertake and fulfil, who they report to on a general basis (usually me), who they report to additionally in case an emergency arises (i.e. is there separate first aid/security on site), where necessary facilities are (toilets, refreshments etc) where the nearest exit points are if indoors, where an appropriate meeting point is if outdoors. It is also very important that it is made clear that there would usually be ad-hoc activities that would need to be undertake by all members of the team (this usually would include audience queries, supporting artist requests, signposting, evaluation etc.).

The decision on how many volunteers is made well in advance of the festival dates. It will be made on reflection of the capacity and availability of the team here and whether there is a learning opportunity for volunteers to undertake. Of course, the more volunteers are available the easier the strain on the core staff, but it may also become an issue to manage larger groups. The other consideration would be whether essential aspects such as evaluation need more people to help facilitate. For example, as a Stage Manager, it is useful to have volunteer support with Artist Liaison to ensure the well-being of those we are working with. However, the volunteer in this role may also be asked to support with site setup, evaluation (artist or audience) and take down.

Ultimately, volunteering can be worth it for both sides. It is where so many budding festival managers gain their first authentic taste of 'real world' situations. The work on the ground will heighten their passion and desire for the roles that they seek. If it does neither of these things then it ultimately proves that the sector may not be for them. Organisations will only gain from this in the long term, as fresh faces enter the industry volunteering provides an avenue to those who will take organisations and productions to either the next level or another level entirely.

Oli Page, Assistant Producer with Artreach

Here are some more detailed issues you need to consider relating to the 'soft content' of your festival plan.

Artists, riders and staging: operational management implications

Some of the operational management issues you will have to deal with will be determined by the artists you book and by their technical and contractual requirements. This is the case regardless of whether your festival is focused on the visual arts, media arts or performing arts. It is true that technical requirements for a festival of literature are likely to be simpler than for a new media festival or indeed a rock music festival. But, nevertheless, each artist or creative practitioner you book will have particular technical preferences and needs, some more demanding than others.

In planning your festival, you need a clear idea of why you are doing it and from that, what your creative content will be. The introduction to this book looked at different types and models of festivals. So, are you a single artform festival or a multi-artform one? You also need to consider your creative content in relation to the venues at your disposal or that you are going to build (i.e. temporary structures). You need to get the price of the artists in balance with the capacity of the venue and the technical requirements of the artists in balance with the venue facilities and ability to accommodate the equipment.

To access this information and get the match right you are going to need to talk to the artist's agent (in many cases you are unlikely to talk to the artist directly until the day of the event). The agent will specify a fee and quite probably will produce a contract specifying terms. They will also be able to provide you with details of the artist's technical requirements. This may well form part of the contract and be a document called 'the contract rider'.

Contract riders are legendary, can be fearsome and sometimes expensive. They can also be very practical, specifying equipment without which the artist cannot perform. They can also request things that aren't completely necessary and, if the contract rider specifies something that it turns out is not used or needed, who pays? You do of course. So, it is well worth costing the contract rider and then going through it line by line with the agent.

Industry example: The rock band's rider

There is a famous story of a well-known 1980s American rock band whose contract rider specified, alongside hot drinks and food, a bowl of M&M sweets with all the brown ones removed. Here's what the actual rider looked like:

```
Fruit
      Fresh fruit platter, including apples, oranges, grapes, pears, melons,
         kiwi fruit and whole bananas

Hot Drinks
      Hot coffee (brewed, not instant)
      Hot water (for tea)
      Lipton tea bags
      Natural and herbal tea bags (e.g., Celestial Seasonings)
      One (1) lb. Tupelo honey
      Twelve (12) fresh lemons (with knife and cutting board)
      Cream and sugar

NOTE:  Water and coffee must be kept hot continuously with electric hot plates,
         urns or other suitable devices.

Munchies
      Potato chips with assorted dips
      Nuts
      Pretzels
      M & M's (WARNING:  ABSOLUTELY NO BROWN ONES)
      Twelve (12) Reese's peanut butter cups
      Twelve (12) assorted Dannon yogurt (on ice)
```

Many people thought this was either ridiculous or a 'power play' to show how important they were and what they could get away with.

In fact, it later emerged that there was a method behind the apparent madness. The band were touring when rock PA and lighting systems were far less high quality that they are today and when health and safety practices and regulations were far less rigorous. To perform the best show they possibly could – the aim of all artists – they had particular technical requirements that were set out in a complex and detailed technical specification in the contract rider. But they were also aware that venues were lax and sometimes didn't read the specifications, let alone act on them. So, the bowl of M&Ms with all the brown ones removed was a Trojan horse. If the band turned up at a venue and there was a bowl of M&Ms with all the brown ones removed, the tour manager could be pretty sure that the rest of the technical specifications had been fully met. However, if the bowl of M&Ms had the brown ones still there, the tour manager knew he needed to do a detailed check of the rest of the rider requirements including all the technical specifications, and if there was no bowl of M&Ms there at all, it was a signal there was a major potential problem and they might have to cancel the gig.

So, think about the technical requirements of the artists you want to book. Talk to the agents and look carefully at the contract riders.

Stage equipment

It is worth noting that some performances will require particular types of additional staging you may have to bring in. In particular some types of theatre and music performances require risers. These are smaller pieces of staging that raise the performers higher on the stage. In music it is usually for the drums and occasionally other instruments too, like horn sections. In the case of theatre or dance the risers may only be needed for parts of the show and will be wheeled into the wings at other times. In the case of music, they will be onstage at all times. Agents will probably specify the size (area) of risers needed to accommodate the artists and/or their equipment.

Specialist venue requirements

Some artforms have even more specific requirements. If you are putting on theatre, opera or ballet they may need to fly scenery. This requires a venue with a fly tower and mechanisms that lift scenery above the stage and drop it in at appropriate moments and technicians with the skills to do this. Actors and dancers require a venue with wings – side stage areas from where they generally make their entrances. Occasionally a production will require a trapdoor to the bowels underneath the stage. Dancers require a 'sprung stage' in order to perform. This is a wooden stage with some 'give' in it so they don't damage their ankles. The give is either built into the permanent stage or it is an overlaid 'dance floor'. The former is preferable.

Opera and musicals will usually bring or require a pit band, anything from half a dozen musicians to an orchestra of 30 or more. These perform in a music pit mostly underneath the stage, but partly below and to the front, so the conductor can see both the musicians and performers and ensure the music and performance are synchronised.

If you are putting on an orchestral or choral concert, they will be above ground on the stage itself. But often a thrust stage will be added. This completely covers the orchestral pit and brings the performers closer to the audience. Rock bands tend to play on the stage. If they are on the thrust, you need to check the thrust will carry the weight of any equipment they bring and also whether you risk a stage invasion if the band is too close to fans.

All of this means looking at the chosen venues and at the performers that have been booked and checking they are suitable. It is possible your creative team will have done some or all of this already.

Artist backstage needs

The needs and desires of most performing artists are fairly reasonable. Some food and drink before or after they perform, a nice quality changing space, and the feeling they are being looked after. Contract riders can however go well beyond this. We have known riders to require hotel rooms that the artists have then not used, and to require specific food and drink that they have not touched. So, it is worth checking with the agents if there is room for manoeuvre, maybe by making a counter-offer.

In addition, some riders can set very specific equipment requirements. If they seem unusual – for example a make of bass amplifier which is no longer in production – contact the agents and offer a reasonable alternative. At the end of the day, you, the artists and their agents all want the same thing: equipment and an environment that enables them to perform at their very best.

Case study

A classical music festival in a church involved one performance requiring an orchestra of 35 players, a violin soloist and a choir of at least 60 singers and the church organ. The choir offered to bring over 100 singers which was scaled back to around 80 after some discussion. The festival manager and the orchestra were concerned whether a big enough space could be created to accommodate orchestra and choir. It required several meetings and careful measurements being made. In addition the festival manager had to identify how to accommodate over 100 performers and adequate 'backstage' gathering, changing and secure storage space for the various groups, and the violin soloist, in a venue not designed for this. Some careful planning made it all work.

Pyrotechnics and special effects

Some artistic performances may involve pyrotechnics (fireworks) either as part of the performance, or as a closing sequence at the end of the festival. As festival manager you will need to be especially careful that pyrotechnics are handled and are set off properly and safely. If these are part of an act's performance, then the road crew that they bring with them should have one or more people with the requisite expertise to supervise this – as it will be part of their nightly show. If the pyrotechnics are part of a separate event that you have planned, then the responsibility is yours. You need to ensure you have read and comply with the Pyrotechnic Articles (Safety) Regulations 2015, or relevant legislation where your festival is taking place. In the UK these regulations are downloadable online at http://www.legislation.gov.uk/uksi/2015/1553/pdfs/uksi_20151553_en.pdf

Environmental issues

If you are working in an outdoor environment, you need to think carefully about drainage. If there is substantial rainfall prior to or during the event, where will the rain go? Will it merely sink into the ground making it soft and boggy? Will you need to provide some form of tracking (metal or wooden sheets) to ensure vehicle movements are possible and your audiences can move about easily?

Are you in a 'grass bowl' where rain will form into a large pond? Is that where you have put the camping area? Or is the site partially on a slope and, if so, what is the impact of the water draining down the hill? What's at the bottom of the hill or hills? There is no getting away from rain in Britain. For outdoor sites, some careful site planning will pay dividends to ensure you avoid the worst of the effects.

Case study

A jazz and blues festival at Lanhydrock House in Cornwall took place a little way from the house with the stage at the bottom of a nearby hill. This meant that a large contingent of the audience could sit on the upper reaches with a good stage view, watch, listen and eat their picnics, whilst others could go down close to the stage and enjoy a good dance. One year, prior to the event, it rained quite heavily and the audience space at the bottom of the hill became quite boggy. Dancing wasn't that safe but to fence the area off would have created a huge gap between the band and the audience and ruined the atmosphere. The production company had to move the stage about 20 yards forward where the ground was less boggy which left less flat ground for the audience. The compromise worked but it could have been far worse in other circumstances.

Logistics

This word simply means getting all the equipment and people to the right place at the right time. Your project plan should have a timescale showing activities you need to undertake on a daily or weekly timeline. If so, you are halfway to the addressing the logistics. But this also needs some care and attention. Logistics also involves time, people and access. Some of this may be your direct responsibility, some may be in the hands of external contractors, however, it's your job or the job of your team to check that everything arrives on time and will fit.

Greenfield sites require a much longer set-up and build time than a fully equipped theatre. But the access issues can be a lot easier. Your site is likely to be well away from built-up areas, therefore you can set up away from prying eyes and interference, and only open when you are ready, which is hopefully when you said you'd be ready. But what size of trucks vans and lorries will be bringing the equipment in? What width are the gates into the site and what is the turning angle like? Small things like this can make the difference between being on time and well behind schedule.

Indoor venues can be just as problematic. What is the access like? Once the equipment is unloaded do the vehicles need to be kept nearby? If so, where will they park? If artists are staying overnight, where is the hotel in relation to public transport (they may be coming by train) and in relation to the venue?

Venues like churches can be open to the public and therefore you may not be able to close them for the fit up and rehearsals. You will have to work around liturgical commitments and churches were not designed with secular performances in mind. If you want to bring in lighting and sound, you need to take careful note of their power supplies which may not be sufficient to meet modern needs.

> **Case study**
>
> An outdoor performance of Carl Orff's Carmina Burana with full orchestra and choir plus stage and lighting at an historic fort with spectacular views in Cornwall nearly came to grief. Forts were designed to keep people out rather than let them in. Their gateways are often narrow and low. The lorries carrying the stage and lighting equipment got in with inches to spare thanks to careful forward planning by the festival organisers who notified suppliers about the restrictions so they could ensure they picked the right sized vehicles.

Environmental impact

We live in a world of increasing demand and diminishing resources. Every festival staged has an environmental impact, all of it resulting from human activity. The growth of outdoor festivals has emphasised this impact. From the 1970s onwards, large scale outdoor festivals have left behind a wasteland of trampled ground overlaid with a sea of litter. The human race is very good at bringing supplies to the party and very poor at taking the residue away. The British media reported an estimated 60,000 tents were left abandoned after a 2018 British rock festival. (Metro, 2018)

Figure 5.5: *Reading Festival* – The aftermath (Source: Metro, 2018)

There has been a growing movement to assess and reduce the environmental impact of festivals, especially on greenfield sites, and to minimise the human footprint they create. In Britain this has been spearheaded by Julie's Bicycle (www.juliesbicycle.com), a London based charity set up in 2006 to support the creative community to act on climate change and environmental sustainability. The organisation seeks to help festivals embed sustainability into festival planning and monitor environmental impacts.

Richard Fletcher (2015) recommended that festivals should incorporate environmental measures into their regular reporting systems and licence applications just as they do finances and audience data. The environmental impact of your festival mainly includes the following:

♦ Energy use

♦ Waste and waste disposal

♦ Water quality and volume

♦ Land impact and contamination

♦ Transport to and from the event

Some of this is predominantly related to greenfield festivals, but some affect indoor venues too. These issues need thinking about as you may be asked for an Environmental Impact Statement as part of your Event Management Plan (see Chapter 7).

There is a lot of detail surrounding the above issues and much expert advice available. Here are a few factors to consider:

Energy use

Are the lights and power sources you are using the most energy efficient available? Traditionally, power supply on greenfield sites is provided by diesel generators, however there are companies building and renting solar powered generators. Alternatively, it may be possible to power generators with an eco-friendlier biodiesel.

Waste and waste disposal

An eco-friendly festival will have a policy on the use of plastics and recycling. It will encourage its suppliers to source degradable or recyclable plastics. It will aim to collect as much recyclable materials as possible, especially aluminium cans and plastic bottles. It will have sufficient waste bins on site to reduce post-event litter clearance to a minimum and ask festival attendees to act responsibly and clear their waste away or take it home. Your festival's waste policy could also source potential beneficiaries for abandoned usable items such as wellington boots, clothing, tents, sleeping bags, rucksacks and umbrellas. A partnership with a local charity would be better than sending such items to landfill. Regular waste collections during the event will maintain the site integrity and reduce your workload after the audience has gone home.

Water quality and volume

Where camping is involved, you need to ensure the water quality is fit for purpose. Camping is also likely to involve showers and toilets and that is where you can seek water efficiency through limits on water flow through showers and to toilet cisterns.

Land impact and contamination

The impact of thousands of people on a greenfield site can be quite destructive, especially when vehicles are involved. You need to assess vehicle routes and ensure that existing tracks are used where possible. Where vehicles will be moving across grass or fields, you may need to lay tracking or matting especially if rain is likely. Land contamination is likely to arise from diesel spillage or contractors disposing of cooking oils or other substances direct into the land rather than into sealed containers. You need to specify eco-friendly policies in your supplier contracts.

Transport impact to and from the event

This is a site selection consideration. How close is your site to public transport hubs (bus and train stations)? Can you encourage people to travel by public transport and train rather than by individual cars? Could you incentivise this in your ticket prices? Can you lay on a shuttle bus service from public transport hubs to the festival site? Can you supply enough buses to meet the demand? *Latitude Festival* provides good examples of how this can be done even by a commercial festival. The first student-focussed *Beach Break Live Festival* used a series of coaches to bus the audience from the nearest public transport hub to the Festival site. The aim here is to reduce two environmental impacts: one of thousands of cars driving to your event, thereby reducing vehicle pollution; and the second the land impact of thousands of cars on a greenfield site.

If you are just starting out and your festival is small or if your event is town and venue-based, then some of the above details will not apply. But the principles apply to all. How can you minimise potentially negative environmental impacts that your festival might cause without reducing the quality or the enjoyment that it will bring?

Summary

Every event, be it a conference, a product launch or a festival comes with in-built uncertainties. It might be a piece of equipment that fails at a crucial moment or a group of people who are just having too much of a good time and put themselves in a risky situation.

Good festival planning will both help deliver your objectives and enable you to react quickly to any such uncertainties. Planning starts with being clear on what you are trying to achieve and then working out, in a methodical way, the things you have to do to deliver the outcomes. It's all about the detail. If you hate the detail, find someone who eats and breathes it. They may drive you mad occasionally, but they will save your backside one day.

There are several different planning processes and systems you can use which this chapter has detailed. Each has its merits. Find the one that you feel most at home with and use it. The other factor in planning your festival is time. There's never enough of it and you may run clean out of it at some point. A good festival plan will include a timeline so you know how long each process will take and you can ensure you are on track. Some things may take a lot longer than you envisage. Over time you will get experience of just how long various activities take. But if it's your first festival and you think you can plan and deliver it in, say, six months, you might be prudent in adding a month or two for comfort.

As well as the planning process, 'the hard shell', festival planning and management also has to deal with the 'soft content' inside it. These are the people you will work with, including agents, artists, suppliers, technicians, volunteers and ultimately the audience. The experienced ones should be a joy to work with. But they may also have their own particular ways of doing things. Again, you will learn over time how to work with them and possibly one or two whose working style doesn't suit you and your aspirations.

The planning process is all about delivering the right things to the right place at the right time. If it works well, all that hard work will be virtually invisible, meaning you will get considerable satisfaction, but probably little direct thanks. But if you haven't planned properly and things are not in the right place at the right time, then you, the festival operations director, will be in the firing line. It's not a comfortable place to be. So, invest heavily in your plan and look after the people working on and at your festival. That way if the unexpected does happen you will be well placed to deal with it and people will rally to help you solve any problems that arise.

Lastly, if you want people to come back and work with you again, there are two words that cost nothing but mean a lot to artists, paid staff, technicians, suppliers and volunteers, some of whom may be working long hours in less than pleasant conditions. Those words are 'thank you'. Don't forget them.

References

Association for Project Management (n.d.) The core components of project management https://www.apm.org.uk/resources/what-is-project-management/ [Accessed on 29 October 2018].

Barrow, C., Barrow, P., and Brown, R. (2018) *The Business Plan Workbook: A Step-By-Step Guide to Creating and Developing a Successful Business*. Seattle: Amazon Media.

Croft C. (2018) https://www.youtube.com/watch?v=qkuUBcmmBpk (accessed 23 Sept 2018).

Evans, V. (2015) *The FT Essential Guide to Writing a Business Plan: How to win backing to start up or grow your business*. London: FT Publishing International.

Events Industry Forum, The (2015) The Purple Guide to health, safety and welfare at music and other events Online at: https://www.thepurpleguide.co.uk/ [accessed 22/9/2018].

Fletcher, R. (2015) Festivals in Transition: Greenlight Festival Leicester. In: Newbold, C. et. al. Focus on Festivals: Contemporary European case studies and perspectives. Oxford: Goodfellow.

Foreman P. (2013) Doing Things Differently Mind Map Available from: https://commons.wikimedia.org/wiki/File:Doing-things-differently-mind-map-paul-foreman.png [Accessed 29 October 2018].

Genadinik, A. (2015) Business plan template and example: how to write a business plan: Business planning made simple. Seattle: CreateSpace Independent Publishing Platform.

HM Government (2015) [online] The Pyrotechnic Articles (Safety) Regulations 2015 Available at: http://www.legislation.gov.uk/uksi/2015/1553/pdfs/uksi_20151553_en.pdf [Accessed 29 October 2018].

HSE (1999) *The Event Safety Guide,* Norwich: HSE Books, downloadable from: https://www.qub.ac.uk/safety-reps/sr_webpages/safety_downloads/event_safety_guide.pdf

Julie's Bicycle https://www.juliesbicycle.com/

Metro (2018) *Thousands of tents left behind at Reading Festival that will now go to landfill,* 29 August, https://metro.co.uk/2018/08/29/thousands-of-tents-left-behind-at-reading-festival-that-will-now-go-to-landfill-7891779/ [Accessed 29 October 2018].

Newton R. (2016) *Project Management Step by Step: How to Plan and Manage a Highly Successful Project.* London: Pearson.

Stone, P. (2002) *The Ultimate Business Plan*. London: How to Books.

Further reading

Association for Project Management (nd) *Planning, Scheduling, Monitoring and Control* Princes Risborough: AfPM.

Conway D.G. (2009) *The Event Manager's Bible*. London: Robinson.

Croft C. (2013) *Project Management: Plan and deliver successful projects on time and to budget*. Poole: Chris Croft Training.

Festivals and the Law

by Paul Kelly

After reading this chapter you should:

■ Understand which legislation affects festivals and what detail you need to know

■ Understand the principles of licensing

■ Understand what sort of event licence you need and how to apply for one

■ Understand the principles of copyright and how it affects your festival

■ Understand what insurances you will need by law

■ Understand the principles of contracts.

Introduction

In order to run your festival, you will need to comply with a range of legislation, obtain a number of licenses, and get permissions of some sort from various authorities. The nature of those permissions will depend entirely on the type of festival you are running, the country you are in and the types of locations you are using. If your festival is selling drink you will need an alcohol license and if it is taking place on public or private land it may well need a licence from the local authority. In a venue, like a theatre, which already has a creative programme it is likely that it will come with many of the permissions you need. If your festival is on a greenfield site, it is quite possible it will have none and that you will have to obtain all these permissions for yourself.

The legislation determining what you can and cannot do breaks down into two convenient categories:

♦ Legislation that you need to know and understand

♦ Legislation that you need to be aware of, but not necessarily in detail.

Although the detail will vary from country to country, the areas where the law will have an impact on your festival are generally:

♦ The ability to use a venue for public performance and venue capacity – the number of people you can cater for

♦ The sale of food and drink

- ◆ Processions – as in carnival processions
- ◆ Staff employment
- ◆ Copyright and payment to artists for the use of their works.

Health and safety forms a part of venue usage and the sale of food and drink and will be an important factor in gaining permissions, however these may not be legal issues in their own right. In addition, you will find it useful to be aware of the law in relation to contracts as you will almost certainly be encountering these both in relation to artists and possibly in relation to sub-contractors. You also have to deal with the law in relation to insurance.

This chapter will cover the basics of all of these matters. We have based it on the law in England and Wales as it stands today, but you need to be aware that over time new legislation is introduced and more importantly, far from being set in stone, the law is subject to interpretation. You would be well advised to find a friendly local solicitor, invite them onto your management committee and seek updated advice where required. If your solicitor is not an expert in the matters concerning festivals and events they might to be able to call on someone in their firm for low cost or no-cost (pro-bono) advice.

This chapter aims to familiarise festival managers with the general principles in law, permissions and licences required to run a festival, it must be emphasised however that it is always the responsibility of the festival organiser to ensure that they conform, in full, with all relevant statutory and other national and local requirements.

Key legislation

There are two key pieces of legislation affecting festivals which you need to be have a good knowledge of. One was the direct outcome of festivals activity. The two pieces of legislation are:

- ◆ The Public Order Act (1986) updated by the Criminal Justice and Public Order Act (1994)
- ◆ The Licensing Act (2003).

The Public Order Act regulates public gatherings of anything more than 20 people. It came about partly as the result of increasing tension in the 1980s between a convoy of counter-cultural activists known as New Age travellers and landowners, local authorities and the police. The New Age travellers travelled the country in repurposed buses and vans, staged impromptu festivals on common land, gathered at the annual solstice celebrations at Stonehenge and attended festivals like *Glastonbury*. It culminated in the Battle of Beanfields, a violent encounter between the convoy and the police as the travellers attempted to get to Stonehenge in 1985, resulting in damage, injuries and arrests (Worthington, 2004).

The outcome was the passing of the Public Order Act (1984) to regulate assemblies of more than 20 people, requiring them to obtain police consent. This had a two-fold cultural effect. It led to the commercialisation of music festivals and the development in the 1990s of underground rave culture. Although the clampdown was specific to England and Wales, it points to something all festival producers should be aware of. Governments, however liberal, are alert to the potentially disruptive effect of large gatherings and tend to want to control them. So, wherever your festival takes place there will probably be legislation that means you have to ask the authorities for permissions of one sort of another.

There are two key aspects in the Public Order Act (1986) that affect festivals in England and Wales.

Processions

Organisers of public processions of any kind – political, cultural or otherwise – need to give the police at least 6 clear days' written notice, including details of the intended time and route, and the name and address of at least one person proposing it.

Assemblies

The police have the power to impose conditions on outdoor assemblies of 20 people or more "to prevent serious public disorder, serious criminal damage or serious disruption to the life of the community". The conditions might specify the greatest number of people who may take part, the location of the assembly, and its maximum duration. This means that if you want to stage an outdoor event for more than 20 people, the police can ban it. In 1994 the Public Order Act was amended to add rules against covered trespass, squatting and unauthorised camping. If the site you want to use is private you will need the land owner's permission, and, you will need to think about how your festival might affect the surrounding residents, and what to do in emergencies. These are the issues local councils and the police and emergency services will want to see you address in your licence applications.

Licensing Act 2003

The police powers outlined in the Public Order Act (1986) are rarely used today in relation to festivals and events owing to a streamlining of the licensing laws. In respect of festivals, licensing is permission from someone in authority for an organisation to sell alcohol and provide entertainment in a public place. If you don't have a licence for these you may be acting illegally.

As Pick notes, there are four major ways in which festivals and other cultural events can be subject to licensing control:

Governments may:

♦ License the audience

♦ License venues and public spaces

♦ License the artwork itself (censorship)

♦ License the professional artist

(Pick, 1988: 76-8)

In Britain the government has chosen to focus on licensing venues and public spaces.

Most licensing issues concerning festivals are dealt with in:

♦ The Licensing Act 2003

♦ The Live Music Act of 2012 and

♦ The June 2007 Guidance issued under section 182 of the Licensing Act 2003 and Amended in June 2013.

Within the UK government, the Department for Digital Culture Media and Sport (DCMS) is responsible for entertainment aspects of licensing and the Home Office is responsible for alcohol aspects of licensing. However, those bodies merely supervise the policy and advise on any necessary legislative changes.

The 2003 Licensing Act combined all licensing activity into a single responsibility and re-allocated responsibility for the consideration and granting of all licences to local authorities. This meant alcohol and public entertainments licences can be applied for and dealt with at the same time in England and Wales. Our advice is to contact your local authority to find out who has responsibility for licences and ask their advice. In principle, in democratic countries licensing authorities are not trying to stop you running an event: they just want it to happen in a way that keeps participants safe, and doesn't disrupt other citizens too much. It is in their interests to help you to understand how best to do this in advance.

In fact, the 2003 Act is a good example of this. It is primarily concerned with public safety and has four objectives towards that end: the prevention of crime and disorder, public safety, the prevention of public nuisance and the protection of children from harm. Its scope covers:

♦ The sale of alcohol by retail outlets

♦ The supply of alcohol by clubs

♦ The provision of 'regulated' entertainment

♦ The provision of late-night refreshment

Under the 2003 Act, local authorities are responsible for all aspects of licensing. By law they have to consult with the police, the local fire authority, representatives of local licensed premises (places that sell alcohol like pubs, bars, restaurants and clubs), and representatives of businesses and residents in the area. The local authority is also encouraged to work in partnership with other relevant agencies.

So, the implication is, if you are planning to stage a new festival, especially one in an area of high population, it is worth consulting with local residents, community groups and the local Licensed Victuallers Association, if you are seeking an alcohol licence. At the worst you can start to identify objections and try to find work-arounds, at the best you might get positive support, all of which will be valuable when making your application.

Under the Licensing Act 2003 every local authority has to produce a local licensing policy and to review it annually. You will find this policy on their websites. It may be generic, but you may find useful indicators, words and phrases to help your approach and application.

The Licensing Act 2003 covers:

- ♦ What activities are licensable
- ♦ The role of licensing authorities
- ♦ Premises licenses
- ♦ Clubs (private members clubs)
- ♦ Permitted temporary activities
- ♦ Personal licenses
- ♦ Offences
- ♦ Closure of premises (that fail to comply with their licence terms)
- ♦ Racial Equality
- ♦ Live music, dancing and theatre
- ♦ Personalised Licenses
- ♦ Open spaces, and
- ♦ Responsibilities – officer delegation

You will find that the 2003 Act itself is written in legal language you may find hard to understand. However, the guidance under section 182 is written in plain English and worth reading carefully. You will find it on the DCMS website at https://www.gov.uk/government/publications/explanatory-memorandum-revised-guidance-issued-under-s-182-of-licensing-act-2003

There were some key changes in emphasis over previous legislation including:

- ♦ **Public order in city centres**: It sought indirectly to reduce drunk and disorderly behaviour in town and city centres
- ♦ **Licensing hours – extended drinking times**: It extended drinking times beyond the 11pm closure that had been the norm until then

- ◆ **Staggered closing times**: It sought staggered closing times, with some at 11pm and some later, in order to avoid everyone spilling onto the streets at the same time.

- ◆ **Single licence for liquor and entertainment**: A new streamlined system

- ◆ **'Cumulative impact'**: The local authority has to consider public order and safety issues. But this should not inhibit the development of thriving and safe evening and night-time local economies.

- ◆ **Children in licensed premises and in cinemas**: The licensing policy should not seek to limit access to children (so long as they are accompanied by an adult), unless there is a threat of moral or psychological harm.

- ◆ **Cultural strategies and tourism**: Local licensing policies should encourage and promote a broad range of entertainment, particularly live music, dancing and theatre for the cultural benefit of communities.

- ◆ **Community benefit**: In addition, to ensure cultural diversity, local authorities were encouraged to seek premises licenses for public spaces in the community in the name of the local authority. So, for example, a local park would be licensed by the council, saving the community the trouble of obtaining one. All the local authority has to do is give its permission for use. So, you need to identify who owns any spaces you want to use, and what their underlying purpose is – it might be easier to get permission for a park that already has a licence than a greenfield site that doesn't.

Licensing and entertainment

You need a licence if your event involves 'regulated entertainment'. However live music performed to no more than 200 people does not need a licence.

Schedule 1 of the 2003 Act defines 'regulated entertainment' as including:

a) The performance of a play

b) An exhibition of film

c) An indoor sporting event

d) A boxing or wrestling entertainment

e) A performance of live music

f) Any playing of recorded music

g) A performance of dance

h) Entertainment of a similar description to that falling within paragraph (e), (f) or (g)

In festival terms this means you will need a licence if you employ and present actors, musicians or dancers. Other artists like jugglers, magicians and street performers are not specified or named in the definition.

Entertainment facilities means amenities for enabling persons to take part in entertainment consisting of making music, dancing, or entertainment of a similar description to making music or for dancing. This suggests street entertainers like jugglers and fire eaters might be covered under the definition of 'regulated entertainment'.

If you have entertainment facilities that you offer or the public use for entertainment then you need a license under the 2003 Act. These include:

♦ A karaoke machine provided for the use of and entertainment of customers in a public house

♦ A dance floor provided for use by the public in a nightclub

♦ Musical instruments made available for use by the public to entertain others at licensed premises.

Much of this involves the simple application of common sense and the guidance cannot give examples of every eventuality or possible activity. Our mantra in all cases of the law, is if in doubt, check.

The Live Music Act 2012

As well as control, governments are also keen to support activities they approve of. One of the secondary purposes of the 2003 Licensing Act was to encourage and increase the promotion of live music in pubs and clubs, in order to help the music industry and the creative economy. The fact that you can apply for both alcohol and performance licences at one and the same time from a single place led to expectations this would benefit live music and musicians. Music industry groups, however, felt it didn't work as intended and research and a subsequent campaign led by the singer and music industry executive Feargal Sharkey argued for amendments to the 2003 Act to give more favourable conditions for music performance.

This led to the Live Music Act (2012) and the following changes:

♦ Unamplified live music no longer needs a licence

♦ Amplified music does not need a licence unless the local authority imposes specific venue conditions and

  ❖ it takes place between 8am and 11pm

  ❖ it takes place at a licensed premises or workplace and

  ❖ the audience is no more than 200 people

So, if you are running a small festival using multiple small venues, you will not need licences for performances if they fulfil the above conditions.

In addition, some types of music are generally exempt from licensing. These include: karaoke; busking; spontaneous singing – e.g. people singing along to recorded music in a pub; incidental music – live music that is incidental to other activities not classed as regulated entertainment; rehearsals and sound checks (unless members of the public are charged admittance for the purpose of making profit); and the playing of some recorded music as part of a performance of live music performance. Note: if you are a venue and have a karaoke machine you will need a licence, but the act of karaoke singing does not.

> **Case study**
> Following the passing of the 2003 Act, a restaurant in London was visited by local licensing officers who threatened to close it down for not having a licence for regulated entertainment. The restaurant protested they did not stage live music performances. The officers argued they did: they hosted birthday parties where Happy Birthday was sung. The Live Music Act (2012) clarified that issue.

The following are also excluded from the definition of 'Regulated Entertainment'

- ◆ Education – teaching students to perform music or to dance
- ◆ Activities which involve participation as acts of worship in a religious context
- ◆ The demonstration of a product – e.g., a guitar – in a music shop
- ◆ The rehearsal of a play or rehearsal of a performance of music to which the public are not admitted.

Private events are only licensable if you charge an entrance fee and intend to make a profit. So, for instance, a private event with an attendance of more than 500 people, which charged to cover the costs of the entertainment, and for no other purpose, would not require a license.

Some activities falling outside the 'regulated entertainment' definition are also exempt, such as vehicles in motion (e.g. steel bands on the back of lorries) and visual art exhibitions.

The purpose of detailing these UK licences is to demonstrate the range of areas and conditions the law might intervene in. Specific conditions will vary over time and depending on where you are. But the general principle is that national and local authorities are concerned to find a balance between the rights of people to participate in festivals and events and the rights of residents to not have their lives disrupted, and to keep everyone safe. How they go about enforcing that will vary, but if you think what you are doing might lead to questions about either of those principles, do ask your local licensing officer.

TSchools

The licensing act does not clearly address the issue of events in schools. However a sensible interpretation of Section 182 is that if a performance is for and involving teachers, pupils and their parents, then effectively it is a private event and should not need a licence.

If however it is a publicly advertised event staged by the school for the general public and especially if it is ticketed and seeks to raise money, then it may need a licence. If in doubt consult your local Licensing officer.

Events in churches

The Act says that the provision of any entertainment or entertainment facilities:

(a) for the purposes of, or for purposes incidental to, a religious meeting or service, or

(b) at a place of public religious worship,

is not to be regarded as the provision of regulated entertainment for the purposes of this Act.

So, if your festival involves some or all performances in churches you will not need licences for those performances.

To summarise: when you need a licence

In England and Wales you will only need a licence:

- If the event is for the general public

- If you wish to sell alcohol

- And/or if you are staging 'regulated entertainment' to 500 people or more

The type of licence you need depends on whether the event and premises will be occasional or regular. The rules are quite complex and there are some other exemptions. Paragraphs 16.5 and 16.6 of Section 182 of the 2003 Licensing Act set these out clearly (DCMS 2018).

If you are staging an event in a park or an open space and the event is for the public, you will probably need a licence unless the local authority owns the land and has licensed it already. A call to the licensing office will determine this.

Types of licences and how to apply

Now we move on to an important area: what sort of licences will you need. There are two different types of license: those for permanent premises that operate 365 days a year and Temporary Event Notices (TENs) designed for occasional events. Temporary events may range from relatively small local events, like traditional performances of a play, which may last for five days, to major rock and pop festivals lasting only one day.

Permanent premises licenses

These are usually for pubs, clubs, theatres, concert halls, etc. Large rock and pop festivals are temporary, in that they usually take place over three or four days, but they have to apply for a full premises licence, with, if anything even more paperwork owing to their size and complexity. Fees for premises licences are based on the ratable values of venues and in 2018 range from £100 to £635. Full full details are on the DCMS website https://www.gov.uk/government/publications/alcohol-licensing-fee-levels. Large events attracting over 5,000 people have to pay the Premises Licence Fee plus a supplement, which in 2018 were between £1,000 and £64,000 plus additional annual fees – full details are on the DCMS website https://www.gov.uk/government/publications/alcohol-licensing-fee-levels/additional-and-other-fees

Temporary Event Notices (TENs)

These are effectively for community type events in unlicensed venues (where alcohol is not regularly sold, if at all). There are restrictions on how many Temporary Event Notices may be given for any particular premises – 12 times in a calendar year. But one individual can only apply for 5 of those 12.

There are also limitations on the length of time a temporary event may last – 168 hours (7 days).

Individuals can apply for up to 5 TENs a year, or up to 50 if you hold a Personal License to sell alcohol (an advanced Bar Manager certificate).

The attendance at an event with a TEN is restricted to 499. So, if you hope to attract an audience bigger than that you will have to apply for a full Permanent Premises License.

If you can work your way round the various obstacles and restrictions, TENs can be quite quick and cheap to obtain. Most TENs have to be applied for 21 days in advance. Each costs £21. But you can apply for up to 10 Late TENs a year – 5 days before the event (10 if you hold a Personal Licence).

If your event is large, outdoor or unusual, speak to the police operations department. They will have seen all sorts of events over the years, will be pleased to hear from you in advance and may have useful advice to give for your licensing application.

Child performers

If you are staging a festival that involves child performers then they will fall under the provisions of Children (Performances and Activities) (England) Regulations 2014. This piece of legislation is designed to enable talented children to take part in professional performances, sport or modelling, but to protect their health, welfare and education, and prevent them from being exploited. The law applies to all children from birth until completion of compulsory schooling at the age of 16. The licence is applied for not by the child or his or her parents but by the event organiser.

A child may perform without a licence for up to four days, but only if:

♦ It is unpaid
♦ No absence from school is required
♦ The child has not performed in the previous six months

Performances arranged by schools, scouts, guides, and youth clubs are exempt from licensing and no application is needed. However, if a child is absent from school for rehearsals or performances, then they must be licensed.

Local authorities and applications

Licences for alcohol and entertainment are issued by District Council or Unitary Authorities (usually cities). County Councils (like Leicestershire, Oxfordshire, Cumbria, Dorset etc), do not have a licensing remit.

Child Performance Licences will be dealt with by a Local Authority's Education Department. That is a function of a County Council or Unitary Authority. District Councils do not deal with Education.

Insurances

In broad terms insurance is an agreement where you pay an insurance company money and they pay your costs if you suffer an accident, injury, loss or someone claims against you for the same. The insurance company will issue you with a policy which usually lasts for one year. The policy will contain all sorts of detailed terms and conditions. If nothing untoward happens they will keep your money (known as premiums) and you have peace of mind knowing if anything had gone wrong you would have been covered. Insurance premiums can range from £100 or so to several thousands and depend on the nature of the risk being insured. A premium of £100 may cover you against several million pounds of losses or claims.

There are several types of insurances required by law. The ones you will or may need if you are running an event are:

♦ Public liability insurance
♦ Employer's liability insurance
♦ Car or vehicle insurance

These are explained further on.

You can buy your insurance through a large insurance company directly, through an insurance broker who will deal with specialist market areas or generalist insurance brokers who will shop around and sell you the best deal.

Types of insurance

There are many types of insurance and not a lot that cannot be insured. But there are also four basic categories of Insurance policies that cover:

♦ Third party liabilities: things like injury to persons or damage to property (someone other than you)

♦ Physical effects for loss or damage (to you)

♦ Business interruption or cancellation of one or more performances or activities

♦ People: either as key people to a production in which their non-appearance would force its cancellation, or for those involved in hazardous work, or because they are travelling abroad.

Public Liability Insurance

Public Liability Insurance is a legal requirement if you are staging live events. You will not get licensing approval for your event if you do not have this. It is usually purchased for a year. The minimum cover needed is usually set at £5 million but local authorities reserve the right to require a higher limit if deemed necessary. The sum insured is the maximum single payment that the policy will pay out. But you should always check the policy small print.

Employer's Liability Insurance

The Employers Liability (Compulsory Insurance) Act 1969 (ELCA) makes it compulsory for employers to have employer's liability insurance. So, if you employ any staff, you will need it. This provides cover against claims by employees who have suffered an injury, accident or illness in the course of their work for you.

The definition of employment is a contested one with some companies like the taxi firm Uber claiming its drivers are self-employed, not employees. This gig economy status is being challenged in the courts in a number of areas. The downloadable ELCA guide (http://www.hse.gov.uk/pubns/hse40.pdf) includes details of what counts and exemptions. However, this is shifting ground so make sure you get proper up-to-date advice.

If you employ staff it is compulsory to have at least £5 million of Employers' Liability Insurance, and some say £10 million.

Other forms of insurance

There are many other forms of insurance, some of which you may wish to consider and some of which are a legal requirement (e.g. car insurance). These include:

Buildings and equipment insurance

Buildings insurance will be based on the value of rebuilding the premises and contents insurance is based on the value of the contents.

Trustees and directors indemnity insurance

This will protect your trustees or directors from claims against them.

Business interruption or cancellation insurance

This will cover business interruption or cancellation of one or more performances caused by cast illness or withdrawal or headline act withdrawal

Car insurance

To cover you against accident, loss or claims against you resulting from an accident. Any employee using their own vehicle needs to ensure that their motor insurance provides cover for business use.

Weather insurance

This is usually known as 'pluvius' insurance (after the Roman god of rain). Pluvius insurance pays an amount should a certain amount of rain fall that affects the viability of your event. It would be purchased, for example, by organisers of outdoor festivals to compensate for losses if an event has to be called off. It can be very expensive!

Key person insurance

This can be taken out to cover you if a key member of your team goes sick or dies at a time that adversely affects the business. For example, if your production manager falls ill and genuinely cannot be replaced causing you to cancel the event, you could receive compensation. The precise details and the level of compensation would be negotiated when the policy is taken out.

Copyright

Artists generally make money in two ways: from the sale of their work directly to the public, or through the use of the work they have created – their intellectual property – by others. The former might include fees from live performances or the sale of a painting or sculpture. The latter is through royalty payments from the use of their work by others – this is generally known by the shorthand of copyright income or just copyright.

The precise nature of copyright depends on the artform involved. Copyright royalties are generally low when the artwork cannot be copied and at their greatest when mechanical reproductions of a work of art sell to thousands or millions of people. As a result visual artists don't tend to earn very much from copyright as they make original one off works of art. So, the sale price of those works tends to be high.

Actors only earn significant royalties if they appear on television or films where the work is repeated or mechanically reproduced on DVD or released digitally. They will also earn a copyright fee if the work is broadcast on television or radio or shown in the cinema.

Musicians earn copyright royalties from writing the work, live performance and from mechanical sales (vinyl, CDs digital downloads, etc.). If you write a top selling piece of music, you will get royalties from live and broadcast performance. If you just perform on a top selling piece of music, you will get some royalties. If you have written the work and you perform on it, you will get even more royalties, both from live performances (by you and your group or by others) and from broadcasts (radio and TV). Royalties are nation specific, so you should get separate royalties from the UK, America, Australia – wherever the song is performed.

For playwrights and dance choreographers, royalties come to them mainly from performances. The royalty costs will be built in to the cost of hiring the scripts or choreography necessary for the production.

Copyright collections agencies

As a festival manager your main dealings with copyright will be with bodies who collect royalties on behalf of artists and then distribute them to their members. If you are a music festival then the main collection agencies you will deal with are PPL and PRS. In the past Performance Phonographic Limited (PPL) collected music copyright fees from broadcasters for music airplay and the Performing Rights Society (PRS) collected copyright fees from promoters for the live performance of music. The two bodies have now merged but their functions remain the same. PRS for Music has around 130,000 members who are all composers. Other collective management organisations cover theatre, video etc. You can find out more from the UK Government's Intellectual Property Office (https://www.gov.uk/guidance/licensing-bodies-and-collective-management-organisations).

If you promote music then by law your venue will need a PRS licence which entails a fee which is dependent on size and function, you will also have to pay a proportion of ticket income to the PRS and give them a set list of the works performed and the composers involved. For classical music, the PRS fee is 4.8% of ticket income. For popular music concerts it is 3%. Full details of how to obtain a PRS licence and their royalty schemes is on their website: www.prsformusic.com.

Other legislation you need to be aware of

The previous sections have dealt with legal aspects you will have to comply with. This last section concerns legislation or legal issues that you may not have to deal with directly, but that you need to be aware of. There are two areas: health and safety and contracts.

Health and safety

In law it is well-established that event organisers have a duty of care to the workers, participants, spectators and the general public, as Lord Chief Justice Taylor stated in his report on the Hillsborough disaster, "public safety must transcend all other issues". There is a large body of health and safety legislation and you may be puzzled why we have placed this in an awareness rather than a compliance section. The answer is, whilst you will be required to demonstrate in your licensing application that you have thought about the health and safety implications of your event, principally through a detailed risk assessment, you possibly do not need to possess an in-depth knowledge of all the acts governing this area (a detailed approach to health and safety is set out in Chapter 7).

However, if you are a festival manager, you really should have a good working knowledge of the Management of Health and Safety at Work Regulations 1999. The processes in this will cover a wide range of situations. You need to make sure your festival has the appropriate type level of insurance, any subcontractors have this as well and that you have copies of their paperwork. If you are providing all the services yourself, then a closer reading of health and safety legislation maybe useful, especially if you are involved in large-scale production and set-building. Stranks (2006) provides a valuable guide to the legislation. However, if you are contracting out services like production, catering and the like, then you need to sure that your sub-contractors are up to speed and compliant with prevailing legislation. Caterers, for instance, must comply with the Food Safety Act 1990 and the Food Safety (General Food Hygiene) Regulations 1995 and any amendments thereto. A useful contact in these sorts of areas is the local authority environmental health officer who can advise on many aspects from catering to site clearance.

Contracts

The other legal aspect which you need to be aware of, but where there is no defined government requirement, is contracts. As a festival manager you will inevitably come across contracts at some point and possibly with great regularity. They may be contracts with artists, with external contractors, with suppliers or even with consultants.

You are or will be running an event. Interestingly, as Becker points out, there is no legal definition of the word 'event'. If you cannot define it, then no one can 'own' an event. So, every event comprises a set of negotiations and agreements. As the diagram below illustrates, these negotiations and agreements may cover a very wide range of activities.

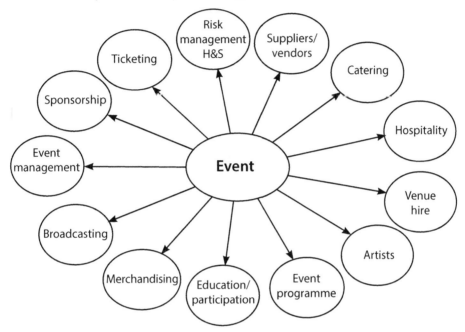

Figure 6.1: Negotiations and agreements (Becker, 2006: 3)

You may choose, and it may be wise, to define and formalise some or all these agreements in a contract. An event says Becker "usually has an objective and theme of some kind, and this gives it an air of formality" (2006: 2). The purpose of contracts is to record the rights and obligations of the various parties involved in the event. The most fundamental reason for having a written contract is to set out the exact terms of the arrangement between the parties, so that the rights and obligations of the parties are clearly defined (ibid).

Events are inherently risky. If the terms of the arrangement are vague, you increase the risk. Events can also go wrong and people have been known to sue event organisers if they are adversely affected. Clear contracts can help identify both responsibility and liability. Large events now often involve large numbers of sub-contractors. So, without contracts between the various parties, the event is at great risk (ibid).

The purpose of contracts is to record the rights and obligations of the parties involved in the event. The most fundamental reason for having a written contract is to set out the exact terms of the arrangement between the parties, so that the rights and obligations of the parties are clearly defined (ibid).

There are three parts to any contract

♦ An offer

♦ Acceptance of the offer

♦ A 'consideration'

The consideration is the legal term for the fee or the terms of the contract. It's what one of the parties will give to the other in exchange for their agreement to the contract – which might not be money!

There are also contract terms. These are details that can cover a multiplicity of matters. Suppose you are writing a contract for an artist to perform at your event, you need to think about the headings you have in the contract. At the end of this chapter is an example contract drawn up for the employment of artists by a local authority and checked by that authority's legal team. It has been used many times. However, you may want to draw up your own contract template and get it checked by a friendly solicitor.

Drawing up contracts

If you are booking an artist, do you send them a contract or do they send you the contract? It depends on scale and reputation of the artist. If it's a local artist, you will almost certainly deal with them directly and you will send them a contract. If it's a nationally known artist, they will have an agent and/ or manager. The likelihood is that they will have a standard contract that they will send you. You may be able to negotiate some of the details. Contracts are normally signed by each party as a record they have both agreed it. In this digital age, electronic signatures and scanned exchanges are becoming acceptable.

If you are going to be in control of your contract, make sure it is in plain English and that all people involved in the contract can understand it. Ambiguity or misinterpretation is very easy. So, if you are drafting a contract, read and re-read it to make sure that the terms cannot be misunderstood. Check it with others. There are five steps in constructing a contract:

1 Intention – initial offer is made

2 Negotiation – discuss, make addition tailor to needs

3 Initial acceptance – agreement on main points and what is to be exchanged for what

4 Agreement on terms – forming legal contract with details

5 Signing – contract established

This process can take some time, so be prepared and start the process as early as possible. It can be a very good idea to get a lawyer to look over and comment on a contract – from someone else or one you have written, especially if you have access to an in-house lawyer. But lawyers cost money. It's much cheaper to get their comments than to get them to write a contract.

Key common contract clauses you will want to think about including are:

♦ The parties details (who are they, and how they can be contacted)

♦ The services or products to be contracted

♦ Definitions of terms to be used throughout the contract

♦ Duration of contract

♦ Remuneration (consideration)

♦ Obligations of all parties

♦ Exclusivity of service

♦ Termination prior to expiry – such as failure to provide product

♦ Force majeure - 'act of God' circumstance outside of anybody's control

♦ Liability and damages – for non-performance, insurance cover, and dispute resolution

♦ Barring clause preventing the artist performing within an agreed distance and time of your festival.

As already stated you may find you are discussing contracts for a wide range of activities including performances, sub-contracting services and suppliers. In each case you need to define who is supply what to whom, when and on what terms and remember to include any critical quality benchmarks that you are expecting.

Contracts and working with international artists

One headache to be aware of when working with international artists is your country's regulations relating to foreign workers, and the costs and delays that involved in sorting out visas. Most countries operate visa systems that restrict who can enter, how long people can stay for and what they are allowed to do when they are there, particularly if they are coming to work rather than on holiday. This applies to artists and their supporting crew, too. Applying for visas is usually an artist's responsibility rather than the festival producer's, but it is wise to stay in touch regarding how the application process is going if you don't want to be left with a gap in your schedule. Artists should apply as soon as possible to avoid upsets, meaning contracts have to be in place earlier than might otherwise be the case. As visas can be expensive, agreement will need to be made about meeting these costs.

In the UK there are two main routes for artists to use in order to work. These are called Tier 2 (general) and Temporary Workers Tier 5 (creative and sporting) visas.

Tier 2 allows UK companies to employ non-residents workers if they have advertised the role for a set period and are unable to fill it from within the resident labour market. Alternatively, the government deems some jobs to be generally difficult to fill. The list of these Shortage Occupations is available on the Home Office website. It includes: artists, dancers and choreographers, musicians, arts officers, producers and directors. A full list can be found on the government website: https://www.gov.uk/guidance/immigration-rules/immigration-rules-appendix-k-shortage-occupation-list.

Workers on Tier 2 visas have to be employed for a minimum of 30 hours per week and be paid a salary above a minimum considered to reflect the market in the industry. An alternative more suitable for visiting artists is a Tier 5 visa. The Tier 5 (creative and sporting) visa is suitable for artists wanting to visit the UK to tour or play a few festivals. It is open to entertainers, artists and musicians who want to give performances; take part in competitions or auditions; make personal appearances and take part in promotional activities; attend workshops and give talks; or take part in cultural events or festivals on the list of permit free festivals. Artists will need a contract and certificate of sponsorship from the organisations they are going to appear at.

Festivals that have been established for more than three years, and have a track record of employing non-resident artists can apply to be included on a list of events that can invite performers without a certificate of sponsorship. This is a bureaucratic process requiring names, dates of birth and nationalities of all non-resident performers who have appeared in the previous 3 years, plus copies of festival brochures, press coverage, accounts and supporting letters from the Arts Council or local authority. This may seem daunting, but if you are going to promote international artists regularly it is worth finding out the requirements sooner rather than later and keeping records from the first edition. More details can be found at: https://www.gov.uk/browse/visas-immigration/work-visas

Industry example: ArtReach producing festivals nationally and internationally

ArtReach (www.artreach.biz) has a 20-year track record as a cultural consultant and creative producer, with its producing work focused on the development and delivery of large-scale, free access arts festivals. Initially ArtReach acted as a commissioned agent, devising and developing to delivery, a number of festival programmes on behalf of local authorities e.g. *Three Cities Create and Connect* (2005-2008) for Derby, Leicester and Nottingham City Councils. This work had an international dimension, which led to partnerships with a range of Latin American Embassies and with Canadian Government Offices, and an opportunity for ArtReach to lead and curate work in its own right.

Since 2010 ArtReach has evolved *Night of Festivals* (www.nightoffestivals.com) as a powerful "exploration and celebration of the values of freedom and democracy through great art" and has delivered 17 editions of the event in different locations – Nottingham, Leicester, Boston (Lincs), Lincoln, Slough, Barking, Hounslow and London (South Bank in Southwark and South Bank in Lambeth). The largest *Night of Festivals* event was presented on the South Bank by Tower Bridge in August 2016, aligned with the opening weekend of the Rio Olympics. It was attended by audiences of 160,000. *Night of Festivals* has also achieved European Union funding through Creative Europe and ArtReach has delivered elements of the Festival in Hamburg (Germany), Gabrovo (Bulgaria), Sibiu (Romania) and Rome (Italy).

In 2013 ArtReach initiated *Journeys Festival International* (www.journeysfestival.com) as an annual ten-day festival programme in Leicester, in order to "provide a platform for exceptional refugee and asylum seeker artists and to share the refugee experience through great art". Since 2016 the Festival has also been delivered for ten days annually in each of Manchester and Portsmouth. In 2017 ArtReach secured Creative Europe funding for an associated programme in Hamburg, Rome, Palermo and Budapest. Following a special European Union Call-Out, this was one of only 12 refugee arts focused projects funded across Europe.

We have found that delivering festivals with an international dimension brings a range of challenges, which can be broadly categorised as: budgeting and funding; communications and delegation; logistical arrangements; and marketing.

Budgeting and funding

In the UK, delivery of free access festivals has become increasingly challenging because of the lack of resources available to local authorities to provide any funding support. This has meant an increasing reliance on Arts Council England and private sources of income.

ArtReach has addressed this challenge by focusing on European partnerships and funding, primarily through Creative Europe. It has involved a creative approach, dove-tailing activity delivered with and through European partners with mainstream UK Festival delivery, so that discreet European projects sit inside and contribute to ArtReach UK festival delivery. Of course, this may all change with BREXIT.

The ArtReach solution, looking forwards, is to utilise excellent partnerships already estab-lished, so that in future ArtReach is an associate partner benefitting from applications sub-mitted by others, rather than being lead organisation controlling the application and deliv-ery process.

Delivering projects funded by the European Union brings many budget and reporting challenges – the required methodology for providing budgets does not match well with a typical arts organisation approach to budgeting; the EU requires fully evidenced documen-tation for all expenditure, however small, including certified time sheets and salary slips for core staff members and boarding passes from flights; some elements of typical expenditure e.g. taxi fares, are not allowable; and as lead organisation, ArtReach is required to have an independent external audit encompassing the financial reports provided by partners (a challenge when material is submitted using Bulgarian templates and language!).

Communications and delegation

International festival delivery requires excellent and empowered partnership working. ArtReach has developed a methodology for partnership meetings that bring together rep-resentatives from key players for two to three days at a time (hosted in different countries to ensure equality). The time is spent in intensive, formal meetings, but also in social activ-ity, attendance at artistic events, and shared meals. This approach is essential to ensure effective relations and clarity over development requirements (with clear, detailed meeting notes, that highlight action points, essential). However, ArtReach has still encountered chal-lenges when language differences, resulting in misunderstanding or lack of understanding, have not been apparent at the time of meeting, especially in relation to budget issues.

There are also occasions when cultural differences, especially with respect to approach to conflict resolution, bring challenging breakdown of communication.

Essential also to the international collaboration/partnership approach has been willing-ness to delegate artistic control. This is risky and on occasions has led to delivery by part-ners that has not met expectation. However, more commonly the outcomes have been different to expectation, but surprisingly satisfying and appropriate.

Logistical arrangements

Clearly there are challenges in logistical preparation (including permissions) and delivery simply between interpretation and approaches in different UK locations. Delivering in a range of international locations exacerbates this challenge.

The requirements for infrastructure review and structural survey; for free-standing or fixed structure permissions; for street processions and road closure; for flyposting and publicity distribution have as many variations as there are countries, despite the apparent consolida-tion provided by European regulations.

Visa requirements and direct artist communication/arrangements can also bring unex-pected challenges. To bring artists from Haiti for *Night of Festivals* required those artists to drive to the Dominican Republic to visit the British Consulate, and then have passports shipped to and from Kingston in Jamaica. The artists concerned had no money to pay for this process and so funds had to be transferred in advance. Only the intervention of the High Commissioner ultimately facilitated a process in time for the event. By contrast the Namibian Government paid in full for transport and visa costs for an 8-piece visiting band to take part in an ArtReach festival.

Marketing

Working with European partners, ArtReach has encountered radically different approaches to and understanding of audience development, evaluation and marketing. Our partners have much less sophisticated understanding of audience segmentation, direct and relationship marketing, and of approaches to reaching, engaging and cultivating interest from those from protected characteristics. Data collection is also an area of marketing where UK organisations have a more advanced approach. As a result, ArtReach has been asked by the Creative Europe Unit in Brussels to give advice on approaches to evaluation given the quality of reporting that can be evidenced from *Night of Festivals* and *Journeys Festival International* events. It is to be hoped this stands the company in good stead when it seeks further support in a post BREXIT world!

David Hill, ArtReach

Other legislation to consider

Other areas to be aware of are the concerns and provisions of the Environmental Protection Act 1990 – which deals with waste management amongst other things; the Disability Discrimination Act 1995 – which covers access, venue design and layout, promotional materials, and use of technology (loop systems); the Equality Act 2010 – which includes wider equality (for example, you cannot exclude someone from your festival on the grounds of old ag) and indirect discrimination; Security Industry Act 2001 – this covers licensed security staff activity such as screening and searching persons entering events, crowd control and ejection.

Summary

The law can appear frightening, but it need not be. Clarity of intention is everything. As a festival manager your engagement with the law will principally be around licensing, insurances, health and safety, contracts, copyright and, possibly, child performers.

The first time you have to deal with these issues it may seem daunting. So, allow yourself enough time to get to grips with the detail. Once you have done it once or twice it should become progressively easier and may in time become routine. Always seek advice and don't be afraid to ask; there are plenty of people and organisations out there whose job it is to help you make your festival a success, such as the local authority events department, the licensing officer, police, etc. Establish a good working relationship with them as soon as possible.

This chapter has made every effort to ensure that the guidance offered here to the festival manager conforms with the general laws, permissions and licences required to run a festival, it must be emphasised however that it is always the responsibility of the festival organiser to ensure that they conform, in full, with all relevant statutory and other national and local requirements.

References

Becker, D. (2006), *The Essential Legal Guide to Events,* Cape Town: Dynamic Publishing.

Pick, J. (1988) *The Arts in s State.* Bristol: Bristol Classical Press

Stranks, J. (2006) *The A-Z of Health and Safety.* London: Thoroughgood.

Worthington, A. (2004) *Stonehenge: celebration and subversion.* Heart of Albion Press.

Web links

DCMS (2018) Revised guidance issued under section 182 of Licensing Act 2003. https://www.gov.uk/government/publications/explanatory-memorandum-revised-guidance-issued-under-s-182-of-licensing-act-2003 [Accessed 1 November 2018].

HM Government (2018) Immigration Rules. https://www.gov.uk/guidance/immigration-rules/immigration-rules-appendix-k-shortage-occupation-list. [Accessed 1 November 2018].

HM Government (2018) Licensing bodies and collective management organisations Available at: https://www.gov.uk/guidance/licensing-bodies-and-collective-management-organisations [Accessed 1 November 2018].

HM Government (2018) Visas and immigration. https://www.gov.uk/browse/visas-immigration/work-visas [Accessed 1 November 2018]

HSE (2018) Employers' Liability (Compulsory Insurance) Act 1969 A brief guide for employers. http://www.hse.gov.uk/pubns/hse40.pdf [Accessed 1 November 2018].

PRS (2018) Here for Music and its Makers. www.prsformusic.com [Accessed 1 November 2018].

CONTRACT

Between on the one part (name of Festival) and «Name» of «Address» on the other part (the performer).

1. **Engagement**

The Festival engages the performer to perform as follows:

Date: «Gig_Date»

Venue: «Venue»

Billed As: «Billed_As»

Performance Times: «Times»

Fee: «Fee»

Payable: «Payable»

Special Terms (If any): «Special_Terms»

2. **PA System, Staging and Lighting**

The Festival will provide a PA system, operator adequate,staging and lighting which is adequate in the absolute discretion of The Festival, for the performer's needs and the nature of the event.

3. **Stewarding and Security**

The Festival will provide stewarding and security adequate, in the absolute discretion of The Festival, for the nature of the event and to assist the performer to set up on stage and clear the stage at the end of the performance.

4. **Arrival Time**

The performer and other members of the group undertakes to arrive at the performance venue at least 45 minutes prior to performance time. They should notify their arrival to a steward or the PA operator.

5. **Equipment Requirements**

The performer undertakes to notify The Festival as soon as possible and no less than two weeks in advance of their performance of any special instrumentation and PA and/or technical requirements.

6. **Electricity Supply**

The Festival undertakes to provide a safe and reliable electricity supply for the PA system and performer's instruments and related equipment.

7. **Car Parking**

The Festival will exercise reasonable endeavours to provide car parking close to the stage for the performer's vehicles for the duration of the load-in, and load-out.

8. Performing Rights Society

The performer agrees to supply The Festival with any necessary information required to enable The Festival to comply with and complete returns to the Performing Rights Society or similar bodies.

9. The Performer shall indemnify and keep indemnified The Festival from and against any and all loss damage or liability suffered by The Festival resulting from any breach of the agreement by the Performer or from the negligence of the Performer or its employees or agents in the carrying out of the performance and/or any matters ancillary thereto.

Signed for and on behalf of The Festival   ....

Date   ....

Signed for: «Billed_As» ....(signature)

Name in full (capital letters)...

Address (in capital letters) ....

......

Date   ....

Fig 6.2: Sample Contract

7 Festival Operations

by Paul Kelly

After reading this chapter you should:

- Understand the role and importance of festival operation
- Understand the processes and key operational documents will you need to satisfy licensing authorities and run your event safely and efficiently
- Understand the processes and people involved in licensing
- Understand the Health and Safety issues involved in running festivals and what you need to do to meet them
- Understand the importance of communications with your team and third parties

Introduction

In our previous chapters we have covered festival planning, logistics and the different types of licensing and insurances that you might require to run your event. This chapter assumes that you now have a viable festival plan and it focusses on how you put that plan into practice in the run-up to your festival and during the festival itself.

We will start by looking at the purpose and principles of operations management, then turn to the processes of getting the necessary permissions and the paperwork you will need to assemble. We will then look at the permissions you will need to run your event and how to obtain those. We will outline the sort of health and safety documentation you will need including risk assessments. We go on to cover issues of first aid, crowd management, security, staffing and communications. Our experience of these systems and processes is from the UK, and we have used that throughout this chapter. Other countries and territories will have different arrangements, but the principle that your event will probably need some form of authorisation should alert you to the importance of identifying whom you need to talk to and what factors you should consider.

An Event Management Plan (EMP) is a key document enabling you to run your festival smoothly and effectively and demonstrating to others that you can do so. But the EMP, however good, will not run your festival for you. Only you and your team can do that. The success of your festival will partly be down to the quality of your planning and partly down to the effort and vigilance you put in whilst it is running. But a good EMP and a simpler Operations Plan will help you hugely to run your festival smoothly and will be a vital support if you encounter problems.

What is operations management?

The basics are really quite simple: festival operations management is about getting the right things to the right place at the right time. That includes both equipment and people. The reality is more complex, as there are a wide range of factors to consider and manage, and there are also a large number of human expectations to deal with, which can range from the outright demanding to the so-subtle that they are easy to miss. These factors include:

♦ The requirements of the artists

♦ The nature of the performance environment

♦ Stakeholders – like councils and sponsors

♦ Permissions and paperwork

♦ External contractors and

♦ Physical logistics

Running a festival's operations aspect goes hand in hand with the event's creative design. It is the fulfilment aspect in terms of the artists, the audience and the festival's creative director and management.

Operations management is the crucial and largely hidden aspect of festivals management, it is the linchpin of a successful festival or event. Everything is expected to run smoothly and effectively, and if it does you will probably get little thanks because nobody should really know you are there and doing it. It's only when things go wrong that operations become visible and festival-goers and artists will then certainly let you know they are unhappy.

Permissions and process

Operations management has an inward facing aspect and at the same time has to deal with external bodies, it has to look both ways at once.

You need a good internal plan showing what is needed where and by when, how it is going to get there, and who will be delivering it by when. You also need a body of documentation that will satisfy the authorities concerned that you have thought of all eventualities and have the necessary insurances. This will be needed to obtain your event licence.

The level and type of documentation required will very much depend on the nature and duration of your festival and the type of venues you are using. If it's a one-day festival in a fully serviced venue like a theatre or arts centre then your Event Management Plan could be quite simple. If, however, you are using outdoor public spaces like town squares or roads that require closure, or greenfield sites involving traders, stages and technical installations, then you will be expected to provide a lot more documentation.

The licence you are seeking will ultimately be decided on by a local authority Licensing Committee. You may get to meet them. But they are likely to be advised, in turn, by a Safety Advisory Group (SAG) who will comprise quite a large number of people which will probably include:

♦ The council's licensing officer

♦ The council's environmental officer

♦ The council's health and safety officer

♦ Maybe a council parks officer if public parks are involved

♦ Members of the emergency services (Fire, Police, Ambulance)

♦ The council's events officer

You may be asked to attend a pre-meeting prior to your licensing application. At this you may be asked questions and given advice. Treat the SAG as your friends. They have lots of experience and good advice to give. They will probably want to see your festival take place just as much as you do. But they will also focus on public safety and the risks your event may pose to that. If they appear to be putting obstacles in your path, then it is perfectly reasonable to ask them for advice on how to address their concerns. They may tell you anyway. The SAG may just want reassurance on points of detail and once you have that, the way may be clear to getting your Event Licence. The Health and Safety Executive's website has useful information on the role of SAGs. (http://www.hse.gov.uk)

Once you have satisfied your local SAG then you are on course to being issued with a licence. The issuing of it may never actually go to the Licensing Committee. It may be delegated to the Licensing Committee chair in consultation with a senior council officer. The full Licensing Committee may only hear large or contentious applications. If you are planning a festival that aims to take over a town centre or bring a 20,000 capacity festival to a local park, you may have to meet and present to the Licensing Committee in person. But your key contact is likely to be a council events officer and/or the SAG.

Event Management Plan: the paperwork

The information you will have to put to the SAG and the council is likely to be listed in council documentation and the requirements probably available online. You will almost certainly be asked for an Event Management Plan. There are quite a number of readily available EMP templates online detailing what these should contain. Many of these have been put together by local authorities. So, they have done some of the work for you as their templates will contain everything they want to know and expect to see. Different local authorities may have slightly different requirements or may like information presented in a particular way. So, it is worth checking with the local authority where your festival is taking place whether they have published EMP guidelines and whether there is a format they particularly like.

The EMP will be a lengthy document – or compilation of documents – which could run to 50 pages or more. Below is a list of headings from one randomly selected local authority EMP template. It may seem a large undertaking to gather all that information and, in some cases, some of it may only be available days before your festival starts when you and your team are working flat out to pull all the final details together. But take it seriously as it will show that you have done everything to run your festival properly and safely and if things don't go to plan or something serious and unexpected happens, it will be your bible for managing unplanned and unwelcome activities.

Sample Event Management Plan Template

Event overview
Event description
Location
Dates and duration
Entrance and exit points
Attendance
Audience profile
Temporary structures
The event organisers
Roles and responsibilities
Contacts
Catering and hospitality
Welfare provision
Litter/cleansing services/grounds maintenance
Entertainment
Licensing
Noise management
CCTV

2. Crowd Management
Security/stewarding arrangements
Barriers
Management of attendee numbers

3. Communications
PA system
Radio
Loud hailers
Telephone
Signage and public information
Media handling

4. Traffic Management

5. Medical and First Aid Cover

6. Fire Risk Assessment
Fire extinguishers

7. Police

8. Risk Management
Risk assessments
Incident recording
RIDDOR
Health and Safety Enforcing Authority
Insurance
Weather

9. Incident Management
Extreme weather
Emergency vehicle access
Event evacuation plan
Hand-over procedures

10. Lost Children / Vulnerable Persons

11. Debrief and Event Review Arrangements

Some of the above headings may need some interpretation. Most templates also come with advisory notes.

It is important to remember the EMP does not just cover what you are doing; it also covers what any external bodies who are part of your event are doing. So, if your festival involves PA companies, lighting companies, production and staging companies and traders, you will need their insurance details and risk assessment forms as well as your own. If they are doing lots of events, this should not be a problem for them. They will have done this before and should have the paperwork to hand. You need to check their insurance policies are in date, and will be for when your festival takes place.

You should also read their risk assessments to ensure they haven't missed anything, especially in relation to your festival.

If you, or a member of your team, don't check the documentation, then you could be held accountable if something goes wrong, even if it's not your fault. For example, if someone gets hurt at a trader's stall or is hit by falling piece of equipment and their insurance is not in date, then you or your festival may well be held liable as you had not checked their insurance properly.

Liaising with emergency services

The emergency services (Police, Fire, Ambulance), will get to know about your event as, if it requires a licence, they will be asked to comment on your application. For outdoor events, whether in an urban location or on a green-field site, it makes sense that the moment you have secured use of the site and know what you are planning, you contact the emergency services and let them know your intentions. They may be able to advise you at that stage of:

♦ Any other major events in the vicinity which could cause problems (a major sporting fixture, for example)

♦ Any other concerts they might know of, or advice they would wish to consider.

In addition, when they get to see your licensing application, it won't come as a surprise, they will know about it.

The sorts of things the emergency services will want to know include:

♦ Emergency access – if there was a fire or major incident could fire engines and ambulances get access to the site easily?

♦ Security provisions

♦ Emergency evacuation procedures

♦ Communications and decision-making protocols

Some of the above are covered in more detail further on.

Remember, you hopefully won't need to call on the emergency services. But they are a very useful source of advice and are crucial to you getting you event licence. A good working relationship with them is a must. If they require something, it's probably for a good reason.

Operational Plan

Your EMP could be a very large file of important documents. In July 2017 the leading festivals promoter Festival Republic Dublin staged a three-day outdoor festival called *Longitude* at Marlay Park, Dublin to an audience of about 60,000 people. The EMP's appendices alone run to 116 pages.

EMPs are vital but not very accessible to your operations staff and contain information that your staff don't really need to know. What you need in addition to the EMP is a much simpler Operational Plan for day to day use for yourself, your team and volunteers. What they will need to know at the very least is:

♦ The detailed programme plan for the venues they are working on showing get in and get out times for all equipment

♦ Programme times for public and artists

♦ Contact details for key festival staff and possibly for artists or their road managers

♦ Emergency procedures including fire, evacuation and first aid

♦ Lost and found children procedures – if the event is open to children. These procedures can also be used for vulnerable people.

That should be a few pages of information which should be venue-specific. Put it on a clipboard (a hard copy is vital when your team's phone battery with everyone's contact info dies suddenly) and your team will have all the key information they need to manage the event they are working on.

Access and special needs

You also need to bear in mind throughout your operational planning how you can accommodate people with learning and physical special needs. This can be challenging in outdoor environments, but has been achieved. The organisation Attitude Is Everything seeks to improve deaf and disabled people's access to live music and is an excellent source of advice, much of which can probably be applied to other artforms.

They advocate that there are five things you can do to make your activities accessible:

♦ Describe your access

♦ Add a viewing area

♦ Offer free tickets for personal assistants to deaf and disabled people

♦ Sign up to their Charter of Best Practice

♦ Train your staff

Their website is full of good advice: www.attitudeiseverything.org.uk

Health and safety

The other significant piece of information that the SAG will want is a Health and Safety policy and a risk assessment. Health and Safety is and large and important subject, it tends to be approached with a mix of derision and dread.

The derision stems from many stories of health and safety 'experts' requiring things that seem silly – like trapeze artists having to wear crash helmets when they perform. In fact, many of these stories are simply untrue.

The dread comes from the breadth of the subject and the volume of requirements you may have to meet. But it's your job, as part of your duty of care, to make your festival a safe, happy and successful event, isn't it? You want to run a festival, not ruin it. A thorough approach to health and safety will help you achieve that.

This section cannot hope to cover all the detail in the many regulations and requirements. What it aims to do is flag up what you need to be aware of and where you can get further guidance and information.

In Britain, Health and Safety in the workplace (which includes festivals and events) is overseen by the Health and Safety Executive (HSE), a national governmental body which oversees health and safety issues throughout industry. The HSE says its aims are "to reduce work-related death, injury and ill-health" – aims we are sure you support.

For all the thousands of events that have been run safely and successfully, there have been quite a lot of distressing and well-publicised accidents that have taken place at live events (see the case studies on p. 153). Sadly, it is the events where people are injured or killed that tend to stick in the mind. An important part of your job as a festival producer includes ensuring that nothing like this happens at your festival.

Creating a Health and Safety framework and policy

Health and safety precautions and practices include the following:

- The construction and operation of stages and associated equipment
- The safe use of electricity
- The safe us of vehicles on-site
- The safe use of chemicals and flammable liquids
- Safe practices when working at height
- Noise at work
- The safe use of theatrical effects, lasers, pyrotechnics, smoke and vapour effects
- Fire safety
- Crowd management

There are Acts of Parliament, regulations and guidance on best practice on all of the above. In the UK the principal Act of Parliament governing health and safety is the Health and Safety at Work Act 1974. Stranks (2006) lists and gives guidance on 47 Acts of Parliament or sets of regulations governing health and safety. This is a daunting list. Not all will apply to you. But some of the chief ones you need to be aware of include:

♦ The Employment Rights Act 1996,

♦ The Electricity at Work Regulations 1989 and

♦ The Health and Safety (Information for Employees) Regulations 1998.

As the HSE's Event Safety Guide advises, there are five things your need to do to ensure effective Health and Safety Management:

1   Create a health and safety policy

2   Ensure the policy is put into practice

3   Organise an effective management structure and arrangements to deliver the policy

4   Monitor health and safety performance

5   Audit and review this performance (post-event)

(http://www.hse.gov.uk)

Under the Health and Safety at Work Act 1974 it is a legal requirement for employers with five or more staff to produce a written Health and Safety policy. Detailed advice on what this should cover can be found on the HSE's website. But essentially the policy should state which organisation the policy is for, what it covers, who it seeks to protect, how it will be applied and who is responsible for supervising it.

Your health and safety policy should demonstrate your approach to this issue. It should include who has overall responsibility for health and safety at your festival and how you will let your staff and external bodies know about your approach. It should say who is responsible for doing what, when, where and how.

The Health and Safety Executive has produced a simple template for a health and safety policy which you can find on their website http://www.hse.gov.uk/. It will need some adaptation and you can probably either find other versions online, or you could contact other festivals and ask for copies of their H&S policy. But remember, as the HSE says, a health and safety policy will only be effective if you and your staff follow it and review it regularly.

Even if you are not the festival promoter and have been contracted in to manage someone else's festival, you will still need to establish who has the overall responsibility for complying with the Health and Safety at Work Act. Even if your festival is too small to require a written health and safety policy, you will still have the responsibility of managing contractors and volunteers on site. The HSE advises a written Health and Safety policy will give you a valuable framework to work with, and we very much agree.

All staff working on your festival have a responsibility to adhere to safe working practices. If you have a staff team, whether paid or unpaid, your policy should include a management structure that defines the "hierarchy of health and safety responsibility for the duration of the event" (HSE, 1999: 4). The duration starts with the planning process and finishes when all equipment and structures involved have been removed and returned.

Health and safety is about the risks to:

♦ You and your staff

♦ Contractors working for you – including artists and performers

♦ The public attending the event or using the site's facilities. If the event is in a venue, they may be there for a coffee in the restaurant or bar.

Your health and safety policy needs to cover all three.

If you are constructing a festival on a greenfield site or using buildings not regularly used for live entertainment, then you will have to comply with a rather more extensive set of regulations. These will probably include

♦ The Building Regulations Act 2000 (stages)

♦ The Construction (Design and Management) Regulations 1994

♦ The Construction (Health, Safety and Welfare) Regulations 1996

♦ The Control of Noise at Work Regulations 2005

♦ Highly Flammable Liquids and Liquefied Petroleum Regulations 1972 (Generators)

♦ Lifting Operations and Lifting Equipment Regulations 1998 (Stage roofs and Lighting and PA rigs)

♦ Management of Health and Safety and Work Regulations 1999

♦ Manual Handling Operations Regulations 1992 (Moving heavy objects)

♦ Personal Protective Equipment Regulations 1992

♦ Reporting of Injuries, Diseases and Dangerous Occurrences Regulations 1995

♦ Safety Signs Regulations 1980

♦ Work at Height Regulations 2005 (flying lighting and PA rigs)

Health and safety and construction

Even this reduced list may seem very daunting. However, you probably will not need to read the full detail of all the regulations. You will however need to understand the principles of their intentions and how to comply with them. In addition, quite a bit of your site build will probably be done by external contractors who should have expert knowledge in their specialist area (eg.

stage building). So, your job is then about checking that they have the requisite knowledge, safety policies and practices and insurances.

One point worth noting is there have also been some recent changes in emphasis regarding health and safety and construction, so if you are using an older H&S policy as a model it might be out of date. In the past there has been a bit of an historic divide between the construction industry, who have to deal with these issues all the time and the arts and entertainments industries. From 2015, the building aspects of the arts and entertainments industries (i.e. stage building) have been brought within the remit of The Construction (Design and Management) Regulations 2015 (CDM). So, if you are building stages for performance, or are employing someone to do this, you will need to ensure your processes comply with these regulations.

RIDDOR

In the course of dealing with health and safety you may come across something called RIDDOR. This is an acronym for the 1995 Reporting of Diseases and Dangerous Occurrences Regulations.

To comply with these regulations, you will need some form of accident book or accident record to ensure that any accidents are duly noted. This will enable you to comply if there is a subsequent enquiry or insurance claim. You will find full details of what and how to record accidents on the HSE website.

Risk management and risk assessments

Whilst the term health and safety has become the industry norm, the associations that have grown up with it, have started to strip it of its intention and meaning. We think a better term is 'risk management and assessment'. Many events involve risks. If you are in charge of festival operations, you may not be directly associated with the creative risks, such as, what if that much vaunted new play you are putting on turns out to be terrible? But you are/will be responsible for the safe execution of performances, both from an artist's perspective (see the Curtis Mayfield example in the case study box) and that of the audience.

It is unlikely your festival will be entirely risk-free. So, your task is to ask "where are the risks in this event and what can I do to minimise them?". What you will be required to do, by licensing authorities and others, is to produce a risk assessment document. This may be slightly laborious but it's actually not difficult to do. A risk assessment identifies the various risks associated with the festival, assesses the level of risk and identifies what measures you can take to eliminate the risk or reduce it to a minimum.

Some festival risk assessments we have seen take matters to the extremes and have included scenarios that involved aircraft crashing on the event and similar. What you actually need to focus on the issues that are within your control or influence. Thermonuclear war doesn't really fall within that! Other matters like earthquakes, floods, famine and plagues of locusts etc. are referred to as 'Acts of God' regardless of which God you worship and whether you are even a believer.

Industry examples: Health and safety event disasters

Electricity

In 1972 the up and coming rock guitarist Les Harvey (brother of rock band leader Alex Harvey) was fatally electrocuted whilst performing at the Top Rank, Swansea. In a break between numbers he touched a microphone at the same time as his guitar strings. The microphone wasn't earthed and Harvey was killed by the full force of the electric current.

Stage safety

In 1990 the soul singer Curtis Mayfield was performing at an outdoor arena in Brooklyn, New York. Some stage lighting equipment was ineffectively secured and fell on him. Mayfield survived but was paralysed and required a wheelchair. After a successful career with a number of influential records to his credit, Mayfield recorded a final album – a few bars at a time. However, his health gradually declined and he died in 1999 aged 57.

Crowd management

In 2010 at the *Love Parade* electronic dance music festival in Duisburg, Germany, 21 people died of suffocation and 500 were injured through overcrowding of a 240 metre entrance tunnel and ramp leading to the event space. This was the first time the *Love Parade* had been held in an enclosed space. The space had a 250,000 capacity but over one million were expected based on previous years' attendance.

Human stupidity – climbing trees

There is no accounting for human adventure, or human stupidity. A small two-day Eco-Festival was staged on a greenfield site. The surrounding area included some woodland and some of the performance areas were surrounded by mature trees. One of the festival attendees decided to climb one of these trees. In the course of this, he fell, hurt his head and was taken off to hospital for treatment, fortunately his injuries were not serious and he was able to return to the festival. Could the festival organisers have foreseen this? Should they have put barriers around all the trees or signs on all of them saying 'Do not climb the trees'? Or were they correct in thinking that climbing trees is not an expected activity by festival-attendees?

Festival Risk Assessment			
Area/Issue	Risk	Level of risk High = 10 Low = 1	What you will do to minimise risk
Electrical supply	That the electrical supply is unsafe and this affects the audience and the performers	2	Ensure only fully qualified electrical personnel are engaged to provide, operate and maintain power supply, that they can supply all necessary paperwork to demonstrate this [you may want to research and add in qualifications of safety standards here] and that they have £10 million or more public liability insurance.
Crowd management	That the [unticketed] marquee venues become overcrowded and as a result people are put at risk through this.	8	Assess the marquee capacities using the 'Event Safety Guide'. Put stewards on all entrances with clickers to monitor numbers inside and restrict entry once capacity is reached. Have a visible but low-key security presence in each marquee to be able to manage crowding issues.

Figure 7.1: Sample risk assessment

Debating point:

Why do you think we have assessed the level of risk in the way we have? See our answer at the end of the chapter. But don't look until you have added to the above!

The Health and Safety Executive also has a sample risk assessment statement on its website.

First aid

You have specific legal requirements for first aid for the people you are employing. Beyond this there are no legal requirements for first aid at events, though licensing authorities may still require this and people may expect to see it, especially at outdoor events. The level and nature of cover will depend on the size and nature of your festival. At the very least you will need to have a first aid kit and a trained staff member available. But normal practice is to bring in an external body such as St. John's Ambulance, your local Ambulance Trust, if they have the capacity, or you could look for an independent paramedic service to manage first aid cover. This will inevitably cost, so you will need to get estimates and budget for it. For outdoor events you will need to organise a designated covered space for first aid, ensure it is well signposted and has good vehicle access in case an ambulance is required.

Crowd management and security

Quite obviously crowd management falls within health and safety. However, it is worth a short section on its own as it is about dealing with people who have both come to your event to enjoy themselves and have probably paid good money do to so. So, it requires a slightly different approach to more inanimate aspects of health and safety management. It also benefits from a bit of understanding of human psychology.

First it is worth noting the whole notion of 'crowd management' may well be offensive to a group of, possibly young, people who have come to an event to escape daily humdrum routine and to 'get away from the everyday', and yet safety is crucial to enable them to do that. Large crowds of people packed quite tightly together can sometimes run counter to that.

Human beings can sometimes act irrationally when gathered together in large groups, especially when the expected nature of things change. There will be a legal limit to the number of people who can be in your venue or on your site at one time. The former will be dictated by the number of fire-exits you have and the latter by the size of your marquee or event area. The Event Safety Manual recommends 0.5m per square metre per person at outdoor events (HSE, 1999: 22). So, if you are staging an outdoor event with an audience area of 50 metres x 50 metres that's 2,500 m2 which gives you a theoretical audience capacity of 5,000. But that will also be something dictated by the size and number of exits and is something that will be confirmed or otherwise in your licence.

There are significant differences in crowd management issues in internal and external venues. In internal venues the issues are as much about things running to time. There is an expectation of format – when events will start and end. If a concert is deemed to start at 8pm and doesn't, people can become unsettled? (see case study) At popular concerts there is now a time-honoured ritual of performing an encore (no matter how deserved). If a band ends without one the audience can leave feeling less than satisfied and it is small instances like that from which bigger crowd issues can develop.

In outdoor venues, timings format can be an issue, but tend to be slightly more 'elastic'. The issue in outdoor venues, which tend to be larger, is the impact of 'people flow'. What are the issues of getting large numbers of people into and out of the marquee or arena space safely and securely, especially at the end of an event (see case study). In addition, if there is a big emergency what access is there for the emergency services? There is plenty of detailed guidance on these issues in *The Event Safety Guide* (and the online Purple Guide (https://www.thepurpleguide.co.uk/ 2015)

If you are using multiple stages and are expecting large crowds, it is possible to split your crowd by staging acts at the same time on different stages. If you can ensure that performances end at different times then you reduce the risk of everyone spilling out of venues at the same time, which can be vital for safety and security, especially when the walkways between different stages have limited capacity.

Greenfield sites can include urban environments like town and city squares or piazzas. These can be even more challenging as access and exit points can be narrow and create choke points. In addition, urban outdoor events often have to be free to the public, causing capacity management issues as it can be hard to estimate and restrict the number of people who turn up.

Several things can play a key role in helping you manage these issues. These include the way you schedule the artistic programming, engaging security staff and communication. If you are working in an internal or external venue where crush and capacity could be an issue, you need sufficient quality and experienced security staff both to communicate issues and to manage them where required. Security staff now need certification and should be trained and hold a certificate from the Security Industries Authority (SIA).

If you are putting on a popular concert where crowds are likely to want to create a 'mosh-pit' or rush the stage, then you will definitely need experienced security staff in front of the stage to extract those members of the audience who are likely to be at risk through these and also to create a barrier between the performers and their adoring fans. This has not yet been known to be a requirement in theatre productions, dance performances, operas or literary readings though.

There is another dimension to communication. Large crowds tend not to respond well to uncertainty. If your event is not going to the expected plan, whether it be for artist or technical reasons, a good compère can help calm the atmosphere either through explanation or entertainment. The person who commands the microphone has power and control. So, if there is uncertainty or unease, having someone authoritative and reassuring on the microphone, whether unseen or on-stage can be vital to crowd management, especially in the unlikely event that a site or venue evacuation is required.

Accreditation and ticketing can also play an important role in crowd management and security. If you are using wristbands then a sophisticated design will reduce the risk of illegal copying and fraud. If you are using tickets, then a bar code on the tickets are the equivalent and enable ticket scanning to determine exact numbers on site. Knowledge of precise numbers attending and more detailed data that a bar code scan can give you can also help post event analysis on things like trader commission, percentage of audience that actually attends (some people actually purchase tickets and then fail to get out of bed), the average arrival time (and what day – if applicable). All of this is useful for future planning.

The general public normally have one or two types of wristbands. But there can be a much wider range of passes for backstage work dependent on the job role and what access required and, if applicable to your festival, these could include:

- ◆ **Main staff** – Access All Areas (AAA) and permitted from a certain dates (early admission)
- ◆ **Traders** – Early admission but not full access across site, just Front of House (FoH) areas
- ◆ **Artists** – AAA for their set day only, and possibly access to other stages so they can see and meet other artists.

When designing wristbands for ticket purchasers, it's important to do it alongside the site map and zone the wristbands as access points. If you have several access points this will help you manage audience flow and avoid overcrowding at 'pinch points'.

Case study: Internal crowd management

A city centre venue promoted a concert by a large musical group led by an eighty-year old musician who was a bit of a legend. The hall was licensed to seat 300 people and was packed to the rafters and hot. The concert was advertised as starting at 8pm. But the band weren't ready at 8pm. They weren't ready either at 8.15pm, or 8.30pm. In fact, they didn't actually take the stage until 8.45pm. The combination of the delay, the packed, hot and slightly uncomfortable auditorium could have caused significant audience dissatisfaction and possibly more serious crowd management issues. The one thing that kept the crowd in calm anticipation was a commanding and genial compère who would pop out on stage every 10 minutes or so, give the crowd an update and both raise their tolerance for the delays and their expectation of the music to come. By the time the artist finally took the stage the audience was at peak levels of expectation with any resentment at the delay forgotten. The compère and his communications were crucial to managing the delay.

Logistics and your role on the day

By the time the event starts, you should have done all your planning, have secured your event licence, have a clear and effective Event Management Plan, have briefed all your volunteers and have everything in place and as ready to go as you can.

Logistics, as we said earlier, is getting the right things to the right place at the right time. However, one of the things you will find about events, including festivals, is they seldom go entirely to plan. You need to be prepared to expect the unexpected and ready to fix snagging issues, that is things that are not quite where they should be or are not quite running as they should be.

This brings us onto a key function of your operations role. Your job on the day is:

◆ To have an intimate knowledge of the festival plan and any critical points that are crucial to its success

◆ To keep monitoring that everything is going to plan and keep an eye on what is coming up next and whether you are on schedule.

◆ To keep an eye on the audience and ensure that they are safe

◆ To make sure that your staff team are not only doing their jobs effectively but also that they get periodic breaks and, if it's a long event, that they get fed and watered, so they can keep going to the bitter end (and if they don't the end may be very bitter).

You may, in the course of this, catch a bit of some of the performances. But don't be under any illusion about this. If you are doing your job properly, you won't see much of the creative activity. If that's a key motivation of yours in staging the festival, then you are probably doing the wrong job. We have seen festivals where key members of staff seemed to spend the entire day or night corralled backstage seemingly waiting for the next thing to happen. It may seem glamorous to have exclusive access to places, but your job is to make sure the public has the best possible time, so it's not a very good use of your time or authority. You should be out there with your schedule looking for the next problem to happen and fixing it before it does.

The key logistical issues usually come down either to equipment failure or timings, particularly in relation to artists. The audiences will usually find their way to the designated venue in time for the event. After all, they have probably paid to be there and anyway it's the marketing team's job to get them there. But are the artists at the right place, at the right time and ready to perform? If you are running several venues at the same time, you may have multiple timelines to manage, though each venue should also have a dedicated stage manager to look after the detail. If you are running a programme with multiple events and the programme timings start to slip, what are the implications and is there anything you can do about it?

The other thing you need to think about is if there are any particular technical requirements that are critical to performances and which may be potentially difficult. Some outdoor events or spectaculars can involve some or a lot of this. You will have done all the safety checks in advance, but on the day has anything happened to change the environment or your pre-event assessments? Sometimes weather can play a major role in this, especially at outdoor events (see case study).

Also, be aware of the mood of the crowd, if at all possible, get out there with the crowds. How do things feel? What are you hearing or picking up as you walk about? As we said earlier large gatherings of people can act unpredictably. But it is possible to smell or feel the mood of unease or irritation and if you can feel it, you are there in time to take measures to calm it.

Whether your event is in an indoor venue or outdoors, it is quite possible you will find yourself doing a lot of walking; from backstage to front of house, between different events, between venues or sites. So, make sure you wear comfortable shoes. If your festival venues or sites are so far apart that you have to drive, have a car and driver in your production budget or take taxis. You haven't time to negotiate the traffic and park. Carry a small rucksack with you, you never know what you will pick up on your travels. A clipboard for your production plan with essential timings can be useful.

To stay in contact, you may be on the phone a lot and may also have a VHF radio with you. If your mobile has a swappable battery, carry a spare and carry a phone charger (that's why the rucksack is useful) and try and charge it in down times. Also, carry a pen and notebook, you'll want to make notes of all the things you want to avoid next time.

Case study: External crowd management

A fringe festival was staged for several years adjacent to a rock/pop festival whose main arena held at least 25,000 people. One of the main entry and exit routes for the main festival site was through the fringe site. This wasn't a problem when people were arriving at the event as inevitably they wouldn't all arrive at quite the same time. It was however seen as a crucial when people left at the end of the night as a good portion of the 25,000 or more people at the main festival would exit through the fringe, and the fringe site wasn't big enough to accommodate anything like that number. So, the festival management decreed that the fringe programme had to finish 15 minutes before the end of the main site programme so that people would walk through an empty fringe site and not be tempted to stop. That sensible move also created some interesting programme scheduling challenges as if the whole fringe programme didn't run to time then there was a risk that the fringe headline act would have their performance time cut which would irritate both them and their audience.

Stakeholder and management relations

Whose event is it? You have done all the hard work, so quite naturally you think of it as your event and you'd probably expect everyone else to think the same. But to make your event work you may be dealing with a lot of stakeholders. These might be sponsors, stallholders, artists, external technical contractors, licensing officers. You might think and expect them to respect all the hard work you have put in to make things happen, but human nature doesn't always work like that and just occasionally people, including contractors, have different views. So you need to think about who your stakeholders are and how you manage your relations with them. It's not always easy. We have known situations where television has been involved and some aspects of the event have shifted to 'network planning' i.e. the TV schedule. We have also known situations where external technical contractors have seemed to think they were running the event.

Sometimes the issues are understandable and you have to give way. In some cases you may need to stand your ground. But remember, whilst you were probably there from the start, everyone professionally involved has a stake in your festival's success and it needs teamwork to make it happen. It's a very good idea to get all the key players together a few weeks in advance of the festival (if not earlier) for a meeting where you can build relationships, identify and resolve concerns and address issues and uncertainties. That way you will also get to know the various characters you will be dealing with.

Communications, staffing and stewarding

Smooth and effective operations management is the linchpin of a successful festival or event. That means, whilst it may be neither very visible nor glamorous, a great deal hinges on it. Of course, all the other section leaders and teams will make this claim, the creative team who devise the festival and bring in the artists, the marketing team who sell the events to the public and the financial team who raise the money and manage the budget and they are right, too. But none of these would really work on their own if the festival wasn't well planned or run. Take away good operations management and you run significant risks. In fact, without good operations management you probably would not get the permissions and licences necessary to run your festival.

So, good planning is vital. But there is one other thing that is also important and that will grow in importance as your festival grows and that factor is staff, volunteers and communication.

Staffing and stewarding

Unless your festival is tiny, you can't run it on your own. You are going to need some help, at the very least on the day. You may be lucky and have paid staff. You may have a committee or a team. But if not you are going to need to find some help on the day. If you haven't got this organised two or three weeks in advance, then you could find yourself in difficulty and under quite a lot of pressure. Potential sources of stewards are:

♦ Friends and family
♦ Friends of the venue – they may have a membership or supporters scheme

- Interest groups – if you are putting on a dance festival, dance enthusiasts or dance students
- Event management students – they always benefit from things to put on their CV
- Local Rotary and Lions clubs

Be clear on whether they are volunteering or you are paying them. If they are volunteering, try and give them something to remember the event by as a thank you. You will want them to stand out as stewards, so a unique festival t-shirt or badge is often welcomed. But t-shirts take time to make and can be costly, so plan and budget that carefully.

Communications and briefings

You may have brilliant and meticulously devised plans, but if they are not well communicated they won't work in practice. If on the day you don't have good communications across your team and site, you will not be able to react if you encounter queries, enforced changes to your plans or something more serious goes wrong.

To ensure good festival communications requires four things:

- A plan of who is going to be where and doing what
- The circulation of that plan, so everyone knows what the essentials are and what their role in the plan is
- A clear command structure
- A communication system that enables you to keep in contact and communicate changes if they are needed.

The dissemination of the plan is normally done through one or more pre-event briefings. These are important so you need to set them up prior to the event and your staff and volunteers need to attend. This is the opportunity to go through the detail, make sure that people understand what will be happening and their role in it and, most importantly, sort out any ambiguities in written instructions. It never ceases to amaze how apparently clear instructions can be misinterpreted, so make sure your team and volunteers know what you plan actually means.

Communications command structure

This doesn't sound very festival-like does it? A command structure sounds like something out of a military or political dictatorship. But what happens if you are required to close down an event early, evacuate a building or clear an entire festival site? Who takes that decision and how would it be communicated? Where, as the Americans say, does the buck stop? It is highly unlikely that you will find yourself in this position. But, just in case, it is vitally important that your plans include this.

Look at your event team, partners and stakeholders. Who has the control and the decision-making power? It might be you, but it may be someone else. In one local authority run festival it was the chair of the Leisure Committee. At the 2008 *Live 8 Festival* staged in Hyde Park by Bob Geldoff and Harvey Goldsmith, it was the late Tessa Jowell, Secretary of State for Culture Media and Sport (the Government minister ultimately responsible) who intervened in a heated on-the-day discussion between Geldoff, Goldsmith and the Royal Parks Authority about event timings and who made the final decision on how late the festival could run (Gowers et al., 2005).

If you are not the ultimate decision maker how do you reach the person who does make such decisions in an emergency? And from there, how will the decision be communicated to others on your team? Key contact details like mobile phone numbers need either to be in your Event Management Plan or, if sensitive, at least available to senior festival staff.

Communication systems

If your festival is spread out across several venues or you have a large greenfield site how are you going to communicate with people some distance away? And remember 'communicate with' might just mean periodically checking in to see that everything is ok.

The options available to you include walkie talkies (two-way radios) and mobile phones. Walkie talkies enable many people (each one who has a radio) to hear the conversation or the 'call out' you are making. Mobile phones are strictly 1:1 and can be slower to connect; you have to dial, they have to answer to be able to pass the message.

Large festivals these days will have an Event Control (EC) centre operating on one designated UHF Radio channel – usually channel one. All staff are instructed to radio in to EC with issues. That could be anything from a blocked toilet to a fatal incident. EC runs for the full day for the last couple of days in set-up and then with a 24 hour coverage during the event. EC logs every query that comes in, relays the information to the relevant contractors, staff members, teams etc as appropriate for a resolution. EC then relays the outcome back to the initial radio user once the job is complete. The log EC makes can then be referenced for RIDDOR.

In other cases you will have teams with their own radio channel or network. For example, the technicians and security people may have their own dedicated channel so they can communicate with each other on dedicated issues without others needing to be involved. But at a large event, as festival operations manager you may need to be able to communicate with senior security or technical people. So, you will all need radios that can scan channels and where you can programme the radios to determine which channels to scan. In addition, you will need to think about radio battery life and ensure you have chargers and spare batteries available and a few spare handsets as well, as they can break down. You will probably also want headsets for the radios so operators can hear and talk more privately. Finally, people using them will need to know how the radios work and be given some protocols about when to use them and what to say otherwise you will have endless and distracting chatter. If the event is large enough to warrant UHF radios, then this will need some careful pre-planning and budgeting. UHF radios are now being replaced by digital radios that operate in the same way but use the digital spectrum rather than a UHF frequency. Other newer radios are now using the mobile phone network to communicate.

Public address systems if you have one, are clearly there to communicate with the public, but can also be used to communicate with everyone on the site. Where public address systems are involved in communicating urgent issues, some organisations use codes so that staff will know but the public will not be panicked. For example, a 'code blue' alert might mean there is a bomb threat or a 'code yellow' alert might indicate a minor fire.

Case studies

"June just rains and never stops"

This line from Flanders and Swann's Song of the Weather came true in 2012 and created chaos at the *Isle of Wight Festival* (capacity 55,000). Campsites were flooded and, more significantly, car access to the greenfield site became a muddy quagmire. Cars simply couldn't move and became gridlocked. Many of the audience were travelling to the festival by ferry from Southampton. Such were the transport problems that festival goers in cars arriving on the Isle of Wight were being sent straight back as there was no means of accommodating them. But Southampton was not much better as there was limited 'holding capacity'. We understand that one of the outcomes is that Southampton has since developed a 5,000 capacity car holding area (which could accommodate 10,000 – 20,000 people) in case severe weather ever coincides with the Isle of Wight Festival again.

Lost and found children

A new small festival was applying for a licence for the outdoor aspect of an event that was taking place all over the town. The festival included a lost children policy in its licensing application. The local authority events team replied they wanted an additional found children policy before they would grant the event licence. The lost children policy had detailed how the festival would initiate a search for children reported missing by parents attending the event. The found children policy needed to explain how and where the festival would look after children who had been found until they could be reunited with their parents.

Summary

The aim of this chapter has been to give you a good grounding in operational management issues as they relate to festivals. It's a big topic and there are a lot of issues to consider. Some are very specific to the size and nature of the festival. It is not possible to cover all the details here, but there is plenty of more detailed advice readily available. The HSE's *Event Safety Guide* and the online Purple Book carry a lot more detail and are well worth reading.

Some of the things that your festival may involve and we have not been able to cover here include:

♦ Food, drink and water

♦ Information and welfare

♦ Camping

♦ Special effects and pyrotechnics

♦ Waste management and sanitary facilities

Operations management requires a lot of planning and attention to detail in advance and on the day. The first time you have to take responsibility for this it may seem an impossible challenge. But the more you do it, the better you'll get. And you'll have the satisfaction of knowing that, without your operational management skills, the festival, whether it be yours or someone else's, could be a disorganised disaster and remembered for all the wrong reasons.

Risk Assessment: Debating point answer

Electrical supply: This must, by law, be installed and checked by a qualified electrician, and thus unless the system contains a faulty component, the risk of failure is relatively low.

Crowd safety: People's preferences and habits cannot always be predicted. If a large number of people all suddenly decide to visit a marquee then that creates a risk. The unpredictability factor means it is wise to rate this as a high risk.

Bibliography

Attitude Is Everything (2018) www.attitudeiseverything.org.uk (accessed 24 Sept. 2018).

Gowers, B., Hopkin, N., Maier, M., Popplewell, C., Posner, G., Valentine, R., Watt, M. & Flattery P. (2005) Live 8. [DVD] London. Innocent.

Health and Safety Executive (nd) http://www.hse.gov.uk (accessed 24 Sept. 2018).

Health and Safety Executive (1999) *The Event Safety Guide 2nd edition*. Norwich: HSE Books.

The Events Industry Forum (2015) The Purple Guide. https://www.thepurpleguide.co.uk/ (Accessed 22 Oct. 2018)

Stranks, J. (2006) *The A-Z of Health and Safety*. London: Thorogood.

Stranks, J. (2006) *The Health and Safety Pocketbook*. London: Routledge.

8 Managing Human Resources

by Jennie Jordan

After reading this chapter you should

- Have an overview of the principles of human resource management as it relates to festivals
- Understand and be able to design an organisational structure and job roles and have a grounding in basic legal responsibilities relating to staffing
- Decide when and how to use team-working, and how to best motivate people
- Be confident about your approach to equality and diversity
- Recognise development needs
- Understand the strategic role of HRM within a festival organisation

Introduction

It used to be called 'personnel', or 'personnel management', and now has the title 'human resources management', usually shortened to HRM. Within large organisations it can be the least visible until people problems arise. It has to undertake the dull but vitally necessary tasks of ensuring that an organisation's 'people management' complies with the law and that the company gets the best out of the people it employs. So, what's this got to do with the comparatively small, lively, friendly, funky, chaotic world of festivals? No matter how small and cuddly your festival is, the management of people, whether full time or very occasional, will be crucial to your success. This chapter sets out the principles which will increasingly apply as your festival develops and grows.

What is HRM?

Definitions of HRM vary, but generally include some reference to processes such are recruitment, training and development, incentives, pay, staff contracts, equality and diversity issues, and performance management. Where companies have dedicated HR managers, they are also involved in developing long-term strategies related to people management that help the organisation get the most out of its staff and for staff to feel fulfilled and to achieve at work.

As small organisations, in many festivals these jobs land on the shoulders on managers who are neither HR experts, nor have the time to dedicate solely to such issues. Nonetheless, it is worth spending time trying to get policies and processes right, as when it goes wrong, people management is upsetting for everyone concerned, takes up a huge amount of time and, at worst, can end in costly and damaging tribunal cases.

HR principles and practices don't just apply to paid staff. Your festival will probably need stewards and volunteers to run the various activities and good HR practices apply to these people just as much.

Human resource management in a festival context

The phrase 'people are our most important asset' is one that is heard regularly in business. It is particularly true for festivals. It is the taste of the artistic director that shapes the festival's programme, and individual artists who ensure the work is high quality. The venue or site design and atmosphere are dependent on choices made by individuals working for the organisation. And on the day, customer services staff are crucial. They have to be knowledgeable and approachable, calm and capable to make festival-goers feel welcome and secure. So, the role of HR is to do more than simply recruit the right number of bodies to undertake tasks on the right days. Who you recruit, and how they are trained and motivated are crucial to a festival's success.

Festivals have some specific HR challenges related to the fact that they are projects requiring rapid scaling up and scaling down, a complex mix of professional skills and types of contracts, all working in an intense environment to unmovable deadlines. This may make it sound like an impossible task, but festivals are part of the original 'gig economy' so there are industry-wide systems and processes to fall back on. There are professional norms that operate across subsectors, meaning that there are certain shared expectations of what a staging company or PR firm will do as part of their field of expertise. Some of the workers at a festival may well be freelancers or employed by a different company subcontracted to provide a specific service so these norms and skills become established practices that can be relied upon. There are also industry bodies such as The British Arts Festivals Association (BAFA), the Association of Festival Organisers (AFO), European Festivals Association (EFA) etc. who provide guidance documents for their members, and unions such as Equity (for actors), the Musicians Union and BECTU (for media and entertainment) who can advise on best practice.

That having been said, one of the traditional roles of HR is to oversee policies related to how the organisation manages its own people, those it employs directly. Policies are statements of principle that guide practice and encourage consistency. They have to relate to the company's strategies, so there are some important decisions that can only be made internally. These relate to organisational purpose and ethics.

Organisational culture

Organisational culture is commonly known as 'the way we do things round here'. It is the unwritten rules that members of a group accept and work to. It is made up of beliefs and assumptions about the organisation's purposes and future direction; shared values – aesthetic judgments, acceptable behaviour and quality standards; and norms – behaviours such as time-keeping, communication systems, the ways people interact, dress code and safety practices. Cultures develop gradually as actions are taken and found to be useful or unhelpful so repeated or ditched. Does a weekly catch-up meeting ease good communication, or does it waste time? Each group will come to their own conclusions and so a culture is born (Schein, 2004).

Of course, festivals do not exist in a vacuum, so cultures are influenced by external factors such as wider sector norms. Staff move between organisations and bring best practice with them. Or staff may go on training courses offered by professional bodies like the Theatrical Management Association (TMA) or Arts Management Association (AMA) or one of the festival producers associations. Similarly, service companies that work with a number of arts or festivals will expect a level of consistency in the ways that their clients work. It is important to have some understanding of how the culture operates as it will influence decision-making across the organisation and, particularly, whether people feel comfortable and happy working at the festival.

Motivation

How to keep staff motivated is a perennial management question. It might be thought that because festivals are exciting environments for festival-goers, that festival production is one long party. But it never is! There are lots of boring and unpleasant jobs to be done, whether it's inputting data from the customer survey, or litter picking (and sometimes worse). So, finding ways to ensure workers stay on task is vital.

Ideas about motivation can be split into two camps. There are those that argue everyone is inherently lazy and need external motivators such as pay or threats of punishment to make them work hard. These are *extrinsic* motivation theories. *Intrinsic* theories believe that generally people will work hard at things they enjoy or to feel a sense of achievement. The two approaches lead to very different ideas about how people should be managed to get the best out of them. Douglas McGregor (1966) labelled the two sets of assumptions Theory X (extrinsic) and Theory Y (intrinsic). In general, in the festivals sector, most managers believe that people are intrinsically motivated and will work hard if they are committed to the organisation's goals.

Other theorists argue that motivation is a result of unmet needs. These theories argue that people who are hungry will put effort in to finding food. People who are lonely will put effort into making social contact. Frederick Herzberg (1966) applied this theory to the work place in a series of experiments and concluded that needs could be divided into those that were fundamental to stopping people being unhappy at work (hygiene factors) and those that made people work harder (motivating factors).

Hygiene factors

- Salary covers basic and status needs
- Company policies e.g. health and safety, time-keeping, breaks, progression possibilites
- Working conditions
- Supervision processes
- Relationships with managers and co-workers

Motivating factors

- Job gives a sense of achievement
- Work is recognised
- Work includes areas of responsibility
- Progression is seen as possible and encouraged
- Self-fulfillment in the work processes themselves
- Personal growth

Figure 8.1: Herzberg's Two Factor Theory (1966)

Herzberg found poor hygiene factors caused workers to be dissatisfied (demotivated), but once people had a good relationship with their manager or were paid at a fair level that covered their needs, these factors could not increase effort. Factors that could increase work motivation were intrinsic. In other words, if someone is unhappy because they want more responsibilities, increasing their salary or ensuring company leave policies are improved (although they are unlikely to say 'no') will not increase their work effort.

Goal Theory argues that, rather than worry about why people work hard since this varies from person to person, managers need to understand how best to structure the work place, processes and incentives so they do. Goal setting defines and states the aims individuals, teams, departments and organisations strive to achieve. Goals give people a clear idea what it is the organisation is trying to do and what their contribution should be to achieving the festival's aims. Research into how hard people work, 'task performance', shows that specific and challenging goals, accompanied by feedback about how well workers are performing, contribute to higher and better task performance (Locke and Latham, 2002). One way to remember to use goal theory is to build SMART objectives into the performance management system. SMART is an acronym that stands for:

- ◆ **Specific** – Clear goals that leave no room for ambiguity are more motivating than easy, general and vague goals.

- ◆ **Measurable** – It is easier to know if a goal has been achieved if it can be measured. Setting a measurable goal also reduces ambiguity as everyone knows what the test is that will be applied.

- ◆ A is complicated. Some people say it stands for **achievable**. Others **attainable**, or **acceptable**, or **action-orientated**. All of these are definitely important. In the end, though, the A we decided was most important was **agreed**. Making sure everyone – managers, workers, team members etc. – agrees the goal reduces ambiguity and builds commitment. It becomes a shared goal.

- ◆ **Realistic** – Knowing that it will be impossible to do what is asked is demotivating and a cause of stress. Locke's research showed that difficult goals (sometimes known as stretch targets) are more motivating than easy ones, as attaining them gives a sense of *Pride* and achievement. But people have to feel they can do them if they work hard enough and won't be punished if they try but fail.

- ◆ **Time-constrained** – Just as people have to be clear about what is required, they also need to have deadlines. Goals without an end point are lower priorities than those with a with an end date.

SMART objectives work best when they are part of a system of performance management where line managers and individuals meet to reflect on how well goals are being achieved and to set new ones. Performance management is discussed later in this chapter.

Organisational structures

How the organisation is structured internally is both a reflection of and influences its culture. It is worth noting that although there are industry norms about the kinds of skillbase, pay and conditions of the different professions festivals work with, how a festival is structure internally is a management decision and a management tool. Charles Handy (1999) identified four common structures, all of which have strengths and weaknesses.

Hierarchy

In a traditional hierarchy, those higher up have responsibility for those below. Communications flow up the departmental levels rather than across, and the chief executive has final authority to make decisions. Hierarchies are good structures for building in-depth expertise as people work with others in their specialism. A weakness of this structure is that it can create 'silo working'. Because communication and decision-making and budgetary control run through the departmental hierarchies, there is little incentive to work with people in other departments.

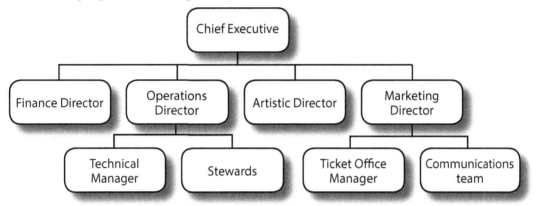

Figure 8.2: Traditional hierarchy

Matrix structures

Matrix structures attempt to overcome the silo problem by bringing people from different departments together to work on projects in multi-functional teams. Teams will be discussed further later on. Structurally this can help to improve communications and is particularly effective on complex projects where different skills bases are needed.

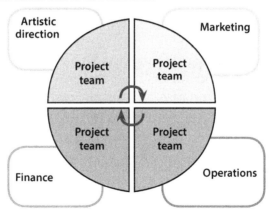

Figure 8.3: Matrix structures

It also helps to build understanding of the thought processes and working practices that form in other departments. So, the artistic team might understand why marketing has set a deadline and be more likely to try and hit it. Or finance will learn about the difficulties experienced by small contractors or artists if they are paid late and begin to prioritise payments for freelancers.

There is, however, potential for conflict built in to the matrix structure as project team members find themselves with two bosses and may have to negotiate competing demands for their time.

Spider's web

The spider's web is a quite common structure in festival organisations because they are small. A spider's web is a sort of formalised team structure, with the team leader or CEO in centre. It is in part a hierarchy, as all communications flow to the centre, where all decisions are made. It is different from a hierarchy in that the person in the centre delegates less responsibility to heads of department for collecting and sharing information from their teams. Instead, everyone is expected to share information between departments and with the chief executive. This can lead to 'turf wars' as there is a lack of clarity about who is responsible for which areas.

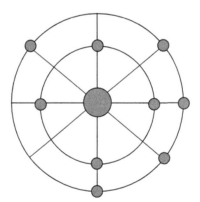

Figure 8.4: Spider's web

Spider's web organisations can be very dynamic and adaptable because power resides with the CEO who can make and implement decisions quickly. This is also its weakness, as it can put a lot of responsibility and pressure on the CEO. How good they are will be crucial to the organisation's success.

Shamrock

The shamrock is a highly flexible structure that is very commonly seen in the festival sector. It consists of a small core team who are employed by the festival. This team understands the festival's core values and manages its strategies. It will generally include the artistic director and people with responsibility for administration, including finances and brand management. These people are employed directly by the festival. Other functions are fulfilled by freelancers and specialist companies who are contracted to undertake tightly defined tasks based on their own areas of expertise. Public relations, security, staging and other technical areas are all often sub-contracted in this way. The advantage for the festival is it does not have to buy and store equipment it only uses for a few days a year or pay staff who may have little to do for six months. The disadvantage is the festival has less control and may lose out to competitors who can afford to pay more for these services.

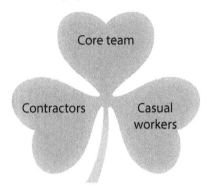

Figure 8.5: Shamrock

Casual staff are the stewards, box office and catering staff who are hourly paid or volunteers. Staffing requirements during the festival period are obviously greater than at other times, so all festivals rely on casual staff and/or volunteers to some extent. There has been much debate about the ethics of employing people on 'zero hours contracts' and about whether volunteering discriminates against people from working class backgrounds. Each festival will have to decide for itself how it feels about these issues, but it is important to note here that workers' terms and conditions and the structures within which they work are a fundamental part of an organisation's culture and motivation policies. If they are at odds with stated values, then actions tend to be considered a better guide to fundamental beliefs than words.

HR planning

In order to be able to find the right people for the job, first the 'job' needs to be defined. What work will be required to produce the festival? When will the work need to be done? How much money is there to pay people?

A staffing plan helps to ensure that the right people are recruited as efficiently as possible, and that everyone knows how these jobs fit into the organisational structure. Organograms, like the hierarchy diagrams above show these relationships graphically.

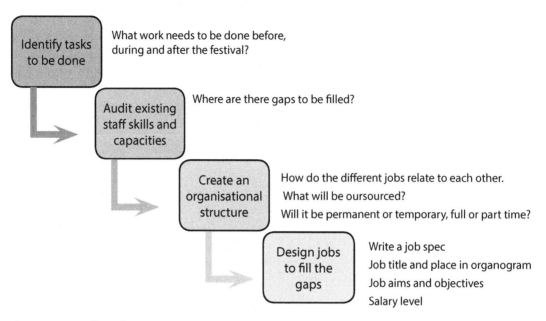

Figure 8.6: Staffing plan

Identifying work to be done

Festival roles and structures often develop organically around the skills of specific individuals. It is easy to overlook the expertise people bring to their roles when they perform them with apparent ease. Taking a little time out to actually look at the work being done, what is essential and what might be 'nice to do' is worthwhile, though, as it simplifies the process if people leave or take on other roles. So how to do that? Well, first, rather than reinventing the wheel, why not take a look at what job roles other festivals have?

In general there are four key festival management functions that are essential:

♦ Artistic direction, programming or curation
♦ Marketing and audience development
♦ Financial management
♦ Operations management

The specifics of these roles can and do vary from festival to festival and are likely to change as the organisation grows. Is the marketing manager responsible for fundraising, for example, or is that the board or the artistic director (who might also be chief executive)? It is important not to allow job roles to be too constricting as this can stifle innovation and demotivate people. But clarity about who is responsible for what helps to avoid conflict. A sample job description could include:

Festival Assistant

X festival takes place annually in [city/venue(s)]. It celebrates [music/dance/visual art/ South Asian culture…]. It has been produced by X organisation since [year]. The festival takes place over [number] days in [month] and incorporates a programme of [performances/exhibitions/workshops/parades…].

The festival is offering the chance for an individual to join the team as Festival Assistant. This is a good opportunity for someone looking to gain experience working on a festival.

The chosen candidate will demonstrate a desire to work within the arts, ideally within a festival or producing/production context.

The festival is managed by a small team, and the Festival Assistant will play a crucial role during the months before and during the festival itself. The Festival Assistant is a varied role incorporating elements of project and venue management, producing and marketing. It would ideally suit a recent graduate or an early career professional looking to gain experience.

The Festival Assistant will:

- Assist the festival director in the run up to and during the festival.
- Be responsible for the delivery of [e.g. the schools programme, managing workshop leaders, bookings and school relationships].
- Assist in the delivery of the marketing and campaign-specific tasks, including print distribution, mailing list compiling and social media activities.
- Act as artist liaison before and during the festival.
- Offer technical and venue assistance during the get in and get outs of the festival and at box office/front of house.
- Assist with administrative tasks including budget management, ticket sale monitoring and the festival evaluation process.
- Undertake ad hoc activities that arise as required by the festival directors.

Person specification

Essential qualities:

- Extremely well organised and able to handle multiple tasks.
- Ability to work under pressure.
- Polite and professional, and able to work alongside people at all levels.
- An understanding of how a festival is put together and the needs of performers, staff, venue and customers.
- Exceptional time-management skills.
- A willingness to "pitch in" as required.
- A knowledge and understanding of the arts.

Desirable qualities:

- Previous experience in a festival environment.
- Arts marketing experience.
- An understanding of social media and its applications to the arts.
- Previous admin experience.

This is a temporary, full-time role for six months from 15-Jan - 15 July inclusive.

Working from our office in [town/city] the Festival Assistant will be paid a pro-rata salary of £18,000 per annum.

To apply please complete the application form available from our website and email it to recruitment@Xfestival.com with FESTIVAL ASSISTANT in the subject line.

Please outline why you are applying for the role, what you hope to gain from it and ensure you cover all the essential qualities as listed above.

Deadline for applications: 10am, 7 November. Interviews: 29 November

If you have not heard back from us by 6pm on 8 November we regret that we have not been able to invite you to interview.

Figure 8.7: Sample job description

A good job description includes a list of the skills, knowledge and experience needed to undertake the role. These are usually divided into essential and desirable.

The list of competencies can include attitudes, such as 'a willingness to pitch in', so that there is 'fit' within the organisational culture, as well as those skills that relate to task objectives. Physical capabilities that are required to do specific tasks (e.g. fitness and strength if delivering print as in the example above) can also be raised. It is worth warning against generalised requirements that might lead to discrimination in recruitment practices that are not driven by real needs of the job. The example above asks for 'recent' graduates, not 'young' graduates, for example, as it wants to support people entering the sector regardless of their age.

Equality and diversity

The terms 'equality' and 'diversity' are widely used as synonyms. However, different people can interpret these terms differently. Equality is a principle that establishes everyone's right to be treated fairly within society, and the requirement to act and behave fairly to others. It doesn't mean treating everyone in the same manner, but it does mean offering the same opportunities. Some individuals and groups may need different provision in order to do their best work. So, if the best person for the job needs to work from home sometimes, or perhaps part-time, the organisation should ask itself if it there is any real reason other than custom and practice why the work can't be undertaken this way.

Diversity is a term used to imply a positive sense of the differences between people. It is about creating a culture and practices that recognise, respect, value and harness difference for the benefit of all. This may sound obvious, but differences can be a cause of tensions, negative feelings and poor behaviour as people's preconceptions and unconscious biases are challenged.

Unconscious bias happens because people tend to feel comfortable around others who share their culture, or look like them. It can also be caused by something known as the 'halo effect', when positive judgements are made about a person for purely superficial reasons; they dress in the same way or use the same jargon as a former worker who was perceived as good. The bias is then justified because actions that reinforce it are noticed and those that undermine it ignored or minimised. Unconscious bias at work can lead to talented workers being overlooked. Worse, if unconscious bias is against a protected characteristic (see below), it can be illegal. For example if during a recruitment process an employer appoints a candidate who is able-bodied when a person with a disability was better qualified, this could breach the Equalities Act.

Unconscious bias is natural, but its effects can be minimised by having good HR policies and processes for recruitment and promotion, and also in relation to training and team-building. Arranging an event in a pub in the evening could cause some people with caring responsibilities in the evening or anti-alcohol beliefs to be excluded. Could the event happen at lunchtime in a café instead?

Why should festival managers concern themselves about equality and diversity? There are three arguments propounded. First, as organisations that promote culture, and often charities in receipt of public money, there are ethical principles at stake that suggest festivals should reflect the society in all of their working practices, from programme selection to employment.

Second, there is a legal argument. In the UK the 2010 Equalities Act identified age, disability, gender reassignment, marriage and civil partnership, pregnancy and maternity, race, religion or belief, sex and sexual orientation as protected characteristics. Members of these groups are offered additional legal protection to ensure that companies do not intentionally or unintentionally put in place policies or procedures that discriminate against them. Breaking the law could lead to the company being taken to an employment tribunal or losing its charitable status.

Third, there is a business case which argues limiting the pool of potential workers through biased hiring practices or policies that make it difficult for some people to work for the organisation, means missing out on talent.

Research into creativity in the workplace reinforces the business case as it argues diverse groups of workers bring new insights that can help in the development of innovation and in communicating with new audiences (Henry, 2004).

Despite the cultural sector considering itself as open and liberal, there is evidence of unconscious biases in operation. Research into hiring practices at orchestras, for example, found that they were much more likely to offer women jobs if auditions took place behind screens (Goldin and Rouse, 2000), and lobby group Arts Emergency found that people from working class backgrounds and ethnic minority groups were underrepresented in all creative industry sectors (Brook et al., 2018). This was made worse by a culture of unpaid internships that discriminated against people who could not afford to work for free. Festivals have a tradition of volunteering that can offer a way into working in the sector – but at what point do genuine volunteering opportunities become a substitute for what should be paid work? Equality and diversity principles suggest a need to think about whether a programme is genuinely open or might actually be excluding some groups. That's where well-developed and transparent processes, such as job descriptions and person specs, help. It encourages recruiters to ask: 'am I basing this decision on emotion or evidence?'. Some job application forms even exclude the names, age and addresses of candidates to ensure that there is no direct or indirect bias at shortlisting stage. If you don't know the age and gender of candidates, you cannot discriminate against them, even unwittingly.

Recruitment and selection

Having written a job description, a vacant role has to be advertised. As with any marketing, it is essential to understand where the target market gets its information from. This will differ depending on the job. For senior roles, advertising nationally in industry press and on key websites can be the best route. For junior roles and casual staff, then local media are likely to be cheaper and as effective and local Job Centres are an important and free resource. Personal networks are also good routes, but be careful this doesn't exclude people from diverse groups who might not have connections to the arts world. The aim of the advert is to generate a good field of candidates with the right skills, knowledge and experience.

Selection

If an advert is successful, it will need to be followed by a robust and fair selection process that ends in the best person for the job being chosen and saying yes! Although no two organisations will run identical processes, and even internally there may be adaptations depending on the role being interviewed for, in general selection involves a variant of: shortlisting from the applicants; testing relevant skills; interviewing; taking up references; offering the job; and communicating to unsuccessful applicants.

In order to ensure the process avoids unconscious bias, shortlisting and interviewing should be based on the person specification. This ensures that the selection panel focuses on applicant's skills, knowledge and experience rather than their skin colour, age or other protected characteristics. One way to do this is to allocate points where there is evidence in the application that the candidate fulfils the essential criteria. Everyone shortlisting or interviewing should use the same point scale.

Essential qualities	Excellent evidence 2 points	Some evidence 1 points	No evidence 0	Example
Extremely organised and able to handle multiple tasks.				
Ability to work under pressure.				
Polite and professional, and able to work with people at all levels.				
Understanding of how a festival is put together & stakeholder needs.				
Exceptional time-management.				
A willingness to "pitch in" as required.				
A knowledge and understanding of the arts.				

Figure 8.8: Selection criteria

Looking at the Festival Assistant role above, some of these criteria will be more obvious in an interview or test, or from references and previous employers so explain in the person specification which skills you expect to assess via the application form, which by a test and so on. If there are still too many people to interview, the desirable qualities come into play and a similar process can be gone through.

Once the shortlisting panel has agreed a list, interviews can be arranged. It is best practice to have more than one person do the interviewing to ensure that there are different perspectives. Ideally it should include the role's line manager. Senior roles in charities often have a trustee on the panel. Sometimes interview panels have been known to include a junior member of staff as they can bring a workforce perspective to the process. Interviews should take place in a room free from interruptions. Planning should include thinking through: who will meet the candidates; where will they wait; will they meet the whole team, or just the panel; will they meet other applicants, or will they be spaced so that they miss each other; how long will each interview last; will there be a test or presentation? Sometimes interviews have all the candidates waiting together. This can be quite awkward, especially if you know one or more of the other candidates, and increases pressure on the candidates. It is unclear what the benefit is of this, unless you want to see how people deal with pressure.

If there is a test or presentation, it should be justified as being the best way to determine if candidates have key skills and helping to distinguish between them. This is also the criterion for the questions, which should focus on the tasks and qualities. Questions relating to protected characteristics, such as age, disability, ethnicity, should only be asked if they are relevant to all candidates' ability to undertake a task. So rather than asking about childcare responsibilities ask about evening and weekend availability if this is essential. Rather than asking about a specific disability, ask whether applicants are able to distribute boxes of leaflets. Take notes during the interviews and allocate points for evidence as for shortlisting. Keep the completed shortlisting and interview selection forms as they provide a good basis for feedback if an unsuccessful candidate requests it, and, at a tribunal would provide evidence the process was criterion-based in an attempt to avoid unconscious bias.

In past times job interviewers quite often asked candidates different questions based on their applications or CVs, questions which could be quite personal. For example "I see you went to so and so school, did you happen to know teacher x there?". Such an interviewing style is potentially discriminatory. It is the practice today to ask precisely the same questions of each candidate and not to refer to personal matters which have no bearing on the advertised job. Under this system it is permissible to ask follow up questions, but only to test their ability to meet the person specification.

Some employers like to ask for references prior to interview, but in general in the cultural sector in the UK references are taken up after an offer has been made as some applicants prefer not to alert their current employer to the fact they are thinking of leaving. So, the offer has to be made 'subject to references'. A disadvantage of this approach is that it means a delay informing other candidates, particularly the person who is second choice, about the outcomes. It is good practice to write to or phone all of the interviewed candidates to let them know your decision as they have invested time and effort in the process and might want to apply again in the future having gained more skills. It's a small world, festival management, so even if they don't end up working for you, you may well come across them in other roles. A bit of consideration and thoughtfulness about the fact they are waiting can go a long way to maintaining good relationships, and your reputation.

Once the chosen applicant has accepted the job, a contract should be signed. By law, all employees, regardless of the number of hours they work per week, are entitled to receive a written statement from their employer within two months of starting work. The statement should describe the main terms of the contract of employment including pay, holidays and the notice period required on both sides and a date agreed for the new staff member to start. You are entitled to the statement even if your job finishes before the initial two months, as long as the job was supposed to last for more than one month and you have worked for at least a month.

Induction

Starting work at a new festival organisation can be disorientating. Most companies run an induction programme to help new starters to acclimatise, meet their colleagues and familiarise them with key systems and processes. Depending on the size of the festival organisation (or the size at that date, as this is likely to change depending on when in the cycle they start), new members of staff might have to meet their direct work team, other teams they work with and key clients. They should be told about meetings they need to attend and important policies and processes. The overall aim of induction is to shorten the time it takes people to learn their way around, acclimatise them to the organisational culture and make them more efficient more quickly, so it is worth spending some time thinking about what needs to be included.

In addition to the soft elements of induction, new starters will also need physical resources such as a desk and a computer. It is usually up to the line manager to arrange for these to be set up and ready.

Teams and team working

As the organisational structures above show, teams are central to the way that festivals are produced, even in hierarchical structures. Festivals are complex projects that have multiple events happening at the same time in a limited amount of space, so different functions have to work together to ensure good communications and a consistent approach. Understanding what teams are best at, how to form and manage them is a core part of a festival manager's role.

When teams work best they do so because they combine complementary functional skills with good social relationships and clear shared goals. At their best, 'hot groups' (Lipman-Blumen and Leavitt, 2001) achieve far more, more creatively and are happier than the same number of individuals working on their own.

But this is unlikely to happen accidentally or immediately.

Tuckman developed a model of group development that shows the stages teams go through before they become truly effective.

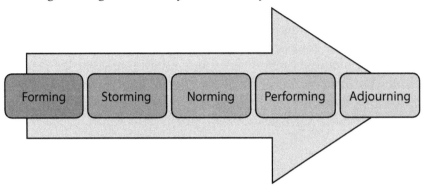

Figure 8.9: Tuckman's small group development model (Tuckman and Jensen, 1977)

Forming

When people come together in any social situation they size each other up and try to work out who is who, who is likely to be a leader, who they feel most aligned to and where they fit in. In a work situation this uncertainty is intensified as members try to work out what the team's purpose is. Some are nervous, others excited. As it forms, team members start to get to know each other's strengths and weaknesses, establish communication structures and so on. The nature of the project is still being scoped out and at this stage people are generally polite. The work at this stage is in the planning stage, so interdependence is not yet critical to people achieving their goals

The person who convened the team has the option at this point of being very directive and retaining the leadership role or stepping back and letting team members decide how to organise themselves to achieve SMART goals. If teams are to achieve their full potential, this is recommended, otherwise they will be less creative and do less to reduce the manager's workload.

Storming

Storming begins when the team starts to take ownership of the project. One or two individuals move to take on leadership roles and others may resist. Working styles and attitudes associated with their professional backgrounds or personalities may grate. A risk-averse finance manager may consider a programmer to be reckless when they push to programme an expensive act with no guarantee that it will increase ticket sales sufficiently, for example. If the team's goals are not clearly enough defined, members will have no rationale to use as a basis for negotiating between them and cliques may form based on personalities rather than purpose. Being a member of a team that is storming is upsetting and can lead to some people leaving the group. Others may become miserable and demotivated. Teams can break apart at this point.

However, awareness of this process means that it is possible to intervene when teams are storming by clarifying the goals and where they sit in the festival's strategies or, if necessary and possible, by removing one or more of the main instigators.

Norming

Assuming the team survives the storming phase, it will move into the norming stage. Norms are generally unwritten shared assumptions and values that form the basis of a sense of group belonging and trust. People understand their goals and know how best to work together. Rather than asking outsiders for help they tend to ask each other, and they ask for and give honest and constructive feedback. Teams that have normed start to work towards the team's goal in a collaborative manner.

Performing

The performing stage is when the team has fully bonded and is jointly working towards its shared goals. Work can be delegated to the team and they will be able to share it out equitably based on a good understanding of who has the necessary skills and time.

Adjourning

Unfortunately, even the best teams can't last for ever, so a plan has to be put in place to manage team members' exit. This should include thinking about what work they will do next, but also needs to take into account the fact that leaving a successful team is an emotional separation as much as a practical one.

Mourning

This is an alternative to Adjourning and especially relevant if your festival is a one-off. Festivals involve a huge amount of human effort and adrenaline. At the end it is common to feel a mix of emotionally flat, exhausted and even quite lost. Festival staff, unless they are contract staff going from festival to festival, will benefit from taking a few days off after the event to reflect and regather. Having 'been to the peak', it is quite natural to 'sink to the depths' for a while once the event is over and 'to mourn the loss', possibly over a well-deserved drink or two.

Performance management

Performance management sounds very formal. And it can be, particularly if there are problems with someone's work or relationships. The purpose of a performance management system is, however, to try and avoid these kinds of problems.

According to the Charted Institute for Personnel and Development (CIPD) performance management is:

> "the activity and set of processes that aim to maintain and improve employee performance in line with an organisation's objectives. It's strategic as well as operational, as its aim is to ensure that employees contribute positively to business objectives" (Gifford, 2017).

Performance management tends to be based around a series of two-way conversations between an individual and their line manager that give feedback on progress towards SMART objectives, successes and problems being experienced. These might happen monthly, or less often, depending on the organisation. Usually these are supplemented by an annual appraisal that focuses more on personal development and goal setting for the next year. The purpose is to make sure the festival happens as efficiently and effectively as possible, so that's the starting point for each meeting: are the organisation's goals being met? What could be improved? What is preventing that from happening? What can the line manager do to improve the situation? What can the worker do to improve the situation?

Training and development aka CPD

A training need might emerge as part of the performance management or appraisal process. An individual might identify a problem undertaking a task, or want to learn something in order to progress. Alternatively, there might be a strategic need for training when volunteers are recruited, for example. As with performance management, from an HR perspective training is only worth investing in if it will improve job performance by developing relevant skills and knowledge, or by increasing an employee's motivation.

There are two elements to this that can be overlooked in a small festival team without an HR function. First, training and development, also known as CPD which stands for continuous professional development, can be expensive, so it is important to budget for it. Second, if it is going to be strategic, there needs to be a process that helps managers to think about whether a training need is essential or 'nice to do'. Some people are very keen to take up training places and others more reticent. The best solution to this is to focus on whether skills necessary to achieve organisational goals and SMART objectives. Others may miss out because they work part-time or have responsibilities that mean they are not available when the course is on. Best practice is to pay casual and part-time workers for their training hours and, if possible to run it more than once on different days and at different times.

One further purpose of training and development is to ensure that managers know the organisation's policies. This can be particularly important when things go wrong.

Disciplinary and grievance policies

Disciplinary and grievance policies should be laid out in a staff handbook that is given to all workers during their induction (it can be on your website). Essentially, these policies lay out the stages a worker or a manager goes through when things go wrong. Disciplinaries happen when a manager feels that a worker is not meeting the terms and conditions of their contract or job description, or that they have broken organisational rules, or even laws. Grievances are when a worker feels they have been treated unfairly, either by a manager or another member of staff. Policies and procedures will vary from organisation to organisation. In the UK, ACAS offers free good practice advice booklets from its website. They advise trying to manage problems early and informally if possible, but not being afraid of the process as ignoring problems will probably make them worse and can be very demotivating for other workers.

Disciplinary procedures are easier to implement where job and behaviour expectations have been clearly established in the job description, induction and staff handbook. That way it should be clear to everyone if the problem is a case of minor misconduct, unsatisfactory performance or gross misconduct.

Good disciplinary processes should:

♦ Be written down and available to all workers

♦ Be fair to all parties and non-discriminatory

♦ Keep information confidential

♦ Be transparent – workers should be told what the complaint(s) are and given any evident prior to a disciplinary interviews. They should also be told what action(s) might be taken against them, and be given the opportunity to put their own case forward.

♦ Be timely. Workers should not be left with this hanging over them any longer than is necessary to investigate fully.

♦ Be clear about who in the hierarchy has the right to implement which forms of disciplinary action.

♦ Give workers a right to be accompanied.

♦ Except in cases of gross misconduct, workers should not be dismissed for a first offence.

♦ Provide for an opportunity to appeal.

♦ Be applicable to all members of staff regardless of status.

Grievance procedures need to follow similar principles of fairness, transparency and sensitivity. Ideally all such procedures should be laid out and available to everyone in a staff handbook, or on an intranet site staff are given or made aware of during their induction. Hopefully they and you will never need it, but the worst time to work out your disciplinary or grievance procedure is during a crisis. Any uncertainty about what people need to do adds to the tension. The time spent writing a pre-prepared policy might feel like a bind at the time, but will come in to its own when things go wrong.

One significant point to note is that, because both disciplinary and grievance interviews, which can be an intimidating experience that can end in someone being dismissed, the person affected has a statutory right to be accompanied. This might be by a fellow worker or a trade union representative. The companion can address the hearing, but not answer questions on the worker's behalf. Full details of legal constraints vary depending on the regulations in place. In England advice is available for employers from ACAS, which has templates and forms and updated guidance on employment law on its website, as well as a helpline. For festivals that are charities or not-for-profit organisations, the National Council of Voluntary Organisations (NCVO), and the Charity Commission both offer guidance.

Unions

As small organisations, festivals may not have to negotiate directly with trade unions about staff pay and conditions, however many workers will be members of unions. Key unions in the sector are those aimed at performers such as Equity and the Musicians Union, and those for technical workers, often BECTU. These unions work with umbrella groups in the sectors like UK Theatre to create collective agreements about terms and conditions, contracts and compensation. These then become agreed standards across the sector and might be written in to funding agreements. Arts Council England, for example, expects any organisation it funds to pay Equity minimum rates.

Unions might also get involved during disciplinary and grievance procedures, advising and supporting their members. However, good union officials are also very knowledgeable about employment law and best practice. They would prefer their members not to be badly managed, so can be a source of information when policies and procedures are being developed.

Compensation and benefits administration

Compensation and benefits includes policies about pay and other conditions such as holidays, bonuses, pensions, retirement pans and career development. In small companies, it also means doing the paperwork related to running the monthly payroll, checking people's hours and making sure they aren't going over their maximum weekly allowances (this is a potential problem during the festival period itself, so worth being alert to) and so on.

The main principles of compensation policies is that they can be divided into:

♦ **Financial** – direct such as wages and salaries, commissions and bonuses, and indirect such as pension contributions, insurance plans, paid leave and so on.

♦ **Non-financial** – interesting job roles that fulfil Herzberg's motivating factors, and a work environment that fulfils his satisfiers.

Some of these areas are regulated and it is essential to know what the laws are in the country or countries the festival operates in. These tend to relate mainly to financial considerations. Key areas to look out for are:

♦ Minimum wage legislation

♦ Minimum paid leave legislation

♦ Maximum working time legislation

♦ Pension auto-enrollment

These items are costs to the organisation and can have a significant effect on the budget or operations is they are not planned for and monitored. What is the policy if a staff member hasn't taken their annual leave and requests time off during the festival itself? What if a key member of the operations staff is scheduled in such a way that they breach the Working Time Directive maximum? As with disciplinary and grievance procedures, HR policies are created to ensure that workers and managers are forewarned and, therefore, forearmed.

Summary

If as many festivals claim, 'people are our most important asset', then making sure you understand how to select the right person, how to design a do-able job, manage harmonious teams even with a diverse workforce must be high on the agenda of all festival managers. This chapter has attempted to introduce the key principles of human resource management on the assumption that most festivals are probably too small to hire an HR officer, let alone a full department. It showed how job descriptions and person specifications can be used to help you think about what jobs really need to be done, and what the skills are required. This helps you to systematically pick the best person for the role, rather than being influenced by irrelevant factors, or the unconscious biases we are all susceptible to.

The chapter has discussed motivation and team theories and linked these to questions of organisational culture and structure, showing how teams, training and hierarchies can be used to ensure people feel enthused by and supported in their work, how to ensure you manage performance and use training strategically to help people develop the skills you need now and in the future.

But sometimes things will go wrong, so it is essential you have planned for the worst. When everyone is upset, a clear set of rules about what happens, who is responsible for managing the disciplinary or grievance process and how long things should take, really helps. You will be glad, then, that you took the time early on to think about HR management.

References

Brook, O., O'Brien, D. and Taylor, M. (2018) *Panic! Social Class, Taste and Inequalities in the Creative Industries.* http://createlondon.org/event/panic2018/. (Accessed 17 May 2018).

Gifford, J. (2017) *Performance management: an introduction.* Charted Institute for Personnel and Development. https://www.cipd.co.uk/knowledge/fundamentals/people/performance/factsheet (Accessed 23 May 2018).

Goldin, C. and Rouse, C. (2000) Orchestrating impartiality: The impact of 'blind' auditions on female musicians. *American Economic Review,* **90**(4), pp. 715-741.

Handy, C. (1999) *Understanding Organisations.* 4th ed. Middlesex: Penguin.

Henry, J. (2004) Positive and creative organization. In Linley, P.A. and Joseph, S. (eds.) *Positive Psychology in Practice,* pp. 269-286.

Herzberg, F.I. (1966) *Work and the Nature of Man.* Cleveland: World Publishing Company.

Lipman-Blument, J. and Leavitt, H.J. (2001) *Hot Groups: Seeding them, feeding them, and using them to ignite your organization.* Oxford: Oxford University Press.

Locke, E.A. and Latham, G.P. (2002) Building a practically useful theory of goal setting and task motivation: A 35-year odyssey. *American psychologist,* **57**(9), 705.

McGregor, D. (1966) *Leadership and Motivation: Essays of Douglas McGregor,* Cambridge, MA: MIT Press.

Schein, E. (2004) *Organizational Culture and Leadership,* (3rd ed.): San Francisco: Jossey-Bass.

Tuckman, B. W. and Jensen, M.A.C. (1977) Stages of small-group development revisited. *Group & Organization Studies,* **2**(4), 419-427.

9 Festival Marketing

by Jennie Jordan and Kristy Diaz

After reading this chapter you should:

- Have an overview of the principles of festival marketing
- Understand the motivations and processes involved in deciding to participate in a festival
- Understand and be able to apply marketing tools including segmentation and targeting, branding, customer relationship management, the marketing mix and marketing research
- Understand the strategic role of marketing within a festival organisation

---

Introduction

Marketing, promotion, sales, communications, audiences, participation – the concepts covered in this section are a fundamental part of festival management, whether your event is a community fête or a globally recognised music festival. The word 'marketing' originated from the simple forms of buying and selling that can be seen in a local street market, but the term now encompasses a range of sophisticated techniques that have developed to help companies decide what products and services to produce and how to persuade people to buy them. This chapter introduces marketing concepts and illustrates how festivals and cultural events can adapt the techniques to develop appropriate experiences for festival-goers, artists and communities.

This chapter will introduce concepts such as supply and demand, segmentation and targeting, CRM (customer relationship management), experience marketing and its relationship to service design, and branding. It will raise questions about the extent to which a festival's artistic programme can or should be led by market demand, whether the relationship between artists and festival-goers is more complex than those expected in traditional marketing models and about the ethics of storing and using data collected on festival-goers' behaviours and preferences.

Definitions of marketing

Although dating back to the late 19th century the acronym AIDA remains an easily remembered and useful starting point in defining marketing. AIDA stands for:

♦ Awareness (or Attention)

♦ Interest

♦ Desire

♦ Action

This neatly summarises what you are trying to do: gain customer awareness that your festival exists, gain their interest in it, turn that interest into desire and finally encourage them to action through buying a ticket and attending (or just attending if the event is free). Arguably in the busy mediatized world of the 21st century the first of these principles has become even more import – we are all in the business of competing for people's time and attention.

Modern marketing is defined as:

"The management process which identifies, anticipates and satisfies customer requirements" (Chartered Institute of Marketing, 2015: 2)

The UK-based Chartered Institute of Marketing's definition places marketing as a management function alongside other core areas such as finance, operations, and human resource management. It has three components: identifying customer requirements, usually through market research, which means understanding what sorts of products or services different groups of people want and need now; anticipating what they might want in the future; and ensuring that the products and services provided are suitable, available and affordable.

Understanding what sort of festival will fulfil customer requirements means having a thorough understanding of why people choose to attend a festival, what processes they go through when making that decision and what they expect to be there. There are some shared basics, such as central places where people can meet, entertainment, and usually colourful decorations and a festive atmosphere that we have discussed in the chapter on festival design. How much people will be willing to pay for a ticket will depend on how interested they are in the social, artistic or comfort elements of the festival you produce. Some people love camping, for instance, while others would prefer to stay in a hotel or go home. Having good research into these preferences will inform your festival's production and programming as well as decisions about core marketing functions such as communications, pricing and promotions.

"Marketing is the activity, set of institutions, and processes for creating, communicating, delivering, and exchanging offerings that have value for customers, clients, partners, and society at large" (American Marketing Association, 2013)

Whilst also being concerned about satisfying customer needs, the American Marketing Association's definition introduces the concept of exchange. At the heart of marketing is a bargain: the company will trade products or services that customers value for something it values, usually money, but in the case of festivals it might be volunteer time or artistic skill. The needs of both the company and the individual must be satisfied.

"The aim of Audience Development Arts Marketing practitioners is to bring an appropriate number of people, drawn from the widest possible range of social background, economic condition and age, into an appropriate form of contact with the artist and, in so doing, to arrive at the best financial outcome that is compatible with the achievement of that aim" (Diggle, 2017)

Keith Diggle's definition of arts marketing broadens the concept, moving it beyond commercial considerations and encompassing public policy outcomes, such as the need to ensure cultural events are not exclusive and that artists' needs are also met.

This definition hints at the complexity underlying the management of many festivals with multiple stakeholders such as local authorities, funding bodies, donors and sponsors as well as audiences, participants and volunteers. The needs of each of these groups have to be understood and strategies developed and implemented to try and fulfil them.

From these definitions it can be seen that marketing is more than simply selling to anyone who turns up at your stall. It involves having a deep and long-term understanding of who your existing and potential customers are, what they value about what you do, where and how they want to engage with your festival(s), how many of them there are and what they are willing to pay. This knowledge has to be communicated to all parts of the organisation in order to inform the decisions taken by content producers such as artistic directors and programmers; staff such as those in charge of front of house operations or the design of the festival site, as well as people directly involved with functions traditionally designated as marketing. These can be seen in Figure 9.1.

In spite of the definitions there can be a significant difference in the way that many commercial companies and arts companies approach marketing. The 'pure' marketing approach is to identify your customer desires and needs and to then design a product or service to meet them.

Marketing audit

What are our products/services?
What is our position in the market (competitors, market share, segments, reputation)?
What is the organisation good at (strengths)? What is it not good at (weaknesses)?
History - what have we tried before? What has worked? What has not worked?

Market research

What do we know about our current customers? Who are they? What do they want from the organisation's products and services?
What do we know about potential customers?
What segments do we appeal to. Why? How do they want to be communicated with?
What needs are not being fulfilled by us or our competitiors that we could serve?

Strategic marketing objectives

What does the oganisation want to achieve? More ticket sales?
Improved brand reputation? New sponsors? Higher profits?
More attendances from particular communities? More volunteers?
Higher showing on social media?

Marketing tasks

Planning - what needs to be done, by whom and when? What skills are required and do we have them? What will it cost and what budget is available?
Sales - ticketing, box office staffing, training and computer systems, direct selling and agencies, webshop.
Communications: press and publicity, social media, direct mail.
Pricing, sales promotions and special offers
CRM - customer database management, loyalty schemes, complaint handling.
Brand management.
Audience development - attracting new market segments.

Marketing tools

Product, Price, Place
Promotion, People, Physical evidence

Monitoring and evaluation

How do we know if our marketing has been successful in achieving our aims?
Collection and analysis of sales data and customer service feedback.
Monitoring of social media. Website hits. Customer surveys.
Monitoring against budgets and schedules.

Figure 9.1: Marketing functions and tasks

The process starts with your customer and then product or service design. However, in some instances, particularly with the arts and often with technology products where the customer probably cannot conceive what technology can do, the process is the other way around. You start with the product or service, and the marketing is the process that persuades the customer that they have to have it and cannot live without it.

In creative spheres you don't usually spend weeks or months researching what your potential customer wants, and even if you did, they probably wouldn't say, "I want a rock festival with some street theatre, poetry and opera thrown in and a paintball fight too." It is often your own or your artistic director's creative vision that is the starting point.

Supply and demand

The concepts of supply and demand are fundamental to understanding marketing. The term 'demand' means the total amount of a product or service that will be bought if there is sufficient supply. Matters such as price and availability will affect demand. Most marketing text books focused on consumer products assume that there is more supply than demand, so companies have to compete by responding to customers' wants and needs in order to persuade them to buy. The objective is to produce just enough of any product to fulfil the demand, minimising waste and maximising sales.

In the festivals market, supply is constrained by a number of factors, such as the availability of headline acts and the capacity of venues. This can lead to distortions in the market. In order to avoid raising prices to levels that many people from their core market could not afford, popular festivals such as *Glastonbury*, for example, have to implement strict policies on how many tickets individuals are allowed to buy so that touts are prevented from profiteering on the secondary ticket market. Less popular festivals can end up with surplus spaces that are then sold at a discount, encouraging savvy customers to wait before purchasing in the hope of bagging a bargain.

> **Debating point:**
> Imbalances between supply and demand provide both practical and ethical questions for festival marketeers. How would you respond if your festival is selling out but there are more people wanting tickets?

Value exchange

Marketing can be said to be an exchange process in which one side parts with something valuable (a festival experience) in return for something else of value (usually money). Both sides are seeking to swap something for something else they value more. The promise offered by the festival experience must be worth more to the buyer than the price of the ticket and the associated costs of attending, such as travel, time off work and so on. The cost of the ticket must also be high enough for the festival to cover its costs of production, and possibly to make a profit. The concept of value exchange is central to marketing, as if customers feel satisfied that they have received value for money they are more likely to rate the festival highly, recommend it to others and return for future events. Good marketing focuses on understanding what customers value about their festival and uses this to create and maintain satisfying exchanges.

The purchasing process

Intervening effectively to ensure satisfying exchanges means being aware of the processes that festival-goers go through when deciding whether to attend a festival, and if so, which one. Engel et al.'s model is useful in thinking through the stages of the process and highlighting where it might be possible to make changes that will lead to more potential participants attending.

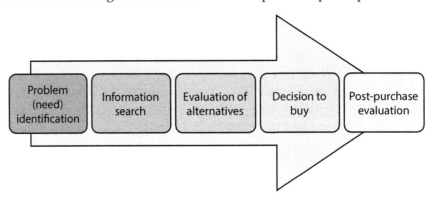

Figure 9.2: The buyer decision process model. (Engel, Blackwell and Miniard, 1995: 153)

Problem/need identification

The first step in deciding whether or not to buy is taken when an individual realises that there is a difference between his or her current state and a desired state. This awareness can be triggered in various ways, by physical discomfort (hunger, thirst); social discomfort (all my friends are going) or by personal factors such as boredom, or the desire to see a favourite band. Advertising, promotions and social media campaigns are often aimed at stimulating a longing for something by highlighting the discrepancy between an individual's current and desired states. A solution's value lies in the size of the gap between a potential festival-goer's current situation and the desired state, plus the relative importance of the problem.

Information search

Once an individual is aware that they have a need, the next stage is to search for potential solutions. The desire to experience a favourite band, for example, could be solved by finding out where they are touring, which might be a number of festivals and non-festival gigs, buying an EP, subscribing to relevant list and forums, or watching them online.

Information sources include

♦ **Personal experience** – how have I solved this problem before?

♦ **Word of mouth** – friends, family, social media groups.

♦ **Experts** – music press, critics, people working in festivals or the music industry.

♦ **Marketing communications** – adverts, ticket agencies, mailings or social media campaigns.

This information is collated and becomes a set of alternatives that will be evaluated. The purpose of much marketing communication is therefore to raise awareness that a product exists and that it can solve the customer's need. Potential festival-goers will not attend if they do not know your festival exists. But even if they do, if they do not know their favourite band is playing and that is their motivational need, they will look elsewhere.

Evaluation of alternatives

Once the information has been collated, it is compared to see which potential solution will solve the problem most effectively. This evaluation can be done in a number of ways. Does the product have the requisite features to solve the problem? In this case, is my favourite band touring? Is it playing that festival? Are there videos on line that I could watch instead?

Each individual will evaluate this differently, and it might be decided that a festival is providing a better fit for solving the problem than watching the band online or attending a stadium gig. But if two or more competing solutions might solve the need, further criteria are used. These might include:

♦ **Price**: of event tickets and associated costs versus price of buying a vinyl version of a favourite album.

♦ **Social and esteem factors**: what are my friends doing? Which option will enhance my prestige?

♦ **Personal preferences**: attitudes to risk, fit between self-image and brand image, emotional factors.

♦ **Product quality and features**: reputation, ease of access, comfort etc.

The options are ranked and a purchase decision can then be made (or, indeed, a decision can be made that none of the options solve the problem adequately and a new search will then be undertaken).

Decision to buy

Having selected a preferred option, most transactions will simply proceed. However, there can be complications. For example, one of the festival-goer's friends would prefer to go to another festival because it has a different headliner, or happens over a more convenient weekend. Or the tickets may be sold out for the first event.

Whilst marketing theorists will describe this in a logical step-by-step process, human decision making tends to be more emotional, intuitive and less logical than the step-by-step process suggests. There is an old marketing saying: 'sell the sizzle, not the sausage.' This is about projecting the benefits that purchasing a product or service will bring you rather than its features. In fact, some people contend that we don't actually buy products or services at all. What we buy are the expectations of the benefits they will give us; today's social media is a perfect way of creating those expectations and selling that sizzle.

Post-purchase evaluation

Having attended the festival, the festival-goer will evaluate the experience. Did it solve the problem identified? Did it solve other problems? Was it perceived as good value?

Post-purchase evaluation is an important part of marketing as satisfied customers, that is those whose problems have been solved are more likely to become repeat attenders. The next time they identify a similar problem, rather than go through the whole decision-process, including exploring the possibility of attending competitor's events, they will remember that the problem was solved by attending your festival and short cut the process directly to the purchase. This is what marketing seeks to achieve through branding. Customers trust that the brand will reliably solve their problem and develop a relationship with it.

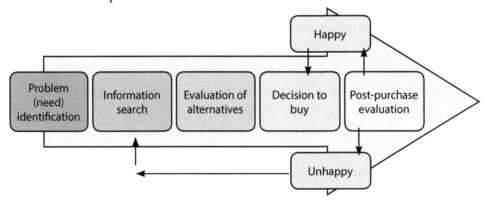

Figure 9.3: Post-purchase evaluation

Relationship marketing

In the past the focus of much festival marketing was on selling an individual ticket or group of tickets to this year's edition. Since the 1980s, marketeers have realised that good practice means thinking about how this sale can be built up into a longer-term relationship in which the festival-goer returns year after year. Selling to someone who has already experienced the event and been satisfied by it, is cheaper than persuading a new customer to try the festival. It also deepens the experience for the audience member, who can compare this edition with last, and might develop friendships with other festival-goers and meet up each year.

This approach is called relationship marketing and requires the festival's marketing department to think about the festival's brand development and customer relationship management (CRM) processes beyond the one-off ticket sale. Research throughout the 1990s highlighted the fact that the costs of attracting new customers, such as advertising, personal selling, social media campaigns, or discounts and promotions are significantly higher than the costs of retaining existing customers, such as maintaining a customer database and producing regular communications. Relationship marketing is an ongoing series of transactions between organisations and their customers (Doyle and Stern, 2006).

Good relationship marketing aims to maximise long-term profitability by building up a series of positive exchanges between the festival organisation and all of its stakeholders. Loyal customers spread positive word of mouth, a prized source of advertising as it is perceived as unbiased, and is perfectly targeted at the friends the festival-goer believes are most likely to be interested.

Relationship marketing is dependent on the development of a customer database. Customer databases can be developed in a number of ways. At their most basic customers can be asked to sign up to a mailing list to hear more about the festival. More commonly customer information is collected during the ticket purchasing process and held in a CRM system. CRM systems hold basic data such as a customer's name and contact details. They can also hold information about which events a customer has bought tickets for, how many tickets have been purchased, in which price brackets and how far in advance of the event. Different marketing approaches can then be designed specifically to appeal to first time attenders, group bookers, early birds or jazz fans, depending on the festival's strategic aims.

Once enough data has been collected, systems can be interrogated to show how effective a specific promotional mailing was or whether residents of some postcode areas are more likely to attend than others. The amalgamation of data from thousands of customers over a number of years can be a powerful source of information for developing new products, services and experiences.

It is important to remember that customer data is sensitive and that any organisation that holds it complies with relevant legislation.

General Data Protection Regulation (GDPR)

GDPR came into effect in the UK in May 2018. It has significant implications for marketing communications. In particular, GDPR gives increased rights to individuals to access information held about them by companies. If an organisation holds personal information about people, for example, name, age, postal or email address, then it must comply or risk being liable for fines. In practice, this means ensuring that people sharing data with you have 'opted-in' and given informed consent, i.e. they know what they are signing up for and are happy for their data to be used in the way you have said it will. When asking people to sign up to your email list, for example, state what type of communication they are receiving, the frequency of communications, and how they can unsubscribe from the service. You should also provide a point of contact should anyone have any queries or concerns. You should ensure you only collect and hold data that you need for specific reasons, and only for as long as you need to hold it. For further reading on GDPR and how to comply, visit: https://www.gov.uk/data-protection.

Customers are entitled to assume that festivals will not keep data that is irrelevant or in accurate. They are also protected from lists of customers being passed to other companies without their express permission. This can be complicated for festivals as there can be debates between a band, artist or theatre company and the promoter (festival) about who the data controller is. The festival may have the ticketing transaction data from the box office, but if a customer has bought tickets to specific shows within the festival, then that company is a data controller in common and has equal rights to use the data, and responsibility for ensuring it is not misused. The Audience Agency has published online guidance on data sharing between cultural organisations (www.theaudienceagency.org).

Other legislation relating to marketing in the UK (other countries have similar regulations, although details differ) includes advertising, which must be fair and accurate, including not having hidden costs.

Whilst initially appearing complicated, adherence to the guidelines is good marketing practice that ensures better relationships with loyal festival-goers who will be given clear, accurate information about events they are likely to want to go to, rather than being spammed with unwanted communications that might otherwise swamp the hidden gems.

Branding

Branding is the process by which organisations distinguish their product or service from their competitors. It is often thought of as the logo, and creating a memorable name and visual image are important in making a brand visible and memorable, but branding also includes thinking about what makes the whole customer experience a unique, distinctive and beneficial one.

A good brand image is important for attracting new customers, as it is a shorthand guarantee that the product or service will be of a specific quality or value. Festival brands can be positioned as exclusive and high quality; as experimental and surprising; as a communal experience; as rebellious; and so on. Each of these identities will influence what acts are booked, how the organisers design the festival venue(s), what the ticket prices are and communications with festival-goers.

Brands are created by adding extras to the core product. For a festival the core product is the social, artistic and/or entertainment experience that the festival-goer considers the central benefit of attending. This is common to all festivals. The core benefit is created by staging events, decorating the site, providing refreshment stalls and a system for selling tickets or managing the capacity of a site. It is essential for any brand's success that the core product is good and right for the market. A festival that cannot programme and stage events on time, pay artists or operate a reliable ticket selling system will not survive very long.

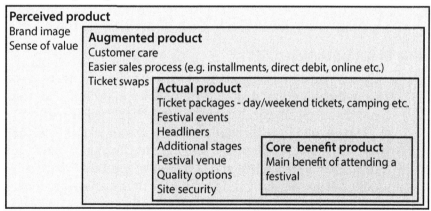

Figure 9.4: Audience value factors

A brand identity is created when this core product is augmented by additional factors that distinguish it from other festivals or concerts experiences. For a brand to be successful, these factors have to be valuable to the customer. Some festivals provide camping facilities, for example, or indoor arenas, family areas or ticket bundles that include transport. Not all augmented features will be valued by all customers. Camping would not be a benefit to a festival-goer who lived close by and could go home, but might be highly valued by a group of people who had travelled from further away.

Understanding which specific factors an audience will value is essential in focusing attention and resources on developing the additional products, services and experiences that create a festival's unique selling proposition.

How much influence marketing can have on each of the product elements will depend on the festival's core purposes. If it is an arts festival that exists to curate the work of a particular art form, the artistic director will have the final say over the festival programme, for example. If the festival exists to serve a specific area in a city, then the festival venue will probably not be negotiable. Marketing activity in these instances will focus on maximising the effectiveness of the augmented product and perceptions of the brand.

Debating point:

What do these festival brands mean to you?

Rock in Rio

Glastonbury

Edinburgh International Festival

Cannes Film Festival

Leicester Diwali

What three things do you think are the most important values to each of these festivals?

What cues have led you to these conclusions?

What do these lead you to expect about price, comfort, quality, safety, or customer service at each event?

Unique Selling Proposition (USP)

To be competitive, especially in a crowded marketplace, you need a USP. This is the thing that distinguishes what you do from the rest. It might be something really major, like a whole new approach, product or service, or it might be something a bit subtler. Your USP will probably be closely linked to your 'why', that we discussed at length in Chapter 2. What is it about your festival that is distinctive and different to the other ones in your genre or locality? If you are struggling to identify that, it might be worth getting 5 or 6 people together and giving them a list of other comparable festivals and your proposal. They may tell you things that you have missed. If they cannot see any differences or distinguishing features, then you may not have a USP and may need to rethink your ethos and your 'why'.

Experiences and service design

Consumer marketing, the basis of most marketing theory, is traditionally concerned with tangible products that are bought by the customer either directly from the producer or through a retail outlet. The change in global manufacturing has meant that developed economies have become increasingly reliant on services such as banking, management consultancy, tourism, leisure and education for their wealth and employment. Services can be defined as having the following characteristics:

- They provide a benefit for the customer
- They are intangible
- They are perishable (they cannot be stored or transported)
- The service provider is part of the process
- Payment does not result in ownership by the customer.

As with other products, services provide core customer benefits. A management consultant helps a business to run better, a car service prevents a breakdown, a meal in a restaurant stops hunger. These core benefits might be augmented by additional features, such as the consultant's research helping to gain a promotion, or being able to meet friends in a restaurant. But if the initial advice was poor, or the meal inedible, the consultant would not be hired again nor the restaurant revisited.

Services as intangible goods. They cannot be touched, tasted, heard, looked at or picked up. There is an exchange of value, but not of an object. The lack of tangibility makes services difficult to market as customers cannot return them if they are unhappy. As a result, many services are augmented by tangible peripheral products that provide customers with physical evidence of the quality of their services. A restaurant might offer samples of its food. A hairdresser's window will showcase the hair products it uses and photographs of models whose hair they have cut.

Because they cannot be stored or transported, services are vulnerable to scheduling and capacity problems. Restaurants have to estimate how long each table will take finishing their meal when taking bookings. Plumbers expecting to give one customer's boiler a simple service might find that the job takes much longer than expected, making them late for the next appointment. Hotels can find themselves turning customers away over a busy bank holiday weekend, but then having empty rooms the following week. Finding ways to manage and smooth out such variations in process and fluctuations in demand in order to ensure customers are not inconvenienced, is an important part of the service marketing manager's role.

Unlike tangible products that can be manufactured in a factory, many services have to be produced in the presence of the customer. Services such as beauty treatments or a visit to a dental check-up have to be done in person. Some services, such as banking, are increasingly being offered online or over the phone, but still rely to some extent on a personal encounter. This makes the individuals involved in providing the services an intrinsic part of the offer. Well trained, skilful people are essential to a successful service.

The experience economy (Pine and Gilmore, 1999), as we saw in Chapter 2, is a development of the service economy that is particularly relevant to the festival industry and thus festival marketing. Experiences are products whose core benefits are individual emotions and memories. Experiences are staged for guests, whose senses are stimulated by spectacular sights and colourful decor, music and aromas. Festival organisers strive to create an ambience that is different from everyday life, an environment of heightened emotion in which festival-goers are absorbed in novel, surprising and personally engaging experiences that have an emotional impact. Although festivals are busy social environments, no two people will have the same experience, which will be influenced by individual expectations, prior knowledge, mood at the time and personal preferences.

Designing memorable experiences

Research into memory development highlights the importance of novelty, intensity, interactivity and relevance (Poulsson and Kale, 2001). In order to be memorable experiences, festival design must consider each of these elements and how they are incorporated into the overall festival experience.

Novelty

First time experiences are more likely to be memorable than repeat visits. Festival-goers who have enjoyed their first visit and return may not be able to distinguish one year from another, particularly if they keep coming back. Festival design – the programme, the venue or site layout and décor, the range of additional events – can be used to ensure that each edition provides new and surprising experiences that ensure each festival edition is equally memorable.

Using a theme that changes each year, for example, provides a memorable identity. *Camp Bestival*, an annual festival that takes place in the grounds of Lulworth Castle in the Southwest of England has used themes such as the Olympics (2012), around the world (2013), circus (2014), wild (2015) and space (2016). The annual theme informs the decoration of the site, the acts and artists who are booked, activities such as children's workshops and the costumes audience members are encouraged wear. As a result, even loyal festival-goers can distinguish one year from another. These memories can be enhanced and triggered by the sale of themed memorabilia and souvenirs that they will value as reminders of a special time.

Intensity

Intense experiences engage participants in the theme through as many senses as possible. The aroma of popcorn at a film festival, or the image of an usher with an ice cream tray will not improve the quality of the film being seen, but do add to the sense of occasion. Themed menus, matching colour schemes and related activities create a sense of festivity. The festival-goer will remember this as a special place, a time away from the everyday.

Interactivity and engagement

Sensory intensity can be enhanced by interactivity and engagement. Audiences might participate as relatively passive spectators at a highly visual theatre or dance performance, or a spectacular light art festival, but active participation will increase the event's memorability. Experiences that involve people in doing something – learning circus skills at *Camp Bestival*, or creating a float for a carnival – engage the senses, but also the mind. Participants think about the festival when they are practicing their new skills or planning costumes, reinforcing their memories of the event.

Some festivals go further, encouraging festival-goers to co-create areas. (Walmsley and Franks, 2011). Co-creation is a process whereby the consumer works with the producer to design and create the product or experience. It both transcends the traditional divide between producer and purchaser and also enriches the outcome or product as it is more directly attuned to what the consumer wants, as they have played a role in creating it. It also enhances the producer's expertise and knowledge base.

Although community festivals and carnivals have traditionally involved residents in producing events, commercial and arts festivals have largely limited volunteer opportunities to stewarding, litter-picking and bar work. With increasing competition to book star headliners, offering festival-goers the opportunity to co-create parts of the programme increases the value of the experience, by giving co-producers prestige within the festival community, as well as privileged access to parts of the festival that are unavailable to others.

Secret Garden Party Action Camps

The *Secret Garden Party*'s website advertised its Action Camps under the heading "Participate". Potential participants were told the festival was a party created 'by you, for you'. 'Campers' were invited to suggest events related to the festival's theme. The event might be a performance, an art work or a participatory experience for other festival-goers to enjoy. The theme for the 2015 edition was 'childish things', with the festival hosting a participatory Games Arena and a Dance-Off.

Relevancy

Co-creation is also helpful to festival producers as it allows participants to develop experiences that are personally relevant to them. Such activities are those that people are highly motivated to take part in, enjoy for their own sake and want to know more about. Market research can help in designing events to a certain extent, but cannot be completely personalised to provide an understanding of individual motivations and levels of interest.

By designing festival processes that give participants control, such as the *Secret Garden Party*'s Action Camps, or by providing a range of activities that happen simultaneously, such as having a number of stages and venues, performances, workshops and refreshment stalls, individuals have the chance to choose the experiences that are most relevant to them.

Memorable experiences are those that adhere to the 3Es – entertain, educate or engage the participant's senses. Highly memorable events are those that provide opportunities for all three.

Experiential marketing and sponsorship

Experiential marketing is based on the concept that a good relationship between a brand and its customers can be created and cemented through sharing enjoyable and memorable experiences. Memories, sensations and emotions are closely linked – think about the way that music can change your mood and remind you of people and places. If a brand can create an association between itself and your favourite group, your feelings for the band will spill over and you will be more likely to think positively about the brand. This is called 'activation' (Anderton, 2015) .

As ready-made experiences, festivals are ideal sites for brands to activate a relationship with their target market segments. This might be through simple name association, such as that between the Leicester Mercury's sponsorship of *Leicester Comedy Festival*'s Comedian of the Year Awards, or through the development of events within the festival. Mercedes-Benz decided to sponsor the Las Vegas edition of the *Rock in Rio* festival that took place in 2015. Rather than just sponsor the Evolution Stage, the company built an off-road test track and allowed festival-goers to drive one of its cars around it. The company aimed to create a once-in-a-lifetime memory that generates a bond between the brand, the festival and festival-goers. For *Rock in Rio*, the sponsors' events add value for its audiences who have more choices about what to do throughout the festival site (see Martin, 2016).

Marketing research

Research is the collection and analysis of data from a sample of individuals or organisations relating to their characteristics, behaviour, attitudes, opinions or possessions (Wright and Crimp, 2000: 3)

Marketing research is the systematic collection and analysis of data relating to marketing problems and potential markets. It includes a range of research methods (see Chapter 10) that are planned and implemented methodically in order to answer specific questions about existing and potential audiences.

The purpose of marketing research is to help organisations make better decisions about all aspects of their marketing mix, to ensure that they are producing the right events, in the right place, for the right people, at the right price. When designing marketing research, particularly if you are asking people to give up their time to answer questions, it is important to know why you are asking a question and what decisions you will take as a result.

Marketing research can be used to provide data about all aspects of the marketing mix (see Figure. 9.5).

Marketing environment	Demographic changes Economic outlook Changes in tastes New product categories
Customer research	What are the factors that determine a decision to buy? What are customers' perceptions of the festival? How do they prefer to buy tickets (online, at the door)? How far in advance do they plan? How far are they willing to travel? , Etc.
Product/service research	What do customers most value about the festival? What features and augmentations would be most appealing?
Pricing research	What are our current markets prepared to pay? How much elasticity is there in pricing?
Competitor research	Who are our main competitors? What are their relative stengths and weaknesses?
Communications research	What are the key messages for different market segments? What are the best channels for each target segment?
Place research	Suitability of the venue Quality of customer service
Stakeholder research	Funding bodies Sponsors Local authorities

Figure 9.5: Marketing mix

Research, as we shall see in Chapter 10, can be secondary (desk) or primary. Secondary research uses data collected for other purposes that has a relevance to the question. It might include research that has been done by the festival in previous years, reports by market research companies such as Mintel, by specialist bodies such as the British Arts Festivals Association, Arts Council England or the Association of Festival Organisers, or from local or national governments, such as Census data.

The benefits of secondary data are:

◆ It is relatively inexpensive

◆ It can be done quickly

◆ There are few ethical issues with published data.

Secondary sources may have copyright and confidentiality issues, be outdated, or not relevant. However, because of the benefits above it is usually better to establish if research has already been done that provides the answers required before undertaking primary research.

Primary research can be qualitative or quantitative, and includes:

◆ Sales analysis

◆ Interrogation of CRM data

◆ Feedback on promotions

◆ Customer feedback

◆ Customer surveys, focus groups and interviews

◆ Observational research.

Technological developments are providing new sources of real-time data about how festival-goers behave and their likes and dislikes. Touch points can be created for festival-goers to use as they walk around a site, perhaps with information on the festival programme, or as part of a festival game. A festival app can provide feedback on what is being searched for. Building marketing research opportunities into the festival's processes as they develop can help to ensure that quality and responsiveness are maintained.

Case study: *Amsterdam Light Festival* Illuminade

Amsterdam Light Festival's walking route consists of light art works suspended along the city's streets. The site is not fenced in or ticketed. In order to know how many people visited the 2015-16 edition, the festival used technology that noted unique mobile phones as they passed four different points along the route. If a phone passed all four points within a few hours, it was assumed that it belonged to a festival visitor. Phones that only passed one point were assumed to belong to non-visitors.

Telephone numbers were not identified or stored.

Segmentation and targeting

Segmentation is "the identification of groups of individuals or organizations with characteristics in common that have significant implications for the determination of marketing strategy" (Jobber, 1995; 200)

Not all festival-goers want the same thing from attending a festival. People who attend a literature event are likely to have different motivations to those who attend a dance music event (see Figure 9.6). It is unlikely that any one festival is going to be able to fulfil the needs of every individual who enjoys going to festivals, so segmentation is used to identify groups with similar tastes, so that organisers can design a festival to suit their specific wants and needs. The aim is to ensure that resources are not wasted on promoting to people who would not attend, or not enjoy the experience if they did. Market research is used to identify shared needs and other characteristics that will enable suitable festival experiences to be designed and communicated.

The shared characteristics that identify a segment are unique to different product categories and event to specific festivals, but are underpinned by an understanding of what motivates people to choose particular cultural experiences. Research into arts audiences indicates that the main motivations are escapism, social bonding, personal development and a desire for a heightened emotional state (see Figure 9.6, an adaptation of Maslow's Hierarchy of Needs).

Physiological	Physical comfort (warmth, ventilation, space etc) Food and drink Sensations (music, food, dancing, lights)
Safety	Well-designed, well-lit site. Equipment is maintained and tested Appropriate levels of policing and emergency services are on hand Secure storage provided
Social needs	Interacting with friends / colleagues Participating in shared ritual behaviours and traditions
Esteem needs	Prestigious, unique experiences Achieving high-profile challenges Exclusivity
Self-actualisation	Personal development and expertise Losing yourself 'in the moment' Experiencing beauty and delight

Figure 9.6: Motivations for attending festivals

Using data from the annual Taking Part survey undertaken by the UK Government's Department for Culture, Media and Sport into cultural participation, the Audience Agency has grouped the UK population into 10 distinct segments based on similar behaviours or shared needs (Figure 9.7). If a festival wants to target family groups with young children, research can be undertaken to find out where the areas are that the 'Trips and treats' segment are most likely to live, or what other places they visit, so that marketing materials can be distributed to those places. Alternatively, research might be undertaken that shows that a new housing development has increase the number of 'Dormitory dependables' in the festival's catchment area, and the programme can be adjusted to include some relevant attractions.

♦ **Metroculturals**: Prosperous, liberal, urbanites interested in a very wide cultural spectrum.

♦ **Commuterland culture buffs**: Affluent and professional consumers of culture.

♦ **Experience seekers**: Highly active, diverse, social and ambitious, engaging with arts on a regular basis.

♦ **Dormitory dependables**: From suburban and small towns with an interest in heritage activities and mainstream arts.

♦ **Trips and treats**: They enjoy mainstream arts and popular culture, influenced by children, family and friends.

♦ **Home and heritage**: From rural areas and small towns, engaging in daytime activities and historic events.

♦ **Up our street**: Modest in habits and means. Occasional engagement in popular arts, entertainment and museums.

♦ **Facebook families**: Younger suburban and semi-urban. They enjoy live music, eating out and popular entertainment such as pantomime.

♦ **Kaleidoscope creativity**: Mix of backgrounds and ages. Occasional visitors or participants, particularly community-based events and festivals.

♦ **Heydays**: Older, they are often limited by mobility to engage with arts and cultural events. They participate in arts and craft making.

Figure 8.7: The Audience Agency's Audience Finder segments (Arts Council England)

Debating point:

Which Audience Finder audience segments do you think each of these festivals appeals to?

The Reading Festival

Glastonbury

Edinburgh International Festival

Cannes Film Festival

Leicester Diwali

The main benefits of segmenting a market are:

♦ To identify existing and potential target markets

♦ To provide a basis for a tailored marketing approach

♦ To support the development of differential marketing strategies and products

♦ To ensure the efficient allocation of marketing resources so that time and money are not wasted creating unattractive events or communicating the wrong messages to the wrong people in the wrong places.

Identifying target markets

Target markets are the segments that a company decides to focus its attention on serving. If a festival can identify groups of customers who share similar needs, it can develop strategies to match their requirements. A good understanding of the needs that are being served by a festival organisation and its competitors might also highlight potential segments that are not currently being served. This might be a community in a particular geographic area, or a segment that has emerged as a result of social or artistic change, such as the GameCity Festival launched in Nottingham in 2006, having spotted the popularity of gaming amongst young people.

Tailored approach to marketing

The 'marketing mix' is term applied to the combination of marketing techniques employed when designing a marketing strategy: the package of product design, price, the venues the festival takes place in and the promotional strategies can be tailored to suit the preferences of each segment. Young, tech savvy adults will look for information in different places and in different formats to retired opera festival fans, who might prefer a glossy printed brochure to be posted to them.

Differentiation

By creating different festivals, or different offers within a festival, a producer can target more than one segment. Festival Republic, a company that specialises in festival production, promotes a number of successful festivals that appeal to different segments. *Latitude* is an arts festival that includes comedy, visual art, outdoor performance and theatre as well as a music programme. It appeals to family audiences and is sold on the variety of artistic options on offer, while rock/metal/punk festival *Download* targets fans of specific musical styles. Each has a clear brand image that is communicated consistently so that the target segments are confident that their needs will be met, giving the festivals an advantage over competitors who are less well defined.

Marketing mix

The marketing mix is the combination of techniques that can be used to achieve the organisation's objectives. As with the tools in a skilled carpenter's toolbox, each is better at achieving particular tasks and it is important to know what you are trying to build before you start, or you might choose the wrong combination. The aim is to use the 7 Ps or 3 Es to satisfy customer needs identified in your research and exceed their expectations; to surprise and delight. The marketing mix is also known as the 4Ps. The 4Ps were first proposed in 1960 by Jerome McCarthy and have been criticised as being too simplistic and not taking services or relationship marketing into account. For this reason, there are three additional aspects to marketing services that aim to overcome customers' wariness. We can also add that there are elements of experiences that neither the 4 nor 7Ps address, the emotional engagement that is central to a festival's appeal.

The 7Ps are:

Product

Product is the core of all marketing. Without the product – the festival experience itself – there is nothing to be done. However, not all festivals are the same. Some are small, local, free and community-orientated, others are huge, international and highly commercial. Some are urban, others greenfield. Some are music festivals, others visual arts, some food, others traditional, cultural or religious. All of these attributes define the product in the mind of the festival-goer.

Even where there are festivals that can be said to be in a similar category, such as greenfield music festivals, there are questions about the type and quality of the headline acts, the number of stages and range of other elements available such as refreshments, market stalls, camping, dance and comedy tents and the choice and decoration of the site itself. All of these peripheral elements are part of the product, and festivals distinguish themselves from their competitors by providing additional features that they think will appeal to their target segments – their particular USP. But even then, it has to be remembered that customers are not buying a festival, but the benefits they feel that attending the festival will bring.

Price

Price is the direct cost of the ticket, plus any other costs the festival-goer accrues. These might be taking time off work, travel costs, childcare, food and drink, special clothing, accommodation and so on. The customer will factor these in to the decision about what the festival is 'worth'. The higher the price paid, the more 'value' the festival has to provide.

Deciding the price to be charged for a product is not, however, as simple as covering the costs of production, or even just undercutting your competitors. Price communicates a message about quality and exclusivity as well. Free events may be perceived as less valuable than festivals that charge a higher price. Whilst most festivals try to keep their ticket prices affordable for the mass market, many offer premium experiences for limited numbers at a higher price. The *Secret Solstice Festival* held in June in Reykjavik, Iceland offers a 'Package of the Gods' available to only six people (three pairs) that includes a helicopter transfer to the top of a glacier (Secret Solstice Festival, 2016).

Place

Place is where the 'product' is purchased and refers to the whole distribution process, from first enquiry to the after-sales service. For consumer products this includes decisions about which retail outlets best reflect a brand's market positioning. In the case of a festival it includes decisions about whether tickets should be sold directly or through ticket agents and bus or train companies who might produce packages. If tickets are sold through agents, it is these agents who have the relationship with the customer, and the festival therefore has less control over customer care. Agencies, however, have their own customer base and can help to promote a festival more widely than it could do on its own.

For festivals, place is also where the product is experienced. The festival site might be a remote greenfield, a prestigious theatre, or an urban square. The place has to be appropriate for the product, and reflects upon its quality.

Promotion

Promotion includes all forms of marketing communication. Promotional activities are those that are highest profile and often thought to be what marketing is. Traditionally it has included advertising (including posters and flyers), public relations (PR), sales promotion (such as bring a friend, or two tickets for the price of one), direct marketing (targeted email, etc.) and personal selling.

Festival promotion relies heavily on public relations, sales promotions and direct marketing. Most festivals, other than large commercial music festivals, have a very small traditional advertising budget as, unless the festival has very well-known headliners, it is difficult for advertising to cut through the media noise and be noticed.

However, the social nature of festivals means that word of mouth is the most effective tool. Potential festival-goers will value the endorsement of those who have been before, which is perceived as unbiased. Festival attenders are also likely to attend with others.

Rather than running expensive advertising campaigns, it is more effective for festivals with a track record to harness the power of relationship marketing by running social media campaigns (see Chapter 11) that encourage those who know the festival to pass on positive messages and act as ambassadors amongst their social circles.

Direct marketing to people who have attended previous editions using information from the sales database is also effective. For example, festival-goers who bought four tickets can be offered discounts on a fifth. Those who book late can be offered incentives to buy their tickets earlier. Well-handled, direct marketing is an important part of relationship marketing with audience members becoming loyal festival-goers, volunteers and participants who will promote the event on your behalf.

Many festivals capitalise on an audiences' positive post-festival feeling to encourage them to purchase tickets for the next event soon after the festival has finished, often at a discounted 'early bird' rate. This secures early sales and builds those long-term relationships, taking pressure off the next wave of marketing.

People

Services, including experiences such as festivals, differ from tangible products that are manufactured out of the customer's sight. A service product, such as a haircut or a festival is intangible and largely created by people the customer is in contact with, often while the customer is present. For this reason, services marketing focuses on three additional elements: people, process and physical evidence.

Festival audiences may come into contact with a range of staff and volunteers at different times. When purchasing of tickets, on arrival at the venue, when being marshalled around a site, during intervals and breaks and so on. Encounters with these customer-facing people can make or break the experience. If they are visible, polite, helpful and friendly then festival-goers will have a positive experience. For this to be the case, customer facing workers, whether staff, volunteers or contractors need to be well-trained so that they know the product and are aware of common problems that customers might face what the options are to solve their problems and to be empowered to implement solutions in line with the festival's marketing strategy.

Debating point:
A customer has a spare ticket for a theatre festival that takes place in three venues across a city because a friend has fallen ill on the day of the event. The customer has a pair of tickets for three other shows during the festival. She asks the ticket office if it is possible to have a refund. Tickets have not sold out and the terms and conditions state 'no refunds'. How would you recommend the ticket office staff respond and why?

The question of people is a complex one for festivals, as it also includes other festival-goers, who are an important part of the festive atmosphere. Encouraging audiences to be friendly and polite, to dress up in 'festive' costumes or participate in activities may not at first sight appear to be a marketing task. However, much can be achieved by training stewards, ensuring the venue design is appropriate and communicating expectations as part of the festival's promotions.

Process

Process is the system for producing the service. It includes decisions about how bookings are made. Can customers book online, over the phone and in person? Does the festival have an app that includes booking options? What information does each provide? Are tickets posted out, printed at home, electronic or held at the venue? What are the transport options for festival-goers? Is there public transport that stops nearby? When is the last bus? If it is a festival with a large capacity, have extra buses been laid on? Is there parking? How easy is it to find and how much does it cost? How long will it take to leave the car park at the end of the festival?

One important concern raised about process is whether the festival retains direct control over important parts of the process such as the car park or the campsite, or the venues' cafes and bars or whether are they managed externally? If these services are contracted out, the festival may find it difficult to maintain the standards it wants and that this will that influence customer perceptions of the product. On the other hand, specialist providers might be able to offer a better service because they have the relevant expertise. Whatever the management strategies, the process factor highlights the need to ensure good integration so that the customer's experience is smooth and that quality is maintained throughout.

Most importantly for festivals with a staged programme of events, the process includes stage management. Do the acts start and finish on time or are their audiences hanging around waiting? Are there other entertainment options for people during crossover periods? Are the refreshment outlets set up to manage the peaks in demand during intervals? Long queues or periods where nothing is happening will frustrate customers and reduce their perceptions of the event's quality.

Flexibility in the design of festival sites, and multiple options about which elements to engage with and when, means that each individual festival-goer can create an experience that suits them personally. Some will want to be at the front of the crowd for a headline band, whilst others would prefer to sit quietly on the sidelines, or visit an alternative stage to see emerging artists. Some people are happy to camp or visit a festival for the day, whilst others will book in to a luxurious hotel. The wider the range of options and the more flexible the operational processes can be, the more likely the festival is to fulfil the needs of individual participants.

Physical evidence

Although largely intangible festivals and other experiences do provide festival-goers with tangible artefacts. Wrist bands, souvenir programmes and other merchandising can both be touched and taken home at the end of the event as reminders of the experience. These tangible objects, things that can be touched, are known as physical evidence. These objects influence customers' perceptions of the event quality. Drinks served in plastic containers suggests the event in less exclusive than one where wine glasses are used.

The physical evidence of the festival venue; its atmosphere, décor, layout, all provide signals about what sort of experience is being offered, its quality and value.

Physical evidence is particularly important in advance of an experience, and for new festival-goers, as it provides essential reassurance that the event is going to happen and that the customer has made the right choice. Tickets, whether physical or online, provide important details about where and when the event is happening, and often give extra information such as maps or what public transport is available. This may sound unimportant, but is one of the first times a festival-goer engages directly with the event and, as such, has a disproportionate effect on their perceptions of the organisation's people and processes.

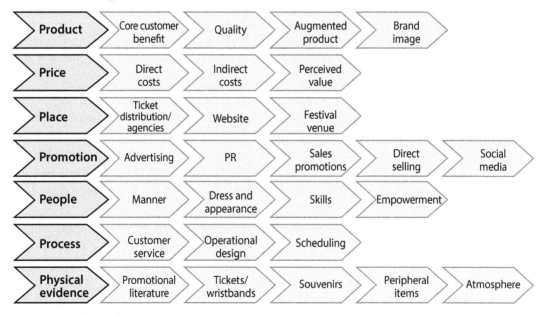

Figure 9.8: The marketing mix

Using the marketing mix

Used in the right combination, the tools in the marketing mix work as a consistent web that ensures that the right audiences experience the right events at the right time and for the right price. For example, an upmarket arts festival would:

◆ Need to stage a programme of excellent performances and exhibitions by world-class artists with high production values in sumptuous or spectacular venues.

◆ Command premium prices.

◆ Be held in exclusive venues with small capacities.

◆ Be promoted using tasteful, artistic imagery in national broadsheet newspapers and lifestyle magazines. Promotional materials will be full-colour and high quality. Well-respected critics, star performers and art experts will be enrolled to give preview interviews and review shows.

◆ Have a high quality, well targeted Digital Marketing campaign (see Chapter 11)

◆ Have customer services staff very well-briefed about the programme and ticket packages, smartly dressed and recognisable.

◆ Have easy and smooth processes for ordering interval drinks or post-show meals. Shows will be scheduled to allow for refreshments or for audiences to be able to travel from one venue to another. Transport will be laid on if necessary.

◆ A lavish ambience, perhaps with live music in the venue foyers during intervals, and the décor and food of a high quality.

A mass-market 'fringe' comedy festival would:

◆ Include new and breakthrough acts of unknown and variable quality, as well as some better known and popular headliners. Use venues where audiences can relax and do not feel they have to dress up.

◆ Be priced competitively. Several comedians may be grouped together in a 'night' with a better-known compere to encourage audiences to take a risk and feel they have had value for money.

◆ Stage shows in pubs, clubs and community venues that are cheaper to hire and less exclusive in feel.

◆ Be promoted by show flyers and posters, in local newspapers and through social media. Comedians with large social media followings will be encouraged to promote the festival alongside their own events.

◆ Have a witty and possibly irreverant, well targeted digital marketing campaign (see Chapter 11)

◆ Have customer service staff who, although generally friendly, might include independent promoters, venue staff and volunteers who may or may not have seen the comedians before. Although there might be a central box office it is unlikely that staff will have been briefed on all of the shows, and many audience members will simply turn up at the venue on the night and buy a ticket on the door.

◆ Have little co-ordination about scheduling, as shows are produced independently, so acts may clash, or be on at venues on either side of the city. Audiences are expected to select their own programme from a range of options with little guidance from the festival's staff.

◆ Might include show flyers of variable quality, depending on the status of the comedians performing. The festival brochure will focus on the quantity of acts included, ensuring that it is comprehensive.

The messages sent by each of these festivals are very different, but consistent and clear, factors that are the key to a successful marketing strategy. Trying to charge a high price for an unknown comedy show in a local bar will confuse potential customers. Similarly offering discounted tickets to an exclusive theatre show starring a well-known actor would undermine the festival's exclusive, highbrow image.

Debating point:
Think about a festival you have been to. How consistently were the 7Ps used? What examples would you use of good and bad practice? Where did you see the advertising? In print online or via direct email?

A shift in mainstream media

Until recently the 'traditional mass media' were important in finding and attracting a large audience. The media include television and radio, newspapers (national and local) and mass market and specialist magazines.

The rise of social media, especially Facebook, has changed things dramatically both in terms of reach and speed of dissemination. Local newspapers have long been a keystone in covering arts and entertainments, but their circulation has dropped significantly and many have merged or closed. They tend to be read by an older audience. Whilst their quality and coverage vary, you need to take a close look at the balance of editorial to advertising. Many now have allied websites, some of which are hard to read because of the volume of pop-up adverts. But these websites may carry a bigger readership than their printed equivalents. However, some local newspapers are hungry for 'good news' stories and will publish high quality photographs with them.

National broadsheet newspapers have been facing similar declining readerships. Many have colour magazines and entertainments magazines in their weekend editions. Editorial in broadsheets is only worth targeting if you have a significant or unique story to tell. It costs nothing to submit your events to national event listings and the Press Association's service is distributed to a number of national publications.

Broadsheet newspapers (*The Times*, *The Telegraph* and *The Guardian*) all have their own websites, some of which are subscription-only. You can advertise on these. Specialist magazines and local lifestyle magazines, for example, *Hampshire Life* or *Yorkshire Life*, have websites and you may reach as many readers through digital marketing campaigns as through traditional magazine adverts and editorial. Look carefully at your festival's target market and think about the sort of media they are likely to engage with. The older the audience the less likely they are to engage regularly with digital media.

Traditional routes to audiences through print media are increasingly going digital. Social media marketing and advertising, particularly Facebook advertising are the new norm and can be very cost-effective. It is possible to target a campaign that can reach tens of thousands of potential customers/purchasers for comparatively little cost. But you will need to get acquainted with Facebook's advertising protocols and be able to produce quality adverts with images and videos. All of this is discussed in more detail in Chapter 11.

Figure 9.9: Strategic marketing planning

Audit

Marketing the festival is part of its management and has to fit with the overall organisational mission, vision and values. If there is a mismatch, the brand and communications will tell a false story and audiences will be disappointed. For this reason, it is important for the marketing strategy to start by analysing the organisation's strategic plans and purpose.

The central questions to be asked in an audit are "where are we now?" and "where do we want to go?"

Where are we now?
- Brief history of the festival/festival organisation.
- Important past events and narratives.

What is the organisation's mission?
- What is it trying to achieve? Is the mission clear and agreed? Do on-going projects and programmes reflect the mission? Do marketing materials and communications reflect the mission? Do festival audiences know what the mission is?
- What marketing resources does the organisation have? Are they sufficient?
- What are the strengths and weaknesses of the organisation and the festival?
- Do the staff, stakeholders and audiences agree on core values?

Environmental analysis
- What are the opportunities and threats for the festival?
- Are there demographic changes that mean the festival's audiences might grow or decline? Are there changes in the popularity of some art forms that the festival programmes? Are there other art forms the festival's audiences might be interested in seeing? Are there opportunities because of the growth of digital media? Are there changes in privacy legislation that will affect how you can communicate with audiences?

What are the consequences for the festival of the analysis?
- What are the challenges and opportunities the analysis highlights? Does the organisation of the skills, knowledge, experience and resources to meet any challenges or benefit from opportunities identified?

Where do we want to go?
- What is the festival's vision? Is there a clear link between the mission and vision? What are the SMART marketing objectives? Do these relate to the stated vision?

Marketing strategy
- What are the key segments to be targeted?
- What are the core benefits for each segment?
- How will the product be augmented to appeal to each segment?

■ What role will price play in the strategy? Will it vary from segment to segment? Will you offer packages and promotions?

■ How will you sell tickets? Are there different distribution strategies for different segments? Will sales be direct via your website, or through agents and ambassadors?

■ Is the festival venue suitable, accessible and in the right place? Is there parking, or good public transport? How will it be decorated to make it 'festive'?

■ How will the festival be promoted? Advertising, social media, offers, website and direct email, media relations, ambassadors? What are the key messages?

Action plan:
■ What will be done?
■ When will it be done by?
■ Who will do it?
■ What resources will be spent?

Evaluation
■ How will you monitor ongoing progress?
■ How will you monitor and evaluate the success of the marketing strategy?
■ What will you report on and who to?

Figure 9.10: Organisational audit

Summary

Marketing is a core part of any festival manager's job, whether or not it is included in your title. Even if it is a free festival and you don't need to sell tickets, without audiences your festival's purpose will not be achieved. This chapter introduced core marketing principles such as value exchange, segmentation and relationship marketing and the marketing mix and showed how they apply to a festival. It positioned marketing as a strategic function that puts understanding audiences' preferences and tastes at the heart of your planning.

The chapter also showed that festivals are experiences, at their best when marketing and festival design work together to create memorable and enjoyable experiences which encourage audiences to feel a sense of loyalty to the event and return year after year.

References

American Marketing Association (2013) Defintion of Marketing. https://www.ama.org/AboutAMA/Pages/Definition-of-Marketing.aspx.

Anderton, C. (2015) Branding, sponsorship and the music festival. In: McKay, G. (ed.) *The Pop Festival: History, music, media culture.* London: Bloomsbury.

Chartered Institute of Marketing, (2015) *Marketing and the 7Ps: A brief summary of marketing and how it works.* https://www.cim.co.uk/media/4772/7ps.pdf.

Diggle, K. (2017) *The A.D.A.M Model.* https://keithdiggle.co.uk/audience-development-arts-marketing/the-a-d-a-m-model/.

Doyle, P., and Stern, P. (2006) *Marketing Management and Strategy.* London: Pearson Education.

Engel, J. F., Blackwell, R. D., and Miniard, P. W. (1995) *Consumer Behaviour.* London: The Dryden Press.

Jobber, D. (1995) *Principles and Practice of Marketing.* New York: McGraw.

McCarthy, J. (1960) *Basic Marketing: A Managerial Approach.* Chicago: R. D. Irwin.

Martin, V. (2016) *Rock in Rio*: The festival. In: Newbold, C., and Jordan, J., *Focus on World Festivals: Contemporary case studies and perspectives.* Oxford: Goodfellow.

Pine, J. B., and Gilmore, J. H. (1999) *The Experience Economy.* Boston: Harvard Business School Press.

Poulsson, S., and Kale, S. (2001) The Experience Economy and Commercial Experiences. *Marketing Review*, **4** (3), pp. 267-277.

Secret Solstice Festival, (2016) http://secretsolstice.is

Walmsley, B., and Franks, A. (2011) The audience experience: Changing roles and relationships. In: Walmsley, B. (ed.) *Key Issues in the Arts and Entertainment Industry.* Oxford: Goodfellow.

Wright, L.W. and Crimp, M. (2000) *The Marketing Research Process.* 5th ed. Essex: Pearson Education Ltd.

10 Research and Evaluation

by Chris Newbold

After reading this chapter you should:

- Understand the importance of a knowledge of research methodology to effective festival management
- Have a good understanding of the range of research and evaluation methods available
- Understand the various uses that the different methodologies can be put to
- Know how to create a viable questionnaire
- Have a good understanding on festival evaluation

Introduction

In this chapter we will demonstrate that research is at the heart of good festival management. Good festival management involves informed decision making, and research methodologies support this at all levels from planning and programming, through the marketing and the running of the festival, to event evaluation and audience development. Research is a key element of the iterative process through which festivals develop year on year via experience and feedback, not only from audiences, but also from artists, staff and volunteers; this information then feeds into the successful planning of the next event and so on and so forth.

The aims of this chapter are to introduce the research process as a whole, give advice and encouragement, discuss the key considerations in carrying out successful research, and identify and describe the main research methods that managers will encounter in running and evaluating their festival. Whilst we will focus on the most often used methodologies of questionnaires, interviews, focus groups and observation, we will also offer some other complementary approaches and discuss the use of digital and online resources in festival research.

Carrying out research is all about making the right decisions. Each method has its advantages and disadvantages, and research can be time-consuming and expensive; this chapter will help you to make the right decisions about the methodologies and their use. Successful research is all about juggling a number of key factors such as cost, time, sample size, response rates and reliability. Research does not have to be either costly or time consuming – indeed a great deal of what festival managers already do could be considered as research, and this chapter will help them sharpen up some of those practices.

Increasingly in the festivals and events sector, external stakeholders are imposing on managers and organisers the requirement to justify their funding through reporting and evaluation. Festivals managers have thus had to become aware of the centrality of using research methodologies as part of their working lives.

The methodologies discussed here are also used by other agencies, such as governments, local authorities, professional organisations or universities, that may not be directly associated with a festival organisation but may be charged with examining areas of its impact, in particular cultural and economic impacts. An understanding of research methodology is important for festival managers even if they do not carry out their own research, in that they need to have a good understanding of how research results are arrived at by outside agencies or by consultants that the festival organisation itself may have employed. This knowledge saves managers from being misled by the statistics presented to them. Key questions of methodological validity, representativeness and accuracy should always be at the forefront of the festival managers' mind.

This chapter is divided into four sections. The first, 'Research and festival managers' looks at the wider considerations a festival manager must take into account when approaching research; the second is about getting started on research; the third takes you through the preparation for your research with crucial aspects such as sampling discussed; and the final area is about 'Methodologies and data collection' and examines the key methodologies themselves, as well as introducing some complementary ones.

Festivals, as we shall see, provide some unique challenges for research because of their transient nature. Many festivals are night events, or reach their climax late into the evening; and a special challenge is that one of the main objects of festival research, the audience, are only passing through, in a heightened state of being, and are likely to be unresponsive to appeals for help with research. This chapter, then, aims to help you develop and achieve effective research.

Research and festival managers

Research leads to information, knowledge and understanding, it provides usable evaluation results, supported applications, and crucially, informed decision making. The key questions in research have always been: Who? What? Where? When? Why? and How? These questions are at the heart of the practice of all research as we shall see, however for the moment they can also help us in thinking about the festival managers' own research universe.

The **who** is important, in particular, who do we carry out research on? Clearly the audience are the major object of research, and all aspects of their experience need to be understood. However, the potential audience is also equally important, especially if a festival is looking to grow its audience. It needs to gain information on the people who are not attending and why they do not attend. Research on your product or the individual components of the festival is important in understanding what works well, what was well received and what needs improving. This could be everything from the programming through catering provision to toilets and parking arrangements. Research on your competitors both near and far is important – what are other festivals having success with, what is their pricing level, and what are the current trends coming through? Often overlooked in research are the performers and artists, understanding their experience is vital to the smooth running of the festival. Finally, never forget your own staff and volunteers. As they are 'at the coalface' (i.e. on the front lines of delivering the festival) they see and experience things you may not be aware of, so their opinions, feedback and suggestions should always be sought.

What kinds of information can festival research provide is also an important question. We can categorise research results three ways: descriptive, explanatory and evaluative. In gaining an understanding of which methods deliver which kinds of information, this can help us in our choice of research methodology.

◆ **Descriptive** research data provides an account of what has actually taken place and could be useful in writing reports or funding bids.

◆ **Explanatory** research data provides information useful in problem solving and thus ensuring the smooth running of the festival.

◆ **Evaluative** research data provides information which assists you in gauging the success or failure of any aspect of the festival and is part of the process of planning the next event. Evaluative information tends to be the most important for festival managers.

We will say more about these later in the chapter.

Where to carry out the research is an important decision for the festival manager. At the event is the obvious option, although not particularly favoured by audiences who are there to relax and have a good time, not to answer probing interview questions or fill out lengthy questionnaires. Indeed, much of the debate about which methodologies festival managers should use is often about which would cause least inconvenience to participants. After the audience member has returned to their home is an option, but this can affect response rates as people move on with their busy lives, and the answers given may be from memory as time often elapses before the responses are provided. Earlier we indicated that research on non-attendees was an important option for festival managers, and this would call for a more traditional market research style of approach usually using interviewers stopping people in town or city streets and busy market places. Another possibility for a research site is a different venue or cultural location, although these could be difficult to access as they may see you as a rival touting for their customers. Finally, research can be organised at a neutral location such as a room in a library, local college or council building.

Alongside these considerations, **when** to carry out the research is another difficult decision for the festival manager, if the aim is to gain evaluative information then after the event is the obvious time. If you are interested in whether the festival changes people's opinions on a topic, such as the environment, then an understanding of the participant's opinions before the festival is crucial to see how their engagement has altered their ideas. If you need some explanatory research carried out, say into why the stock of beer glasses is running low, then you might need to carry out a quick piece of research during the festival, maybe of your collection and reusing system. To gain a rounder view of your audience's experience of your festival then clearly a methodology that encompasses a before, during and after design would be ideal, inevitably though this could prove costly, difficult to keep track of and involve some participant denudation.

Why festival mangers should carry out research and familiarise themselves with the various debates and arguments in research is one of the questions this chapter grapples with. As we have said, research is a management tool:

- ♦ In planning strategies, products and growth
- ♦ In managing people, policies and plans
- ♦ In marketing and evaluation

In all these areas research provides information, knowledge and understanding which leads to informed, better decision making.

Our final research question was **how**? Well, that is what the rest of this chapter is about!

Getting started on research

Successful research is a consequence of effective research thinking, understanding the various methodologies and their uses, continuous questioning and reflection throughout the research process, good research planning and organisation, making the right methodological decisions and asking the right questions.

Asking the right questions means:

- Asking the right questions – in developing the research idea, identifying issues and devising a hypothesis or research question
- Asking the right questions – in selecting the sample of the 'population' to be researched
- Asking the right questions: in your research design, choosing the appropriate methodology/ies
- Asking the right questions – IN the research
- Asking the right questions – of your data, interrogating, understanding and interpreting your results.

Effective research involves questioning every aspect of the research process, from developing your idea to working with your data. At each point you are making decisions which will affect the outcome of the research and its validity.

At this point, it is worth drawing two key research distinctions as these are at the heart of many of the research decisions made. First, a distinction is drawn between primary and secondary data. In primary data, the researcher can be said to be the generator and the first user of the data. In secondary data the researcher is using data from other sources; often this data may have been generated for other purposes than the researcher is using it for. It is still valid material but needs to be referenced.

The second distinction is between quantitative and qualitative data. Quantitative data on the whole is statistical information, presented in figures and percentages, in graphs and charts, and is the most favoured form of data for project scoping, funding bids, and annual reports. Quantitative data has the air of the scientific method, of being mathematical, statistical and therefore 'true'. It derives from the positivist approach to the social world, where 'social facts' are out there waiting to be discovered, measured and generalised into 'laws' of human behaviour. The qualitative approach on the other hand derives from an interpretative tradition where human behaviour can only be described, interpreted, and understood in terms of meanings, and where reality is a social and cultural construct. The results of research from this tradition tend to be written in prose, descriptive and analytical, often producing discussions setting out alternative understanding or interpretations. Data from this approach is used where a more in-depth and analytical report is sought, where the research question posed may well be about the cultural or social impact of a local city festival, such as a mela or carnival.

The first steps in carrying out a piece of research usually involve identifying an area of research, coming up with a research question or developing a hypothesis – whichever way you will need to scope and define your research. First of all, what do you want to find out? What are the aims and objectives of the research? It is worth writing these down as they will help you keep a focus in your research. Consider your problem in terms of its breadth, depth and focus, these may well influence your methodological decisions. Is your research broadly based, requiring a lot of information on a range of topics? For instance, is it about the whole visitor experience from first contact to exiting the festival? If so, a questionnaire would be the most appropriate methodology as it will also allow you to gain a potentially large number of respondents. If your research requires detail on an aspect of the visitor experience, then an in-depth approach is essential and interviewing a small number of respondents may be the way to go. Developing a focus for your research is important; even the broadest research project cannot ask everything so be sure you are focused on what you need to know. Remember, all good research benefits from constant review and revision at each stage.

At this point it is essential to carry out background searches and review all available literature relevant to your topic. Is the data or information you are seeking already available? You may well find that similar research has been done elsewhere and makes your research unnecessary, or helps you focus your own research topic. At any rate, this will help you review and develop your own research idea and give you insights into how other people have used methods and presented their results. Using library resources and the internet to identify reports, research and books (such as this one) is a good starting point. Your own or other cultural organisations may have similar material, local authorities and government departments will have a wealth of useful material, and your local university or college may well have people whose expertise you can tap. Organisations such as The Audience Agency (www.theaudienceagency.org) are designed to help with many of the areas you may be interested in. Ask around and seek help and advice, especially if you are new to research.

Having built up a knowledge base in your area of research, and probably also gained some valuable insights into the types of questions you may well be wanting to ask, it is now essential to define your central terms, to be sure that you (and others) are clear about the key terms and what you mean by them. For a lot of cultural festivals being 'authentic' is important, so if you are asking questions about authenticity, be sure you yourself have a clear definition of what you understand by 'being authentic'.

A central area of consideration at this stage of the research process is cost. Research can be expensive and two of the key dimensions are time and staffing resource, which can both increase your costs substantially. Thus, methodologies such as interviewing are resource heavy and costly, especially if you have an in-depth research design which involves an interviewer spending an hour or so on each interview. Questionnaires are considerably cheaper, especially if delivered via the internet. However, there is a third dimension to this which we will discuss shortly – the importance of response rates, which are clearly going to be higher with interviews than with online question-naires. There are also a great many computer-aided research packages on the market. These can appear to be the answer to your research dreams, but it is not only their initial price tag that festival managers need to take account of, it is also the cost of having staff trained to use them which can be prohibitive.

A key decision for festival organisations is always whether to bring in out-side agencies or consultancies to carry out research or whether to do it 'in house'. The latter option is inevitably cheaper but dependent on available staff and their expertise in this area. The availability of resources such as staff, time, photocopying, materials, or IT expertise may well be a determining factor in the scope and ability of an organisation to carry out research. This chapter is designed to help you carry out the research for yourself, however, if you do take on outside assistance it also helps to understand what your consultant is doing and what they are presenting to you.

Next steps

Draw sample

Defining the population to be covered is the first step, deciding whether this is to be covered in its entirety or partially. There are two aspects to this, first practicality: if the population to be studied is your staff of five people plus ten volunteers then that is entirely possible, but if the population to be studied is the attendees of five thousand people then that is highly impractical. Second, financially, if your population is small then depending on the methodology you choose your costs will be manageable – clearly the larger the population the costlier it will be. Thus, drawing a sample in most situations is the only real option; the key though is that this sample should be representative of the whole population, enabling you to generalise your finding to the entire population. The key questions that determine your sample are about the size, validity and representativeness of your chosen research group. As with so much in the field of research, a distinction is drawn between qualitative and quantitative research. Qualitative research by its desire for in-depth 'rich' data will tend to accept small sample sizes; single or double figure respond-ents would seem reasonable in most festival research scenarios. Quanti-tative research with its requirement to produce data that is reflective of a whole population tends to look for more mathematical precision in drawing its sample size. In social research terms, festival research tends to be on the small-scale survey spectrum, in which case we would recommend a sample size from 1% -10% of the total population. The important thing is that the sample must however attempt to be representative, taking into account the key social variables that may be at play at any particular festival, such as gender, race, age, and social class.

There are essentially two types of sampling: probability and non-probability. Probability is random sampling where every member of the population has an equal chance of being selected and tends to be used in larger scale quantitative research. Non-probability is essentially selecting a quota sample that is representative of your chosen population, which tends to be used by small scale qualitative research.

Within these two types are a couple of approaches that are useful to festival managers. First, for probability there is either simple random sampling or stratified random sampling. In the former, the researcher randomly selects people to approach, the most effective way to do this is to take every 'nth' person (could be fifth or tenth... it doesn't really matter). For stratified, the researcher pre-orders the population by social variable (gender, age, race, etc.) and then takes a random sample from each variable. This approach on the whole provides more accurate information about the population and has the advantage of enabling comparisons between the variables.

For non-probability sampling, the emphasis moves from broad representativeness to a specific focus sample where the researcher selects the sample on the basis of the research question itself, using their knowledge of the research topic (festivals) to concentrate on specific targeted people who are reasonably expected to be 'information rich'. This approach is known as purposive sampling, with the sample usually having something in common, such as their attending your festival, or they are female and attending your festival, or they are female, over 45, Hindu and attending your Mela. You can then take a quota sample of this focused population, using the same counting the 'nth' person suggested above. Or, in such a scenario as just mentioned, an approach called 'snowballing' would be helpful whereby one interviewee introduces you to another, and they to another and so on and so forth.

Inevitably the kind of sampling you use will be dependent on your research question, the type of data you wish to generate and of course your available resources.

Considering response rates

Response rates are the percentage number of completed returns against uncompleted ones, so if you send out 100 questionnaires and get 62 back your response rate is 62%. Response rates should always be given as a number as well, clearly a response rate of 33% sounds alright but when the actual number is 3 out of a total of 10, then that is really not sufficiently a large enough sample to draw any significant conclusions. Be wary of percentage response rates only and always ask for the sample number. Generally, response rates to face-to-face interviews are the highest (especially where the interviewer is given a quota to fulfil), online (using tools such as Survey Monkey or Typeform) comes next, with postal and telephone (unless the respondent has already agreed) tend to have the lowest. Again, cost and staff time are factors here in the decisions to be made about which method to use.

As we have noted, festival research is difficult because of the very nature of festivals. There are, however, a number of things you can do to try and boost your response rates. Essentially these are incentives, the most popular of which for questionnaires is the prize draw, for things such as free entry next time, or for some product associated with the event. For interviews, a voucher for refreshments or a product can help. Straight 'pay-outs' are rare, obviously because they increase the cost of the research overall, however they are used in focus group research where costs, both financial and time, can be incurred by the respondents. Other factors that can influence response rates are things such as the length of the questionnaire, so only ask what is relevant. The shorter the better is a general rule, as interviewers are always asked "how long will this take?" In the case of self-completion questionnaires, make sure it is easy to return with a number of clearly marked return boxes on the festival site or a stamped addressed envelope/postcard. The 'look' of the questionnaire and how user-friendly it is can all play a part. Don't forget, research is a social act and the appearance, approachability, and general demeanor of the interviewer can play a big role. People's decisions as to whether or not to take part are usually made within the first few seconds of an approach.

The key factors in successfully approaching respondents are telling them:

♦ What you are doing

♦ Who you are working for

♦ Why it is worthwhile

♦ That they are important

♦ Their answers will be treated confidentially

♦ How long it will take

♦ Try to establish a good rapport early on.

Finally, it is always worth taking a moment to consider the non-respondents. At a festival it is often the most satisfied and most dissatisfied who will tend to respond, with the majority being in the middle of these two. Noting any identifiable factors for non-responses is always worth doing in the research report.

Gain access

Gaining access to a research site in order to conduct fieldwork is often the forgotten part of the research planning process. Clearly if you are conducting research on your own festival site this is not so much of an issue, however, in any research conducted elsewhere you need to be aware of the ground rules. The best rule of thumb is to always seek permission to conduct research. Settings can be either open or closed, and open settings such as public parks, streets or town squares need little or no negotiation (check first though), whereas closed situations such as other cultural venues will require you to gain permission to research there. Even sites that appear open to the public, such as shopping centres, are often privately owned and you will need permission to do research there. The type and level of access you will need depends on the type of research you are conducting. Questionnaire distribution or 'clipboard' interviewing should be fairly straightforward, however observation style research may require more complicated negotiations, which are often constrained by levels of confidentiality and research ethics.

Ethical considerations

Ethical practices should apply whatever kind of research you are involved in, whether it be face to face, at a distance or online, and a code of ethics should be carefully followed. Below is the Market Research Society's code of conduct, which is an excellent starting point for considering ethical research.

The Principles of the MRS Code of Conduct:

1. Researchers shall ensure that participation in their activities is based on voluntary informed consent.

2. Researchers shall be straightforward and honest in all their professional and business relationships.

3. Researchers shall be transparent as to the subject and purpose of data collection.

4. Researchers shall respect the confidentiality of information collected in their professional activities.

5. Researchers shall respect the rights and well-being of all individuals.

6. Researchers shall ensure that participants are not harmed or adversely affected by their professional activities.

7. Researchers shall balance the needs of individuals, clients, and their professional activities.

8. Researchers shall exercise independent professional judgement in the design, conduct and reporting of their professional activities.

9. Researchers shall ensure that their professional activities are conducted by persons with appropriate training, qualifications and experience.

10. Researchers shall protect the reputation and integrity of the profession.

(Market Research Society, 2014: 4)

It is good practice to note on your questionnaires that you follow the MRS code of conduct to show that you are aware of your responsibilities and the consequences of your research.

For festival research it is important to think ethically at all stages, from design to field work, writing up, data usage and data storage. The latter has particularly become an issue in 2018 with the Data Protection Act and the General Data Protection Regulations (GDPR), the key principle being *informed consent*, which means the participant must have a clear and unambiguous understanding of the reasons for the research and collection of data and must give their consent to the data being collected and what it will be used for. More detail on this is available from the MRS at www.mrs.org.uk and the Information Commissioner's Office at www.ico.gov.uk.

Apart from the legal requirements, it falls to festival managers to conduct research morally and ethically, and to treat all information confidentially and respect people's privacy. In the vast majority of festival research it is unnecessary to reveal people's identities, indeed most data should be collected completely anonymously, and there is no real or practical reason for retaining large amounts of research data.

Triangulation

The next stage of the research process is the crucial stage; deciding which methodology or methodologies are appropriate for your research. In discussing each of these methodologies we will tend to examine them in isolation from each other, looking at their merits and demerits, however the best kind of research will triangulate methods. Triangulation as with land surveying means looking at one object from two different directions. Triangulating research methods provides a more holistic set of results that will not only complement each other but will overcome some of the inherent weaknesses of the different methodologies. A good triangulation design may well be a questionnaire of say 50 participants to provide a breadth of statistical information, triangulated with say five in-depth interviews to provided more focused, qualitative rich data which may well include experiences, opinions and suggestions that the researcher may not have even been aware of when they designed the initial questionnaire. The best research will combine approaches, and good reports will reflect other sources such as in-house documents, reports from other organisations, or even academic work, in order to help support, illustrate and back up what the writer is saying.

The methodologies and data collection

As you reach the stage where you want to operationalise your research question, there are a number of considerations you need to take into account when asking which method(s) are best for what you want to find out, given the resources you have at hand.

This is where the three Rs come in:

- Resources – Cost, time, personnel, material
- Respondent – Sample size, representativeness, response rates, autonomy
- Results – data (quantitative/qualitative), comparability, reliability and accuracy, analysis

The methodologies you are considering can then be assessed on their usefulness for you by considering each in turn and cross referencing them. So, an on-site semi-structured interview scores well as it is fairly good on **resources**, as there are no travel costs and has minimal material implications (just paper and a printer), but there are costs as it takes time and uses personnel. For **respondent** requirements, it is very good in terms of being able to gain a good sample size and assure that it is representative. Response rates would be high as you can continue gathering interviews until you have reached the required sample size, and the open-ended nature of the questions gives the respondents high autonomy in terms of the answers they can give. The **results** should be very good since it can provide both qualitative and quantitative data, which should be comparable between interviewees and across events, they are also very good for reliability and accuracy, that is checking that the responses are as full and honest as possible. The analysis of the data is good since the structured questions are pre-coded, that is, a numerical value is given to each possible answer which can be easily analysed using a statistical package or Excel spreadsheet. The qualitative data, although more time-consuming to compare and contrast, can give you that rich depth of analysis and often provide the unforeseen or unexpected answers that are vital in really understanding your festival.

Questionnaires

It should come as no surprise that questionnaires are the most commonly used form of social survey for festival managers, and they are the basis upon which most types of research are built. In their simplest form, they can be a small number of 'closed' yes/no questions designed to gauge people's responses to a festival and can be delivered on a postcard. In their largest form, they are information gathering exercises on all aspects of the festival – its administration, its facilities, the performances, the staff, and the audience themselves – and can run for pages!

As we have said, research is about making decisions, choosing between different alternatives, weighing up the pros and cons of each element of the method as well as the overall method. One of the key decisions in using questionnaires is how to administer them, and there are basically two alternatives: self-completion or interview.

Thinking through the three 'Rs' is useful here. Self-completion scores well across **resources**, being relatively cheap and requiring minimal personnel; they are straightforward to set up and require fairly simple materials. Interviewing, as we saw in the earlier example, can be costly. In terms of the **respondent**, self-completion is a little weaker largely because of poor response rates, leading to variable sample sizes and no real control over how representative the returned questionnaires are going to be. It is often said that questionnaires are only ever filled in by those who are either very satisfied or very dissatisfied. Self-completion questionnaires by their very nature usually do not provide the space for respondents to have much autonomy, and certainly with no interviewer there to ask the 'why' question, answers can be fairly restricted. There is also the issue that pre-coded questions tend to reflect the researcher's understanding to the world rather than the respondent's. As far as **results** are concerned, self-completion can score fairly high as the data is quantitative and pre-coded, thus accessible to computer-aided analysis, and results are clearly comparable. However, reliability and accuracy are harder to gauge without the presence of an interviewer to challenge the answer or ask for further development and clarification.

Another key early decision then is how to deliver the questionnaire, this can be done in a variety of ways, through:

♦ Self-completion questionnaire - handed out or picked up

♦ E-survey – through a service such as Survey Monkey or Typeform

♦ Text message

♦ Postal – Stamped addressed envelope (SAE) or postcard

♦ Face to face interview

♦ Telephone survey

Clearly a major consideration here is resources and thus the obvious cost implications of the various modes of delivery. These however might be outweighed by the gains to be made in terms of the respondent and the results.

Before you design your questionnaire, there is one final decision that needs consideration in the light of all that has been discussed above, which is whether your questionnaire is going to be *structured*, providing questions that allow only closed answers in a predetermined order, *unstructured*, allowing for open answers in a looser structure, or *semi-structured*, allowing for both. Clearly the structured approach will score well in terms of the results category allowing high levels of comparability, while the unstructured will score well for the respondent allowing considerable autonomy and *Latitude*.

Standardised questions are at the heart of the popularity of questionnaires, regardless of whether they are closed or open. All respondents getting the same questions means that you are able to make comparisons, not only within the same survey, but if you continue to use the questionnaire in subsequent years you can make comparisons across the lifetime of your festival, helping you identify recurrent issues, areas needing expansion, and trends.

Questionnaire design

Many of the rules and approaches used in questionnaire design are equally applicable to designing both interview questions and focus group questions. Regardless of which of these methods your research is using, it is good practice to start with a brief introduction to what your research is about. It is here you can mention the Market Research Society's code of conduct, and also mention your incentives. For example, 'if you want to be entered into the prize draw, fill in your name and contact details (postal address or e-mail) at the end of this questionnaire'. You may then ask for permission to contact them with further news about events, information or special offers – asking them to tick which they would like to receive.

Question order

The order the questions are delivered in is important, the structure we recommend is:

1 Contextual – characteristics
2 Peripheral – activities
3 Central – attitudes
4 Other – anything else?

Questionnaires/interviews should always start with straightforward questions that people will know the answers to. Asking people about their personal characteristics is a good place to start, such as gender, age, where they have come from, etc. It provides contextual information that relaxes people into answering, gives them confidence and increases the possibility they will complete the research. Moving on then to peripheral questions such as their activities, how many times they go to festivals a year, what kinds of festivals, and how much they spend at festivals. These types of questions take a little more thought and prepare the respondent for the central and more complex questions which are sometimes the attitudinal ones that take a little more refection, or indeed the more personal and sensitive questions and issues. Finally, the 'other' question, this is where you can ask, 'is there anything else you might want to tell us that we haven't covered in the above questions?' This is often the point at which the researcher learns something they might never have conceived of when designing the questions, it is often the most revealing answer of them all! 'Other' should always be included in a choice of alternative responses if possible, as this gives the respondent the opportunity for an autonomous answer.

The key to successful questionnaire or interview sheet design is layout. Clearly the order in which you ask the questions is important in that the questions should build on each other and follow a logical flow. The structure should be easy to follow, especially for self-completion questionnaires. The phrasing and length of questions is obviously important, especially for providing clear answers and improving response rates, which we'll say more about in a moment. A too easily forgotten rule of design is leaving adequate space for answers, to ensure full and detailed responses. Finally, and most importantly, keep your instructions clear, especially if you have a complicated structure where people may have to move from one section to another or indeed skip a section if the response is 'no' (then move on to section 5)....

Open and closed questions

We have already begun to talk about 'open' and 'closed' questions. Closed questions are where the answer choices are limited and the respondent is required to simply answer yes or no, or as in the below examples, tick a box.

1. How often do you go to a festival? (please tick one)

Very often (weekly)	( )
Fairly often (monthly)	( )
Quite often (>monthly)	( )
Not very often (<monthly)	( )
Never	( )

2. Which type of festival do you prefer? (please tick one)

Music	( )
Arts	( )
Literary	( )
Food	( )
None	( )
Other	( )

In open questions, space is provided for the respondent to provide their own answers without having a restricted choice.

1. How often do you go to festivals?

_____

2. Which type of festivals do you prefer?

_____

Open questionnaires are more likely to be able to allow you to ask the all-important WHY questions:

3. Why do you go to festivals?

_____

Designing and wording questions

Getting the design and wording of the questions right can be the most challenging and difficult part of the research process. The key is ensuring that all questions contribute to answering the overall research objective, providing informed and informative answers. The wording of questions can indicate types of answers required:

How many...?

Measurable – quantifiable responses

What is...?

Single or multiple factors – descriptive responses

Which...?

Specific factors to be explored - explanatory responses

Why do...?

Unknown factors to be discovered – evaluative responses

There are some simple do's and don'ts that need to be followed in devising questions:

Questionnaire design: Do's:

- ◆ Keep questions focused
- ◆ Keep questions clear and simple
- ◆ Keep questions short if possible
- ◆ Keep questions one-dimensional
- ◆ Keep questions unambiguous
- ◆ Provide enough options in the answer as are needed
- ◆ Distinguish between fact and opinions
- ◆ Avoid questions (unless desired) that can be answered simply by yes or no
- ◆ Be careful of delicate areas
- ◆ All questions must serve a purpose based on hypothesis – research question

Questionnaire design: Don'ts:

- ◆ Ask leading questions
- ◆ For information they might not have
- ◆ For opinions they might not have
- ◆ Be vague or threatening
- ◆ Ask hypothetical questions
- ◆ Use language that is too technical or jargonised
- ◆ Ask two questions in one

Debating point:

Consider these examples of how getting the design of questions right is so important.

Principle	Bad example	Improvement
Use simple language	What is the frequency of your utilisation of the Theatre Royals' internet audience booking system?	How often do you use the online booking system at the Theatre Royal?
Avoid being vague	Do you go out very often?	Have you done any of the following activities within the last month?
Avoid leading questions	Are you against the shocking wasteful expense of the government funding the arts?	What is your opinion of the government funding the arts?

Types of questions

The main types of questions used in festival research can be grouped into about six various approaches:

1 The yes/no answer

Have you attended this festival before? Yes/No

2 Inquire/opinion question

What was it about the festival you enjoyed the most?

3 Agree/disagree statement

The staff were friendly and approachable. Agree/Disagree

4 List options

Please list the activities at the festival you enjoyed the most.

5 Rank in order

From the list of activities provided rank in order the ones you found were the best value for money with 1 being the best value, 2 being second best and 3 being the least.

Inflatables		Big wheel		Wine tasting		Shooting	
Slide		Apple bobbing		Bowling		Face painting	

6 Rating

How significant are the following factors in your choosing to attend this festival? (with 7 being very significant and 1 being not significant)

	Very significant						Not very significant
Ticket price	7	6	5	4	3	2	1
Distance from home	7	6	5	4	3	2	1
Overall programme	7	6	5	4	3	2	1
Headliners	7	6	5	4	3	2	1
Facilities	7	6	5	4	3	2	1

The most often used form of rating is called the Likert Scale, this simply asks your respondents to either strongly agree, agree, neither agree nor disagree, disagree or strongly disagree to a series of statements.

Your festival experience:	5 ☺	4	3	2	1 ☹
Festival site entry was easy and well organised.	…	…	…	…	…
The staff were helpful and friendly.	…	…	…	…	…
The toilet facilities were clean and sanitary.	…	…	…	…	…
The queues were short and well managed.	…	…	…	…	…
Food and drink were reasonably priced.	…	…	…	…	…

Coding

As we said earlier, using questionnaires has many advantages – it is relatively cheap, quick and produces quantitative data, and the results can quickly be analysed by computer packages such as SPSS-X and Excel. Before this can happen, however, the raw data needs to be given a numeric code. There are essentially two types of these:

♦ Answers that are 'real numbers' such as ages – 32

♦ Answers that are given nominal codes such as 'very satisfied' – 1

Most questionnaires (especially self-completion) have a 'for office use only' column on the right-hand side, which is where the researcher enters the appropriate code for the answer in a box or boxes. These numeric codes are then transferred to a computer file, usually through a data entry process, and depending on the size of the questionnaire, this can be quite short or very long. Qualitative 'textual' data, from the open-ended questions on questionnaires or from unstructured interviews, can also be computer analysed in a similar way through 'string' variables, which are strings of letters or characters. The leading software for this is NVivo or ATLAS Ti. A more detailed discussion on how to code and computer analyse quantitative and qualitative data can be found in Veal and Burton (2014: 358 – 413). Clearly the issue with this kind of computer aided analysis is the availability of adequately trained staff. Coding and analysis can be achieved 'long hand' but will inevitably lack the sophistication of computer aided analysis.

Pilot

Piloting is important to all research methodologies, it is where you test the viability of the questionnaire, ensuring that people understand the questions, that the structure is easy to follow, and that the responses you are getting actually help you answer your research question or hypothesis – that you ARE asking the right questions! Piloting will allow you to:

♦ Change and rephrase questions

♦ Rearrange the structure

♦ Reconsider your research question or hypothesis

♦ Maybe redefine your methodological approach, possibly triangulating methods

Pilot and fine tune on a small selection from the sample group, two to four will usually suffice. Ultimately, piloting is the key point for assessing the feasibility of the research. It will tell you if your research design is feasible; then you can take the opportunity to consider if your research timetable is feasible and if the research is financially feasible.

Debating point:

You are concerned that attendances at your festival seem to be falling. Devise a questionnaire which will help you discover why, and what you can do to address and then reverse this.

Hints:

Who are your visitors? – Gathering demographics.

What is the experiences of your visitors? - Information/transport/parking/ticket buying/events/toilets/café/shop/staff.

What do your visitors like/dislike? – Highlights problems.

How did your visitors hear about you? – How effective is your publicity?

What is your catchment area? – Where should you focus your marketing?

What other types of events interest them? – Developing your programme.

Other? – Other information unthought of.

Most importantly, devise some questions for a sample of ex-visitors and non-visitors.

Interviews

Survey research involving questionnaires is excellent for providing a snapshot of the audience, their make-up, experiences and behaviour – the who and the what. If we are concerned in our research about the how and the why, then a more in-depth and probing methodology is required. This inevitably will involve you engaging your respondents in a more face-to-face exchange. All research is to a greater or lesser extent a social process, and personal factors will inevitably play a role in the methodology. The social survey methods we are about to discuss are particularly reliant on good and appropriate interaction between the researcher and the respondent. The first is face-to-face/in-depth interviewing, usually conducted with a single respondent. Interviews can also be conducted by telephone, Skype/FaceTime, or by email or text messaging. The second involves group respondents and these might be in the form of group interviews or focus groups. The previous section on questionnaires dealt with the more structured approach to survey research, and this section will concentrate on addressing semi-structured and unstructured/ open types of social survey. These types of research tend to produce qualitative data and aim to get at the insider's view/interpretation of the world. The questions used can be semi-structured or unstructed and open, with a more conversational approach than a formal interview, indeed, the researcher may only be using an aide-mémoire or checklist of areas/topics to discuss rather than a set of questions - questionnaire style.

As with all research practice, the who, how and where are important. *Who* is your sample; *how* is whether face to face, by telephone, or video conference. The *where* is, in the street, at their home, place of work or a hired room. The latter two are particularly important for group surveys. The conditions for successful interviewing are accessibility – the who, how and where; cognition and motivation – that the respondents know what they are doing and why; and confidentiality – that the information they give will be treated with complete confidentiality. Crucially here, the notion of informed consent is central to research ethics particularly in the social process of interviewing, where the interviewees' words are taken as being 'on the record and for the record'.

Experience has shown that if people are approached in the right way, they have confidence in the researcher, and the importance of their role in the research is emphasised, then they actually enjoy the opportunity to discuss issues, air their views, and reflect in a manner they don't ordinarily do on their life and the world. Research can and should be a very positive experience for both parties.

Face-to-face interviews

A face-to-face interview during your festival onsite is clearly going to be cheaper than one organised on a street or at a person's home, both of which incur considerable expense, although there are still festival personnel time costs involved. The content of the interview will also be different. At a person's home you will be able to have more of a 'conversation' and time will not necessarily be a factor, stopping people in the street usually limits you to between five and ten minutes interview time, and on your festival site might depend on when during the events to try to engage people – clearly during a 'downtime' is best. The big advantage of interviewing over a self-completion questionnaire is that the interviewer can probe the answer, can ask for or give clarification, and most importantly can ask the 'why' question. The in-depth style of face-to-face interviewing allows this 'conversation' to be more free-flowing and wide ranging, often allowing the interviewee to dictate the direction of the interview so that 'their' interpretation of the world is the dominant voice, not the researcher's imposition of their interpretation of the interviewee's world. The disadvantage here is clearly that in building up a body of evidence, the in-depth style of interview has difficulties when it comes to comparing responses from multiple interviews, whereas a semi-structed approach will give you more points of comparison.

The style of questioning here is also going to be different, with the emphasis on allowing the respondent to come up with what is genuinely their own answer, so you would ask more 'open' questions such as: 'What was your favourite thing about the festival?' Here you might get an answer that relates to an impromptu 'happening' or a friend's related activity that you might be able to formalise for next years programme. Talking to people about their experience, any issues they had, their attitudes and opinions, and of course asking if they have any other information they can offer, will provide a great deal of detailed information for you to consider.

Focus groups

Conducting focus groups has become very popular in the past two decades or so, particularly in the area of politics and policy development, new product launching and marketing, and cultural research. It is comparatively cheap as a reasonably large number of people can be 'interviewed' simultaneously in one place by one interviewer. It has advantages as a method in that the interaction between people, their conversations and arguments can highlight issues of genuine concern to them, rather than those imposed by an interviewer. Group dynamics are the key tool in stimulating, eliciting and generating information and discussion, and indeed it could be said that in a successful focus group, the 'interviewer' has to do very little except keep the discussion on-track.

A distinction can be made between small group interviewing and focus groups. Small group interviewing tends to be less than five people and more often than not is family groups or friend groups. In small group interviewing the group is usually known to each other and this makes for a slightly different group dynamic to focus groups who are usually larger and unknown to each other. As we shall see, the methodological considerations are similar for both, however. There are basically three ways of constructing a focus group:

- ♦ Pre-existing group
- ♦ Unknown group
- ♦ Oppositional group

The pre-existing group is as we've just described, families, friend groups or work colleagues, whereas the unknown group is not known to each other. The oppositional group is the most controversial, where a group is constructed from people whose views are known to be different (perhaps from a previously conducted interview).

As the name implies, focus groups are about focusing on specific themes or issues, homogeneous issues upon which the sample – group – are all selected to have an experience of, opinion on or interest in. For this research method, social context is important, obviously in festival research what this group will have in common is knowledge of or experience of your festival. Focus groups are more comfortable for the respondents, as there is not the one-to-one, face-to-face pressure of interviews. This is particularly important as we have seen for families, youth groups, ethnic minorities or employees who may feel uncomfortable or unwilling to participate in an interview situation, especially if the interviewer is perceived to be an authority figure. Interaction and discussion are at the heart of the methodology and everything should be done to achieve this so that it can generate as wide a range of views and information as possible. Through discussion the parameters of a discourse can be revealed, as a group will often search for a common basis upon which they can all debate, formulate meaning and move a discussion forward. These discussions can then stimulate people to think about areas they might not have considered by themselves. The naturalness of the language used is also important here, where people use their own vocabulary and not a false one imposed by an interviewer in an unnatural interview situation.

Focus groups work best, in our experience, when they have between six and 12 members. With fewer than six it can be difficult to get a group dynamic going, with more than 12 you have too many for everyone to be heard and it can prove intimidating to some people. The number of groups you run is ultimately determined by your funds and available time, however two different groups should be a minimum as it provides for good comparative material and checks against the first being a 'rogue' group. The location for the focus group is important – normally if you are doing it during an event then somewhere quiet away from the hustle and bustle is best as it helps people concentrate. If you are carrying out the research after the festival then it should be somewhere neutral, such as a library room or a college room, or at your premises if you have one. A degree of comfort should be ensured with refreshments available and chairs arranged around a central table. A good focus group, as with an in-depth interview, should run somewhere between 45 minutes and an hour; any longer and individual and group fatigue begins to set in. We have always used financial incentives (a token amount, say £10) in focus group work as this ensures a degree of commitment on both parties and is recompense for time taken and travel (if needed).

The 'interviewer' is best thought of as the facilitator of the focus group; their role is to stimulate and then moderate the discussion. Getting the participants confident to speak and relaxed, yet focused on the discussion is the key moment at the start of the session.

Starting the session:

♦ Can start with small questionnaire to gain key facts as people arrive

♦ Welcome self-introductions

♦ Explain the research and focus group process

♦ Outline types of subject they will be discussing

♦ Emphasise the importance of their contribution

♦ Encourage them to speak up, and speak one at a time to help recording

Explaining the research and its importance, getting people to introduce themselves, and beginning the questioning with some uncomplicated non-controversial issues is a good way to start. As with a questionnaire, start with contextual questions about themselves and their activities, move on to their experiences, and then to the central issues, debates and their attitudes and opinions. This structure is essentially funnelling, moving the group slowly towards the key area(s) of concern. Inevitably this means that the researcher has already decided what the key areas might be, but focus groups can also be structured in a more recursive or natural flow, where the participants decide on the direction of the debate as they go along, or they can be structured for narrative or storytelling where a group recounts their experiences of an event/festival from start to finish. The moderator, in moving the discussion along, may refer to an aide-mémoir which just has the sequence of areas/questions on it, may use aids such as flip charts/books, visual aids such as photographs, or indeed products. The nature of the extent of prompting, probing and further questioning may depend on the group dynamics.

The moderator's task is complex and requires some social skills, especially when group dynamics are such an important feature. They not only have to ensure that all discussion topics are covered in the time allocated; they have to handle questioning and anticipate when the next area needs to be introduced, or further probing is required; they also have to control dominating voices, curb the over-enthusiastic, encourage the quiet ones to speak, and ensure that everyone has an equal opportunity to voice their opinions. Sometimes an intervention and a gentle "has anybody else got anything they would like to add to the discussion?" or "we haven't heard very much from this side of the table recently" is necessary. Cross-talking and separate conversations can be equally gently handled by blaming the technology: "I'm sorry, can you speak one at a time as the recorder won't pick up many voices at once and it becomes difficult to transcribe". Research is a social process, and perceptions of interviewer neutrality are important, so the management of verbal and non-verbal clues is vital, as you should not be seen to be taking sides or overly agreeing with one point, while at the same time encouraging people to elaborate or expand another. At the other end of the scale, inadequate or unhelpful responses may need you to reframe the question, explain the question or simply ask supplementary questions. As with interviewing, the ability to test the accuracy of responses by probing and further questioning is one of the advantages to the methodology.

Prompt	Intention
"Uh-huh" (nodding)	I'm still listening
"That's interesting"	Encouraging subject to keep talking - expand
Repeat their last statement as a question – "you don't like going to Jazz festivals?"	Encourage reflection
"Why don't you like going to Jazz festivals?" "What is it about Jazz festivals you don't like?"	Inviting explanations – probing
Raising a finger and leaning forward slightly	The moderator wants to interject
"Let's go back to…"	Back tracking - to bring the conversation back onto the topic
"Can we move on to…"	Initiating a new topic
…	Silence can be useful, listen rather than speaking
"In the little time we have left…"	Urgency – please focus on the issues in hand, we're coming to the end of the session

Figure 10.1: Interviewing interventions

The questions themselves should be open and designed to provide cues for discussion. *Tell me* and *give me* are good ways to start a focus group and introduce a new topic:

Tell me about your experiences of arriving at the festival?

Give me your first impressions upon seeing the festival site?

This can be followed up with the specific areas you are interested in, so *how* and *what* questions will tend to dominate:

How easy was it to follow the parking arrangements at the festival?

What did you think of the laser show?

They can then be followed up with *did, was,* and of course *why*:

Did the colour coding help?

Was the finale all you expected?

That's interesting! *Why* do you say that?

In both interviewing and focus groups, asking for further clarification, for examples and more details, is an essential part of the in-depth nature of the methodologies. They are also ways to check the authenticity and reliability of the responses.

And of course, don't forget the other question:

Finally, is there anything else you would like to talk about that we haven't already covered in the discussion?

Interviewing recording and analysing answers

In both interviewing and focus groups, one of the key decisions is how to record the conversation. Clearly an audio and/or video recording is the best, but of course permission is required to both to use and store the recorded information. Experience has shown that people on the whole are far more nervous of video recording; it is more obtrusive, and less user friendly than a simple audio recorder. Taking written notes is difficult especially in the midst of trying to run a complicated focus group. Admin support could be useful, especially if shorthand were available, however this is another stranger in the room and it can be off-putting. Audio recording is then the recommended method.

The key here is that the act of transcribing the record of the proceedings is essential to this methodology. The same is true for interviewing. Whilst embroiled in the social process of running an interview or a focus group, you do not really get time to think in depth about the answers being given or the group dynamics; only when you sit down and begin to transcribe do you actually think about what has been said. Also, as you are transcribing you are beginning to formulate the structure of your writing up of the data. Inevitably a great deal of data is actually produced by these methods, and computer software has become available for both transcription and analysis, however these packages can be expensive and require a certain degree of staff expertise. They can also vary in accuracy, for example due to different accents, so an element of manual transcription and editing is still needed in many cases.

Analysis of transcripts

The analysis of transcripts from either in-depth interviews or focus groups is a matter of conducting a form of content analysis. Avoid at all cost simply reproducing your transcript in the report, as that is not analysis, and leaves you open to others drawing their own conclusions from your research! Hopefully, as you have been transcribing you have taken notes and probably begun to form a kind of structure for your write-up as common themes have begun to be drawn out of the discussions. As a great deal of ground would have been covered in the discussions, it is important at this point to refer back to your original hypothesis or research question, making sure that your analysis stays focused on this. The key is to group similar themes, topics and discussions together, always taking down significant and important verbatim quotes, as you do so. Put the themes or areas you have identified into a structure – you might order them by frequency, most discussed first, or by oppositional statements and discussions; summarise each area; illustrate and back up with quotations from the participants, and any other references or sources you have; then comment and conclude on each section. Finally, top-and-tail your analysis section with an introduction and then a conclusion and/or recommendations.

Interviewing: Dos:

- Do be well prepared – know as much about your topic as you can
- Do create a comfortable situation
- Do try to listen rather than speak
- Do keep good eye contact
- Do try and keep the proceedings on track and focused
- Do remember to turn on your audio recorder (be sure it's fully charged!)

Interviewing: Don'ts

- Don't try to cover too much
- Don't be too interrogative/aggressive
- Don't get so involved in the conversational style that you are 'led' by the interviewees
- Don't agree or disagree with interviewees
- Don't suggest answers

Observation and participant observation

Participant observation involves the researcher becoming a participant in the phenomenon being studied. Thus, if you are interested in how your audience actually experiences your festival you might pose as a typical festival goer and participate along with everybody else in the activities. Participant observation allows you to witness for yourself how people 'use' your event – information that might not necessarily be revealed though other standard methodologies such as questionnaires.

In non-participation observation the researcher observes the phenomenon from the sidelines so to speak. For example, you might be interested in how your audience moves around your festival, where the bottlenecks are, how effective the sign-posting is, or why one area is becoming particularly boggy.

Observation in its most straightforward sense is used by good festival managers all the time, observing and being aware of what is going on around you is a key management skill. In terms of festival research this again can be quite straightforward. A mela manager of our acquaintance who was keen to understand the ethnic mix of his audience would observe from a vantage point a designated area, and count the identifiable variables of race, gender and age within that area. Clearly, he was going to be making some assumptions and his results were based on his perceptions and observational skills; indeed his, like all research in this methodology, was an act of interpretation.

As a qualitative method, description and interpretation are at the heart of observation and participant observation. Research of this type generates very detailed descriptions, often referred to as 'thick description'. It is based on *hermeneutics* or acts of interpretation; and relies to some extent on *verstehen* or the ability to empathise with others. In the social science world this methodology has been widely adopted by anthropologists, ethnographers and phenomenologists, who all believe that any social situation can be studied using this method as it seeks to understand the world through the eyes of those being studied in their natural setting. The methodology has concentrated on areas of deviant behaviour, youth culture and subcultures, areas of social life where it would prove difficult for more traditional methods to be used. It has also proved a valuable methodology for studying the latent or hidden side of life, examining taken-for-granted assumptions that people make in areas such the professions, classroom interaction, and consumer behaviour. It could also be argued that because of its unobtrusive nature it is an excellent tool for festival research as other methods are intrusive when people are simply there to enjoy themselves.

The evidence gathered through this methodology are the observed actions, interactions and symbolic language of people within their location. For us, the location is clearly going to be our festival and the symbolic language could be everything from the spoken word to body language and dress; the observed actions and interactions will probably be a key issue for festival managers as these may well be a result of some of the decisions we made in planning and designing the festival.

Doing observational research

A number of issues that arise for observers in other social situations are not applicable here. Clearly the issue of entry into the situation (your festival) is not so problematic, and permissions of owners need not necessarily be sought. However, often contingent to this is the overt/covert decision, should the observer admit their role, so that people are aware they are being observed, or as this might alter behaviour, should the observer and their observations go unrecognised, and the observer don a plausible disguise or pose as a typical festival goer in order to blend in and thus observe?

A number of other choices have to be made:

◆ Site(s) to observe

◆ Observation points

◆ Study time period

◆ Continuous observation or sampling

◆ Number and length of sampling periods

◆ What to observe.

The types of things the observer will be looking for will depend on the initial research question that they set themselves, but as a general guide the following is a useful set of headings for field notes:

■ Date and time: key facts

■ Weather conditions: if applicable

■ Location: the physical setting

■ Activities: what is happening?

■ Objects: relevant physical things that are present

■ Symbols: significant visual elements

■ Participants: the people/subjects involved

■ Activities: what the subjects are doing

■ Significant acts: single actions by individuals

■ Goals: what are subjects trying to accomplish

■ Duration: time taken to accomplish acts

■ Language: spoken discourse

■ Feelings: emotions demonstrated and expressed

■ Tensions: moments of crisis

Figure 10.2: Observation field-note areas

Using a series of field note headings like those above help you focus on what you are looking for, and give you headings under which to take notes. Systematically recording your observations is important because memory, even short-term memory, especially in the midst of a festival can be very unreliable. Note taking, in whatever form, is essential, and this is what will constitute your data. Working in small teams can be helpful as you can compare notes and corroborate each other's observations. Having another member of the team to report to can also be useful as they can quiz you about your observations, and probably draw out more information. Some observers working over a long period will keep detailed diaries. Building up supporting material, such as attendance figures, accident reports, or visual records, and gathering other contextual facts, such as weather conditions, will also help build as full a picture as possible.

Observational data and analysis

The data gathered from observation or participant observation may well be useful in serval ways. First, as we saw with the mela example at the start of this section, observations can be turned into statistical data. The mela manager counted the total number of people in his designated area, then counted the numbers of men and women, their ethnicity, age etc. and was able to arrive at percentages reflecting the make-up of the audience. Second, your recorded observations of actions and activities are the primary qualitative data and will form your main evidence, so you might have observed that a great many of the concession stands were missed as people were taking short cuts to the main stage around the play area. Third, experiential data from your participation observations will be central evidence in your research. You may be investigating wheelchair access, and your experiences 'on the ground' of lack of ramps will be key evidence. Fourth, direct quotations gathered from conversations can be used as supporting and illustrative evidence. Last, your own reflections on the experience are valuable data and should always include self-conscious reflections on the research process itself.

There is some similarity here with the analysis of interview and focus group data, in that the transcription of all field notes is a vital part of the methodology, and the point at which you can really think about and reflect on the research. Be sure that you read and re-read all field notes and your diary, identify basic components, themes and issues, look for patterns and relationships between them, compare and contrast different experiences, views, and observations. Identify key quotations that are illustrative of the points you are making or move the discussion on significantly.

Observation and ethics

Clearly all social research methodologies have their ethical issues which researchers have to contend with, however, those of observation and participant observation are particularly acute as informed consent is nearly always absent. The key issue with this method is going to be the 'self-conscious rigour' with which the researcher carries out their role. For Denscombe there are two clear guide lines which must be followed:

♦ First, if it can be demonstrated that none of those who were studied suffered as a result of being observed, the researcher can argue that certain ethical standards were maintained.

♦ Second, and linked, if the researcher can show that the identities of those involved were never disclosed, again there is a reasonable case for saying that the participant observation was conducted in an ethical manner (1998: 151).

Self-imposed discipline is essential to all aspects of observation, not just in the processes of observing and recording, but also in ensuring that you think and act ethically in all that you do. The advantages of observation/participant observation are clearly those of intimacy with your subjects and their actions, of immediacy in being able to record as situations happen and develop, perhaps to see the hidden sides of social behaviour that might not be recounted or recalled through other methodologies. As it is an 'active' methodology, you are able to react to the data as it comes in, so you might change the direction of your research question in the light of new evidence.

The problems and issues that arise from this methodology are many, and do cause some to dismiss its findings as unscientific and biased. Clearly there are the large ethical questions which we have already posed, there are also ethical methodological questions about researcher bias and self-selection. Questions about the observer's presence distorting that which is being observed, issues about keeping covert, and problems – particularly for long term studies – of researchers 'going native' (ceasing to neutrally observe and becoming an active participant). Ultimately the quality of the data gathered depends on the skills of the observer. However, being aware of these issues, and imposing strict self-conscious rigour, the researcher can endeavour to at least minimise some of these issues. The richness, immediacy and quality of the data is felt by its proponents to outweigh the difficulties, and observing audience behaviour remains a key research tool for festival managers.

Other methodologies

There are other methodologies, which we have not had room to discuss here, that are complementary to a festival manager's attempts to gain a full insight into their festival's working, development and success. Amongst these are content analysis, where any form of visual, written or verbal communication can be analysed. It is particularly useful when looking at marketing material, website design or brand images. Like so many methods it splits between quantitative and qualitative approaches. Quantitative content analysis tends to be about counting the occurrences of a set of variables and thus drawing conclusions on their importance. Qualitative content analysis tends to use tools such as semiotics to decode signs and meanings (see Hansen et al. 1998, Chs 5 and 8). In a similar vein, discourse analysis provides the tools to examine how the 'conversation' about your festival is being fashioned by the media and other agencies, and thus enables you to be proactive and to intervene and influence its direction (see Hansen and Machin, 2013). Both of these methodologies are particularly useful in examining media coverage, website and social media content, as discussed in Chapter 11.

Mapping research is a new area for festivals research. It is workshop-based, interactive and collaborative. Participants work together and interact using visual and non-visual material to create a map/representation of their festival experience or journey. The group discuss, debate, ask questions, make observations and come to decisions, which empowers people as capable collaborators, defining and representing issues that are important to them, and is thus a social encounter between the research participant and research facilitator, for whom the evidence is not only the final 'map' but more importantly the whole process of creating it. This approach may well be better suited to a fun festival environment when trying to research a festival goer's 'real' experience rather than some of the traditional methods discussed earlier (see Bradfield, 2015).

Technology in the form of RFID (Radio Frequency Identification) is increasing being used as a research tool to measure how visitors interact with cultural content in the festival programme. RFID sensors in silicon wristbands each have a unique ID tag, and a separate reader – part festival pass, part loyalty card – where visitors touch the reader at each point of a visit. Thus, the festival can track audience's behaviour; how many stops are made and when; account for the attractions visited; analyse time spent at each location; understand what are the most popular attractions. Plus, through special offers for wristband wearers, the amount of money spent could also be accounted for. This technology records what people actually did instantaneously, unlike post-event interviews or online surveys.

Industry example: Festivals, technology and knowledge management

I began working with festivals through audience research and this continues to be an area of interest for many. Often through the audience, we are able to understand a lot about the economic, social and environmental impacts of a festival, not to mention the importance of the central relationship between organisers and attendees. There are very many potential forms of audience data that could contribute to our understanding, from box offices, web traffic, CRM systems, surveys, use of a festival app, social media, photo or video records and more besides. New technologies have been bombarding organisers with exponentially increasing volumes and varieties of data. The same is true of data about other important stakeholders; staff, volunteers, traders, residents, artists and prospective audiences. Now let's make sure we are considering, quantitative and qualitative, current and historic types of data as well.

It is easy to feel overwhelmed and that we are somehow missing many of the opportunities technology presents, but then, neither festival organisers nor researchers have traditionally been expected to have software development as part of their professional skill set. It may also be important to note that software developers, conversely, are not expected to be experts in the types of knowledge or skills that make up festival management.

I increasingly see the potential for Knowledge Management (or KM) theory and practices to be taken up at a strategic level by festivals. These practices no doubt already exist, at least in part, but a fuller discussion can be had through labelling them as such. Festivals and many similar types of events can clearly struggle with organisational continuity and building institutional knowledge; principles which I'm sure readers of this book will have learned or personally encountered. In the public sector, it is more likely that individual organisations will have some of their KM approach determined for them by funding bodies, though networks or sector support organisations have a similar role across all sectors.

This sets the scene, where a conventional research project usually enters the picture, whether this is managed in-house, by external consultants or through an academic-led project. The ambition is usually to answer a relatively prescriptive research question: Who attends? Were they satisfied with the festival? What is our impact on X, Y or Z? It is relatively easy to identify the work involved with data collection and analysis; and to learn more about the tools and practices that improve and simplify this essential research 'legwork'. It is less likely that we could describe these (nevertheless valuable) stand-alone projects as consistently fitting into, or replacing the need for, an overarching strategic plan for Knowledge Management within the organisation.

The 'DIKAR' model (Venkatraman, 1996) is a commonly used way of abstracting the KM process. Briefly this shows the technology-driven side (DI: Data, Information) meeting the business value side (AR: Action, Results) with Knowledge (K) in the middle. Business decisions create demand for knowledge, while data and information supply the raw material to inform knowledge. On the supply side, there are clearly many options to explore and evaluate for collecting data and processing it into usable information. Not all festivals are doing so efficiently or effectively. Given the proliferation of data, it is easy to rapidly amass a wide variety of seemingly authoritative data that does not inform any particularly important business decisions (Action) or generate value, however this is determined (Results). If we borrow anything from software developers, let it be the phrase: "Garbage in, garbage out".

Many technological developments simply add to the supply-side of this model. As a researcher, I happily share my burden of the blame for overenthusiasm about new technology and methods which might not have clear applications to immediate business problems. There will always be room for experimentation, but sustained competitive advantages will be more likely to emerge with the demand-side of this model also in mind.

Some specific tools I have used and would recommend for various purposes are: Open Data Kit (surveys, checklists, forms) Amazon Mechanical Turk (data entry, image tagging) QGIS (geographic mapping), Tableau (data visualisation). Even aspects like ticketing and

CRM are being challenged by more flexible open source options: Pretix and SuiteCRM respectively. Beware any event management platform that claims or appears to be the one holy grail, magic bullet or other mythical cure-all of your choice.

Specific technologies are not inherent to KM practice, though it is hard to argue that reduced barriers have made some approaches possible that would have previously been cost-prohibitive. There is plenty of work and value to be realized from taking a step back to consider how you could simply manage existing data, information and knowledge resources more effectively. Substantial trust is needed within organisations for individuals to relinquish ownership of knowledge, or methods of working, which will likely be encoded in very individualised ways. If nothing else, this can also identify where tacit, personal and flexible decision making should start and where more data-driven or formulaic decision making should end.

In conclusion, a KM strategy tries to not emphasise any one form of data, or research method over any other. Instead, it provides a model for addressing the whole spectrum of knowledge supplying and demanding processes, giving appropriate place and consideration to each. Few festivals would want or need to employ a full-time archivist of course, but this approach is worth bearing in mind the next time you pull together sales reports, survey results or web analytics; with only a vague idea of what organisational knowledge this is actually feeding into, or what demand-side decisions can be informed by this. Equally, you may save considerable time and effort, being reassured that some questions are less urgent than others, or have already been satisfactorily answered by previous efforts.

Richard Fletcher is an independent festival and events researcher and part-time lecturer

Festival evaluation

We started this chapter by stating that research methodologies are central to the iterative process whereby festivals learn, develop and change year on year. Undoubtedly, they are the key tool of any festival evaluation; for Don Getz, evaluation is:

> "an essential management function of information gathering and feedback through which processes can be improved, goals more effectively attained, and by which organisations can learn and adapt" (2018: 2).

A simple evaluation usually involves a consideration as to whether the festival met its aims and objectives, what went wrong – or indeed right! – and what lessons can be learnt to feed into next year's event. Authors such as Quinn (2013) have pointed out that inevitably these evaluations are becoming more essential as the numbers of stakeholders in festivals increase, bringing their own auditing demands. These audits may not be solely economic; the social and cultural impacts may need to be demonstrated by a local authority who have part financed your festival with an expectation of it providing some 'social good'. Thus, whilst some audits may require hard evidence of the kind that quantitative research methodologies provide, others may well be looking for the kind of evidence that the more qualitative methodologies produce.

Interestingly, Fox ex al. suggest that evaluation should go beyond the post close-down phase of a festival and should be part of:

Pre-event evaluation – part of a feasibility study

The implementation stage monitoring and control as part of project management

As well as post-event evaluation
(2014: 13)

Whilst evaluation in all its forms is an important part of festival management, the ability of the majority of festivals to consider this degree of engagement will be severely limited by the availability of staff, time and finances. However, for festival management a number of areas for evaluation are particularly pertinent:

- ◆ Social and cultural benefits
- ◆ Degree of arts engagement
- ◆ Involvement of volunteers
- ◆ Environmental impact
- ◆ Relationship with host community
- ◆ Pedagogic function
- ◆ Stakeholder engagement

Festival managers will have to cut their evaluation cloth according to what is necessary and doable; the same can be said for their use of research methodologies.

Summary

In navigating a huge, complex, and at times highly academic field, we have tried, based on our experience, to give solid and directed advice that will help and encourage festival managers to engage with research methodologies to the benefit of themselves, their organisations and their festivals. Good festival management requires informed decision making and a solid knowledge of research methods, and how to use them is an important part of that decision-making process.

The key methodologies we have discussed all have their advantages and disadvantages. The best and most productive research designs will triangulate these methods, providing festival managers with the best possible array of data. We have also suggested some complementary methods, and would remind festival managers that they already have a great deal of 'research' data in-house, in their sales and finance figures, on their mailing lists (post-codes are useful to discern your catchment area, distance travelled etc.), through their digital communications, and within the many other documents that organisations produce year on year.

Research and evaluation are becoming essential to the work of festival managers, however a good working knowledge of research methodologies will enable them to make the right decisions in choosing which methodology/ies best answer the questions of their festival that they are asking.

References

Bradfield, E. (2015) *Art in Mind: Evaluating the impact of participatory arts on improved mental wellbeing*. Discussion Papers in Arts and Festivals Management DPAFM 15/1. Leicester: De Montfort University.

Denscombe, M. (1998) *The Good Research Guide: For small-scale social research projects*. Buckingham: Open University Press.

Fox, D., Gouthro, M. B., Morakabati, Y., and Brackstone, J. (2014) *Doing Events Research: From theory to practice*. London: Routledge.

Getz, D. (2018) *Event Evaluation: Theory and methods for event management and tourism*. Oxford: Goodfellow.

Hansen, A. and Machin, D. (2013) *Media and Communication Research Methods*. London: Palgrave Macmillan.

Hansen, A., Cottle, S., Negrine, R., and Newbold, C. (1998) *Mass Communication Research Methods*. London: Palgrave Macmillan.

Market Research Society, (2014) Principles of the MRS Code of Conduct, https://www.mrs.org.uk/pdf/mrs%20code%20of%20conduct%202014.pdf

Quinn, B. (2013) *Key Concepts in Event Management*. London: Sage.

Veal, A. J. and Burton, C. (2014) *Research Methods for Arts and Events Managers*. Harlow: Pearson.

11 Managing Festivals in a Digital World

by Kristy Diaz

After reading this chapter you should:

- Understand some of the key developments and theories surrounding digital media
- Understand how digital technology and communication are used in festival management
- Recognise the opportunities they can present, as well as how to manage potential pitfalls
- Know how to use digital marketing effectively, including how to execute a multi-channel campaign
- Gain a set of tools and frameworks with which to manage your festival in a digital world
- Understand the meaning of 'digital culture' in the context of festival management and audience engagement

Introduction

What exactly is digital? Debated by those who are less tech-savvy and those with advanced knowledge alike, the term 'digital' has been notoriously difficult to define. We see it used mostly as a prefix – digital device, digital television, digital divide – but, for the purposes of this book when we say 'digital' we are referring to the use of digital technology and communications.

This chapter focuses on giving you an understanding of how digital technology and communications are used in festival management, and how you can use them to maximise the success and impact of your festival.

So why is digital technology so important? Before looking at the practicalities, it is worth looking briefly at how it has developed and has had a fundamental and mostly liberating impact on both marketing and human communications.

Digital technology has had an impact on arts and culture in the following ways: mass communications, access, rights and ownership (copyright) and networking, power and control.

Mass communications

Prior to digital technology, the primary means of getting your message across to a mass public, or indeed a niche market, was via the printed press or broadcast media. The cost of producing a daily or weekly newspaper, or a weekly or monthly magazine, or setting up a radio or TV station was extremely expensive. This concentrated media control into a small number of hands, particularly newspaper owners, their editors, and public and commercial broadcasters. The cost of getting your message across via paid adverts was comparatively high and access to the public via editorials quite limited, and through a limited number of broadcast outlets. Broadcasting and editorial access via people with the power to choose whether to transmit your message, your brand and support your activity, was also determined by a relatively small number of people, most of them probably middle-aged men.

The growing impact of technology, particularly TV, from the 1960s onwards was accompanied by a development of media theory about the role and relationship of new technology to human communications and indeed human relations. There is a considerable body of literature on this subject, far too much to go into any depth and detail here. However, there are one or two theories that are worth mentioning as they mirror the development of festivals from the 1960s onwards.

The power of the televisual media to influence social thinking and human interaction was particularly noted by the Canadian media theorist Marshall McLuhan. In his 1964 book *Understanding Media: The Extensions of Man*, he coined the phrase "The medium is the message", arguing that the platform used (in this case television) influenced the way we perceived the message. This observation is a forerunner of the way that different social media platforms have been adopted by different user groups.

Access, rights and ownership

The Internet emerged in the late 1980s, and its most visible component, the World Wide Web, came into use in the mid-1990s. The web was conceived and developed as a free educational resource by the British computer scientist Sir Tim Berners-Lee and colleagues. It has since become commercialised and there is an ongoing debate about whether it can and will remain open-access or whether commercial interests will, in time, limit the freedom and access to information that it has generated.

Considerable parts of arts and culture are financed by income from copyright, especially literature and music, and technology has significantly increased revenues from these rights. Ironically, it was digital media file sharing that caused the breakdown of the music industry's business model which had been built on revenues from album and CD sales, leading to a revival of live performance and the growth of music festivals.

The issue of ownership and rights in the digital sphere has been challenged by the American academic and lawyer Lawrence Lessig (2005), who has argued for reduced legal restrictions on copyrights and trademarks and open access to the radio spectrum. In 2001 he set up Creative Commons to encourage the publication of creative works for public sharing and benefit. Lessig's arguments revolve around whether it is better to commercialise information and extract financial value from it, or to make information freely available to the benefit of individuals and societies. This issue started to develop in the 1960s and 70s through publications like the pre-digital *Whole Earth Catalog*, which sought to make a wide range of knowledge, particularly about ecological and ethical products, freely available at low cost to the public, seeking to empower the 'grassroots'. Steve Jobs described it as a sort of pre-digital, paperback Google.

Today's digital equivalent of the *Whole Earth Catalog* is Wikipedia, founded and championed by Jimmy Wales, which for all its open access risks and failings has effectively sidelined the previously highly respected and authoritative Encyclopedia Britannica and other published encyclopedias, which were only available in public libraries or at a high purchase price.

A similar path surrounding access, information and rights has been trodden by music festivals from the 1970s' free festivals, which were comparatively unstructured, uncommercial and disorganised, to today's highly structured, commercialised and targeted music festivals.

Networking, power and control

Even more significant was the research by the Catalan sociologist Manuel Castells, who charted the growth of the digital sector in America's Silicon Valley and formulated the idea of the rise of 'the network society'. He found that in the early 1980s emerging technology companies grew as much through interdependent co-operation as through traditional models of commercial competition. Castells coined the memorable phrase 'the space of flows' to describe the way that technology brings about real-time, simultaneous, high speed, long distance interactions (1996: 467). This was different, he said, to 'the space of places'. Castells concluded his three-volume study *The Information Age: Economy, Society and Culture* (1996-8) by observing that networks constitute a new social morphology or structure. "...the power of flows", he observed, "takes precedence of the flow of power" (Castells, 1996: 469).

This observation was made some six years before Mark Zuckerberg set up Facebook and yet describes the power-shift that Facebook and other digital platforms, especially social media platforms, have brought about. Digital technology, first through computers and now through mobile phones, mean that many societies are now highly networked, and what influences people are not 'commands from above' as much as information flows through platforms like Twitter, Facebook and Instagram. Newspapers and magazines still exist. Their owners, editors and writers still exert influence over public opinion. But digital media platforms have allowed individuals to bypass these traditional media structures, and even bypass governments, allowing the general public to communicate with interest groups large and small at little or no cost, mostly unfiltered by institutional control. Many festivals have become highly commercialised and it is access to digital technology and the 'power of flows' through social media platforms that will allow you to access a mass market at no-cost or low-cost using the tools we set out in the rest of this chapter. The medium is still the message.

The issue of continued freedom of access to digital communications and unrestricted access to your potential market via social media platforms is an increasingly contested area which, as academics like Hannah Fry (2018) explain, is now dominated by how computer algorithms are transforming fields such as health, justice, transport and the arts in an increasingly data-driven world.

Digital technology now pervades all areas of modern life: the way we live, work and play are dominated by it. When it comes to leisure and entertainment, the use of social media, smartphones and apps are increasingly central to the decision-making process, as well as to the experience itself. We buy tickets online, share the events we are attending with our friends, and document the events with pictures and video shared via social media. According to the UK Office of Communication, the "internet is essential to the way in which people in the UK communicate, find information, seek entertainment, shop and participate in society" (Ofcom, 2017:164).

The report found 88% of adults have internet access at home. And it's not just young people who are tech savvy: 53% of over-74s are internet users. Whilst usage habits do change with various factors, such as age and socio-economic group ,the internet can no longer be considered the playground of the young, or those living in urban areas. 76% of adults have a smartphone, and 66% of people use their mobile phone to access the internet.

The digital revolution represents a much wider cultural shift in which we now operate, than simply sending email or having a website for your event, and the implications for festival managers are very significant. It impacts how events are organised across the board, affecting marketing and communications, operations and security, project and financial management, programming, evaluation, customer service and more. As festival managers, digital is ingrained in every aspect of the job!

Are you digital-ready?

Producing a festival in a digital world presents a host of new and exciting opportunities, but it also comes with challenges. A crucial first step is to consider how your organisation – whether you're setting up a community arts festival run by volunteers or a national music festival – is ready to meet, adapt to, and maximise those opportunities and challenges, especially in terms of the new relationship with the audience that the digital world provides.

As Martin and Cazarré state:

"Demanding modern consumers ask for more and more functionality, speed, accessibility, innovation, involvement and engagement – and this last one is directly dependent on increasing participation and interaction of the public with one another and with the event itself" (2016: 36–37).

Digital technology is resource-reliant in terms of both budget and people: not only do you need to have access to the internet, and any associated hardware and software, but you also need to understand them and manage them. You cannot have social media presence without someone to keep it updated. A website is nothing without well-considered and timely content.

You could start by asking a series of questions:

◆ Does the festival management team understand and support digital activity?

◆ Are they clear how digital technology and communications can benefit the organisation and achieve its strategic aims?

◆ What level of digital understanding and capacity does your organisation have in every department?

◆ Who in your festival team has responsibility for digital in their area, and how do the different functions interact?

◆ Is your marketing function up-to-date with digital technology and strategy, and how will it use them?

◆ How does the digital age relate to the artistic direction and programming of your festival?

◆ What budget do you have available? Are you likely to make use of free services and software, or do you have advanced needs which will require additional funding? What are both the up-front and maintenance costs?

◆ What timescales are you operating to?

Understanding your needs, aims and objectives when it comes to digital will be the cornerstone of getting it right. By considering the above, you can avoid wasting time, money and energy on pursuing things that won't be right for your festival. Just because certain digital techniques and strategies exist, doesn't necessarily mean you'll need to use them. For example, if your target audience for a community arts festival is people based within the local area, it is unlikely you will need to invest in an advanced Customer Relations Management system when small-scale print and social media advertising could reach the intended results.

Digital marketing, communications and content

It would be fair to say the area of festival management most dramatically transformed has been marketing. Digital technology presents many new opportunities to reach, develop, engage and communicate with audiences in a more direct way than ever before. With traditional print media increasingly in decline, the nature of advertising has changed; internet advertising now accounts for the largest percentage of advertising spending in the UK, at 46% (Ofcom, 2017: 196). Having an active online presence is now a fundamental requirement for most festivals. The elements that form online presence, including a website, social media, email, mobile and advertising can be considered and adapted as necessary, finding the right mix to meet your festival aims.

What is digital marketing?

Digital marketing can be defined as, "the application of the Internet and related digital technologies in conjunction with traditional communications to achieve marketing objectives" (Chaffey and Ellis-Chadwick, 2015: 10). However, it is important to remember: "it is the results delivered by technology that should determine investment in Internet marketing, not the adoption of the technology" (op.cit.).

You will not suddenly gain new audiences by merely building a website; you need tell people it is there, and the goal is not just to get them there, it is for them to act, to decide to attend your festival, to buy tickets, to share the link with an interested friend. Until you have built relationships and engaged with your online community, social media following is just a number.

The key is to consider digital as a toolbox, with different elements that work together as part of the overall marketing mix (see Chapter 9), which converge and interact to maximise reach and achieve the intended results.

What is multichannel marketing?

Multichannel marketing describes how "customer communications and product distribution are supported by a combination of digital and traditional channels at different points in the buying cycle" (ibid.: 11). Simply put, it is the strategy of marketing your festival across a strategically selected range of channels, including digital ones such as social media and email, alongside 'traditional' channels such as printed flyers or radio advertising. It defines how "different marketing channels should integrate and support each other" (ibid.: 14).

Key areas of digital marketing

We will now focus on the following key areas of digital marketing, which can be harnessed alongside traditional mediums to achieve your festival marketing objectives and its overall strategic aims in an integrated way:

♦ Website

♦ Social media

♦ Email

Website

Most festivals will have a dedicated website, but it is not unheard of for some to host their online presence elsewhere, as a blog, or on social media (a Facebook page, for instance). The scale of your festival will determine what your website requirements are likely to be. The cost of developing websites can be high, particularly if you opt for a more bespoke option that requires the services of a web developer or digital agency.

There are a number of cost-effective services that can create sophisticated and professional-looking websites for those without a technical background. Examples include the WordPress CMS (Content Management System), Squarespace and Wix. These allow you to build your website using a pre-set theme, or from a selection of design options where you can select the colours, the layout, and where to add an image or text box. Different providers will require varying levels of digital skill, some have very simple 'drag and drop' options, whereas some will need to be set up by someone with a competent degree of IT knowledge but without the need to be able to write code.

The decision to hire in technical expertise or to do it yourself will ultimately come down to the following factors:

♦ How much traffic you are anticipating. How many people do you think will be using your site? For example, a national festival with hundreds of thousands of users is likely to have more advanced hosting needs and the support of a technical team.

♦ How much direct control you need over the website design and features, and how bespoke it needs to be. For example, are there any special features you want your website to have, such as animated video or interactivity?

♦ What is your budget? Hiring in technical skills and knowledge is expensive, and a custom-built website (depending on many different factors) will likely start in the thousands.

♦ What in-house digital knowledge you have. Is there someone in your team with competent IT skills who can take care of the website, or do you need the support of someone external? Consider scenarios such as the website going down; how urgently would you need to get it up and running again? Do you have someone who knows enough to be able to talk to your hosting provider and get things fixed?

Working with web developers and digital agencies

If you do decide to engage the services of a web developer or agency, ask around. Often the best recommendations will come through word of mouth. If you have someone in your team who has existing knowledge or responsibility in this area, make sure they join you in any initial discussions. Lastly, try to have a very clear idea of what your exact needs and requirements are, as well as your budget and timescales for delivery. This will make the relationship with your external provider much more productive on all sides and avoid any unwanted surprises, such as a higher-than-expected invoice or a delay in your site going live.

The best way to do this is to provide a brief, which should outline your requirements and serve as a starting point for discussions with your web developer or agency before they quote for the work.

Example website brief

About the organisation
A newly established multicultural food festival in Nottingham, aiming to attract 1000 attendees when it launches in July 2019.

Objectives
The website should be a destination for people to find out more about the festival and the range of vendors that will be present, as well as cooking workshops.
- We aim to reach 500 website visitors per month
- We aim to reach 100 workshop bookings

Target audience
The festival is targeting 25-40 year olds from a range of cultural backgrounds in the East Midlands with an interest in food and drink.

Example user profiles:
A marketing professional with a busy schedule but likes to travel, cook and visit high-end restaurants in their spare time. They do most of their web browsing during their commute using a smartphone.

A student who enjoys weekend activities with friends, especially involving eating and drinking in pubs and bars. They have an adventurous personality and are always on the lookout for novel events and new experiences they can share on social media.

Website requirements

We are looking for a website with a clean, modern and accessible design that will appeal to people who are passionate about contemporary street food. The website should be fast to load, simple to navigate and fully functional on mobile devices. We anticipate traffic will increase sharply in the run-up to the festival launch in July 2019.

The website will be updated regularly by various team members with no technical background, who will need separate user accounts.

Key features will include:

- General information about the festival
- Calls to action to view the list of vendors and book on to workshops
- A list of food vendors with short profiles and images
- A schedule, venue map and visitor information
- Latest news
- Links to social media accounts

Content

We have existing photography available. A festival logo with visual brand guidelines will be provided. All website copy will also be provided.

Budget

We have budgeted in the region of £3-4000, but would like a detailed quote and the opportunity to discuss options where there may be different costs for varying levels of functionality.

Timescale

The festival launches on July 15 2019, so ideally the website and its main elements will be live three months in advance (April 2019). A key announcement - the full list of vendors - will be made on June 15, when this page will need to go live.

Contact

Marketing Manager

Email

Phone number

Figure 11.1: Web brief diagram

There is a famous saying in web development project management: "you can be on spec, on time or on budget: pick two". In an ideal world, you would have all three – and of course, you need to be satisfied with the results – but there is some truth in this received wisdom. If you want your site to be very sophisticated and built quickly, it will be more expensive. If you want it to be very sophisticated, but affordable, it will take longer. If you want it delivered cheap and quick, there will be compromises to be made on your specification and features. Consider your priorities, what you can and cannot compromise on, and agree the best way forward.

Hosting and domains

If you decide to host your own website, rather than to use a managed hosting platform (such as WordPress, Squarespace, etc.) you will need to purchase web hosting. If you decide to use a digital agency or web developer, they will often provide this service as part of the work.

Consider the following:

What will your domain name be?

Your domain name is what becomes your website address. Using your own domain, e.g. examplefestival.co.uk will add credibility to your event and show it is professionally run, rather than using any default address from a hosting platform, e.g. examplefestival.hostingprovider.co.uk.

You can purchase your registered domain from a large number of hosting providers, such as 123-reg, Go Daddy, 1and1 Internet or Namecheap. You can then use this domain to set up email addresses, for example, digital@examplefestival.co.uk. You will, however, need to ensure email addresses are included in your hosting package – most will do this.

Think carefully about your domain name and make sure it is easily recognisable. This is something you'll want to start planning when you give your festival a name – if there are other festivals of the same name, it is likely domains and social media handles will have already been taken. It can also cause confusion and possibly a loss of sales when audiences are looking for your festival but find information for another! It is wise to search both your desired domain and any social media platforms before you commit to either to ensure you can achieve consistency across your entire online presence.

Where will your website be hosted? What level of hosting package will you need?

Web hosting is a service provided by companies to store your website and its content on a server, which allows it to be viewed online. You will pay a fee (for a small to medium company, expect to spend no more than a few pounds per month) for the level of service you need, which will depend on factors such as the number of websites, domains, databases and amount of storage.

Accessibility

It is crucial that your website meets current accessibility standards which ensure it is usable to people with additional needs. For example, people with visual impairments, those using assistive technologies such as a screen reader, or those using a keyboard rather than a mouse.

The Web is fundamentally designed to work for all people, whatever their hardware, software, language, location, or ability. When the Web meets this goal, it is accessible to people with a diverse range of hearing, movement, sight, and cognitive ability. Thus, the impact of disability is radically changed on the Web because the Web removes barriers to communication and interaction that many people face in the physical world. However, when web sites, applications, technologies, or tools are badly designed, they can create barriers that exclude people from using the Web. Accessibility is essential for developers and organizations that want to create high quality websites and web tools, and not exclude people from using their products and services (World Wide Web Consortium, 2018)

The internationally recognised standards in web design are to be found in the Web Content Accessibility Guidelines found at https://www.gov.uk/service-manual/helping-people-to-use-your-service/understanding-wcag-20

In practice this means your website, and indeed all of your digital channels, should be designed to be accessible by people with different abilities. This affects a number of areas of website design, from fonts and colour, image descriptions, and navigation. Ensure that, as part of your brief, you discuss this with your developer. A good one will be well-versed in this practice and will factor it into the web build. If you have chosen a managed hosting platform, many themes are already built with accessibility in mind, but they also provide useful resources and tips to enhance your website's accessibility.

Consider the vast number of people you are likely to exclude from your festival if they cannot use your website. In the same way you would want to ensure that anyone physically attending your festival is well accommodated and gets the support they need to have a comfortable and enjoyable experience on site, you should be aiming for that level of service throughout your online presence. Ultimately, if someone doesn't feel included at this point then it is likely they won't be encouraged to attend.

Mobile

In the introduction, we noted that 66% of users access the internet via their mobile so most of your audience will be visiting your website on a mobile device at least some of the time. Therefore, it is essential your site has been mobile optimised - simply put, can be easily viewed and navigated on a range of mobile devices, including smartphones and tablets. Ensure this is included in your brief if you are engaging the services of a developer.

If you are using a managed hosting platform, most will have a range of templates which are built to be viewed on a range of devices through what is known as 'responsive design' (i.e. the site 'responds' to the browser it is viewed from and is resized accordingly.)

Website content

As we have said, having a dedicated festival website is an essential first step for almost every festival. Your website should be a central hub with all of the information your audience will need. Consider the different people who might visit your website, and what their user needs are.

Example 1: Someone has heard about your new music festival through a friend. They might be interested in attending, but they're not sure if it is the type of music they like.

Provide a festival line-up with information about the artists, containing further links with audio and video content.

Example 2: Someone has already bought tickets for your arts festival and is looking for information to plan their visit. What are they likely to look for?

Provide a full address and map, and details of public transport services, parking, local accommodation providers and information about accessibility.

Example 3: Someone is currently at your festival, and they need some immediate help.

Provide information on where to get help, such as an emergency contact number, or a map outlining where security, festival stewards, or medical assistance can be found.

Every festival will have its own marketing objectives; therefore, the website content will vary according to those, but as a general rule you'll want to make sure you have included the following:

Essentials

The name of the festival, its location, dates and times. These are critical factors in someone deciding to attend and need to be prominently displayed.

Programme and schedule

The programme, or line-up, will be a crucial factor in drawing audiences to your event; for many, it will be their primary motivation to attend. Make sure you have information on the artists performing or exhibiting, including strong visuals. It is important to display the festival schedule clearly, in a way that is intuitive for people to understand – especially if it is over multiple sites, dates and times. There are useful tools that can help with this, such as the Sched event scheduling software which allows you to create a multi-day, multi-site schedule which can be embedded into your site.

Tickets

If your festival is ticketed – i.e. attendees need to have a ticket to enter the festival, free or paid – you need to make it as easy and as obvious as possible where they can be ordered. Potential attendees will want to know how much the tickets cost, and details of any special offers, packages or group bookings. You should sell tickets from your website, either directly from your own e-commerce system (which will need to be factored in to your web brief) or through a third-party ticketing service such as Eventbrite or Ticket Tailor. Some festivals also sell tickets through other outlets, for example, the venue or local retailers, shops or bars. If the festival is not ticketed, and audiences can show up on the day, ensure this information is made clear.

General information

This often takes the form of an 'About' page or section. It should sum up what the festival is about, who is behind it and its purpose or vision. Not all websites will have this, but it is often useful for interested parties to know things such as who the festival management team is, including sponsors and partners. Most sponsors and funders, whether the money is private or public, will expect explicit acknowledgement on all marketing materials, including the website. This is commonly represented as a logo block, but different funders will have their own guidelines as to how they wish to be recognised.

Useful information

Consider what additional information an attendee or potential attendee would want to know about your festival. For instance, a map of the area or festival site, information about the venue, directions and travel, access information and how the festival will accommodate people with additional needs, local accommodation and hotels, where to stay and where to eat.

Press and media

It is useful to have information to be used by the press, such as news announcements, press releases and media such as high-resolution images for use in publications. You should ensure you have the correct rights to use any images, as well as including credits where necessary (see Chapter 6). This should be updated at key points, such as announcing the festival and its programme, or the addition of a high-profile artist.

Call to action

In digital marketing, a 'call to action' is something you want the user to do as a result of visiting your website, or any other channel. Common examples are: make a purchase, share this on social media, book an appointment. For a festival website, this might be 'buy tickets', 'view the programme' or 'sign up for our mailing list'. The key to a good call to action is to display it prominently, make it crystal clear what the user is being asked to do and ensure that the link works!

> **Debating point:**
> Visit a handful of your favourite websites and identify where you see a call to action. Think about where it is placed, how it is worded, and how it is designed in relation to the rest of the page. Would you be encouraged to take action as a result?

Developing creative content and rich media

Whilst getting across the key messages and information to your intended audience is crucial, a good festival website will also be fun and engaging to use. In alignment with your overall brand, you should use your website as a platform to make people excited about your event. Your site doesn't need to just have static text and images, and corporate messaging. Get creative!

Writing for the web

Considering the tone and style of your copy is important. Is the language appropriate, understandable and relevant to your target audience? When writing for the web, it is good to be concise and clear. Keep copy and sentence length short as people are often browsing on the go and can be put off by lengthy text.

Images

High-quality images will bring life to your site and can communicate powerful messages. Think about where they can be used to maximum effect. For your programme and artist entries or pages, images are a must.

Video

Short, engaging videos are popular with audiences and play a very significant and rapidly growing role in digital marketing. According to Wyzowl's *The State of Video Marketing in 2018* report, 81% of businesses use video as a marketing tool (up from 63% in 2017), 72% of people would rather use video to learn about a product or service, and if your audience enjoys the video, 83% would consider sharing it with their friends (Wyzowl, 2018). But keep the length reasonable – under two minutes is a good rule of thumb to keep people engaged. For example, *ArcTanGent* used a short video to prominently display their 2018 festival line up on their website: http://www.arctangent. co.uk/

Audio

A number of music festivals create Spotify and YouTube playlists of their artists' songs which can introduce attendees and potential attendees to the artists they don't know, or build excitement for the upcoming event.

Visual branding

Your website should reflect your visual branding (see Chapter 9) including your logo, fonts and colour schemes.

For example, the *Timber Festival* website (http://timberfestival.org.uk/) uses strong visual branding and design, striking images, interactive elements and a clear call to action.

Produce it once, use it everywhere! Make sure you get the most out of your creative content, as it takes time and money to produce. To get the maximum effect, repurpose content wherever possible, sharing it across your other channels, including social media, email communications and advertising.

Making your website discoverable

Your website, whilst a central resource as part of your marketing strategy, will not necessarily be the way people discover your festival. You should consider it as more of a destination rather than a discovery tool in itself. It is vital that you are signposting people to your website wherever possible – through social media, ensuring your website link is on every channel you use, as well as your print marketing materials, email communications, and advertising.

A common strategy is to employ search marketing techniques. Search marketing, or search engine marketing (SEM), is the practice of "promoting an organisation through search engines to meet its objectives by delivering relevant content in the search listings for searchers and encouraging them to click-through to a destination site" (Chaffey & Ellis-Chadwick, 2015: 668).

Search engine optimisation (SEO) and Pay-per-click (PPC)

SEO focuses on optimising 'organic' search listings – these are listings that appear on Google (or other search engines) when you search for something. They appear as the main body of the text, often below the paid-for (or 'sponsored') results, which usually are designed differently or marked out as 'ads'. SEO aims to increase a website's positioning on search results listings, ideally so it is in prime position at the top of the results.

There are many different ways in which you can adopt good SEO practices, without needing to be an expert in it. Working with your web developer is a good place to start, as a good one will know how to embed this into your website build. Most digital agencies will provide this as an additional service.

Your website content will also play a significant part. Using keywords and phrases in your text, and ensuring all posts, images and videos are tagged correctly will all contribute to better search engine performance. If your content is hosted elsewhere, for example, a blogging (i.e. WordPress) or social media site, often these platforms will have good search rankings themselves.

Whereas SEO relates to organic search results, PPC is paid advertising which shows up as 'sponsored' results. You only pay when someone clicks on the advert's link to your website. For example, Google Ads (formerly AdWords) provides this service by allowing you to build an advert, choose a set of keywords and set a daily budget (https://adwords.google.com/intl/en_uk/home/how-it-works/search-ads/).

Debating point:
Consider what keywords people would search for that could lead to your festival website. For example, think about the location, the artform, the name of the festival and of its key artists; as well as broader searches, such as people looking for things to do in your city or town. Try a few words or phrases to search, and see what results come up.

Social media marketing

Social media has caused a major shift in marketing communications. It is increasingly the first port-of-call for anyone looking for further information about a product, service or brand. The main platforms are intrinsic to marketing strategies for organisations and events of all artforms and sizes; for example, holding an event without using Facebook's event pages is practically unheard of now. It encompasses many different elements of marketing, including advertising, communications and public relations (PR), as well as customer service. Users will frequently turn to social media platforms to make enquiries, comments (and complaints!) due to its swift and visible nature.

People also use social media as a reflection of themselves, to project a certain image of themselves, share their interests and connect with like-minded individuals; their 'tribes' and 'subcultures' (Dahl, 2015). Therefore, when harnessed effectively, social media marketing can be a powerful word-of-mouth tool and have a significant positive influence on both reputation and attendance.

Equally, reputational risks can be high online. News spreads very quickly and is difficult to control. Many festivals have been on the receiving end of sharp criticism on social media. For example, in 2015, a blogger edited the *Reading and Leeds Festivals* poster to only include acts which featured at least one woman, highlighting a stark gender imbalance which gained significant press interest.

The now-infamous *Fyre Festival* in 2017, which was sold as a luxury boutique event in the Bahamas but saw attendees arrive to disaster relief tents, or no accommodation at all, sewage problems and cheese sandwiches replacing the promised gourmet dining, was a disaster that played out in real-time on social media and made international headlines. This fast spread of information means that any festival will need to monitor and manage their social media presence closely – for both positive and negative reasons.

One common pitfall of social media marketing is to share messages using a rather outdated 'push marketing' model, only promoting the brand or product and trying to make sales, rather than engage with audiences and stakeholders on a meaningful level. Consider social media as a conversation; here it is most useful – and don't forget the listening aspect. Listening allows you to get audience information, fast responses and feedback, and evaluate different elements of the festival. Consider all feedback as free market research, and make sure you remember to tell people what you have done in response. When a complaint is dealt with well, customers are 67% more likely to return (Legal Ombudsman, 2013).

Social media platforms

The most prominent and popular social media platforms, particularly in the UK and US, are Facebook, Twitter, YouTube, Instagram, Snapchat, LinkedIn, Pinterest, Tumblr and Reddit.

A successful social media strategy will understand what the different platforms are used for, and tailor its content to specific audiences in that arena. It is important that you have a good idea of where your target audiences are likely to be present, which can depend on factors such as age, profession, socioeconomic group, etc.

It is important to note that you don't need to be active on every platform – use the ones relevant to your audience. If your festival is aimed at an older age group, you could safely assume – or through audience development research, prove – that there won't be a large percentage of your audience active on Snapchat or Tumblr, for instance.

As mentioned in Chapter 9, the Audience Finder tools indicate social media use across audience segments. For example, Facebook Families, who generally have mid-to-low engagement with arts and culture are keen users of Facebook. You can use this to inform your social media marketing strategy.

Don't spread your resources thin trying to do everything, when you could be doing a handful of things well. It is prudent, however, to claim your username (or handle) on all social media platforms in case you decide to use them in future.

Building your networks online

If you are developing a new festival, it can seem daunting to have new social media channels with no followers. To avoid feeling as though you are shouting into the ether, you need to start building a following. This should align with, and be factored into, your overall audience development strategy (see Chapter 9).

- ◆ **Post regularly**. Whichever social media channels you decide to use, make sure they are populated with content regularly, and you are responding to messages in a timely fashion; otherwise it will look like a closed shop.

- ◆ **Target your messages**. Think carefully about the messages you are putting out through social media, and at whom they are aimed. Is it a major announcement, is it a call out for volunteers, or do you have media opportunities with artists? Like any other form of marketing, be clear about the intended audience and what action you want them to take as a result.

- ◆ **Use (but don't overuse) hashtags**. Widen the visibility of your messages through hashtags. A hashtag is a word or short phrase directly after the hash [#] symbol, which makes it easy to track on social media. For example, try searching for #festival on Instagram, and see what results come up! However, do not overuse hashtags as it can dilute the message and look like 'spam' (unsolicited or irrelevant content). Make sure to create your own hashtag for the festival, as it will make conversations easier to track, and encourages people to engage. Keep it short, memorable, and check what is already being used to avoid any confusion.

- ◆ **Follow and engage with your immediate network**, and utilise the following of your partners and stakeholders. Make a list of people and organisations that are likely to be interested, or already have an interest, in your festival. You may have already done some stakeholder mapping as part of your marketing plan (see Chapter 9). For example, your festival team and volunteers, sponsors, funders and supporters, local media such as newspapers and radio, and anyone who has partnered with you for the event. Start with what, and who, you know and build from there.

- ◆ **Use your artists**. They already have influence with your target audience – make sure you're connected on social media and encourage sharing and visibility at every opportunity. Make sure you gather their social media details right from the contracting and booking stage.

- ◆ **Connect with your local area**. Think about the locality of your event and its the key influencers, for example, local media, tourist boards, other arts and cultural organisations, and bloggers or prominent social media users with a high profile. Which accounts do your target audience follow? If they're students, check university and society accounts, if they're families, research family-oriented Facebook groups. Consider reaching out to these groups or accounts, over email or private message, to ask for their support in promoting a new festival. People are often very generous in supporting something which benefits the life of the area the event is based in, and you can offer reciprocal support through cross-promoting their messages, or offering to let them put out flyers at your event, for example.

♦ **Connect with businesses, restaurants, leisure companies, accommodation providers**. These organisations all benefit from increased footfall and tourism in your area, which festivals can provide. Connect and engage with them online and consider partnerships and cross-promotion through social media.

♦ **Develop brand ambassadors and online partnerships**. The power of partnerships cannot be underestimated. Is there an individual or an organisation who has influence with your target audience, whose brand and values align with your festival, who might be willing to help to promote your festival? This is often a paid service which is common amongst online influencers such as fashion bloggers. For example, as part of the 2018 *Coachella Festival*, Absolut Vodka promoted their 'Absolut Open House' through a brand partnership with Rita Ora, which saw the singer post sponsored content through Instagram to her 13 million followers.

♦ **Signpost at every opportunity**. Make it easy for people to find you online: on print collateral, email signatures, presentations, press releases. Put your social media handles on absolutely everything.

Developing your social content

The most essential element in building your network and profile online will be the quality and relevance of your content. You should have a keen understanding of your target audience, their needs and interests, and tailor your social content accordingly. Will they respond more positively to humour, or to cultural commentary, or both?

According to a 2016 report by Sprout Social:

"while brands view Facebook, Twitter and Instagram as broadcast outlets for pumping out promotional content, consumers recognize these social channels for what they truly are: powerful portals for two-way dialogue" (Sprout Social, 2016).

Given the conversational nature of social media, it is important to think 'engagement' rather than 'sales', as the former will take care of the latter. Nothing will put an audience off more than feeling they are being aggressively sold to, or that the organisation has no personality. Social media is inherently human, so speak with a personable tone rather than an overly corporate one and foster genuine relationships.

Much like the website content discussed earlier in the chapter, your social content should be creative and exciting. Make use of the following:

♦ Features such as polls that allow you to ask questions, to encourage discussion and debate, as well as seek valuable audience insight.

♦ Rich media such as video, audio and podcasts.

♦ Other people's content – for example, there are apps that allow you to repost others' Instagram pictures. You could utilise your festival hashtag to find pictures of attendees enjoying the festival and share it to your feed.

Accessibility is important. Make your social content more accessible by using close-captioned videos and image descriptions, and by creating a transcript of any audio.

Tools – and people – for managing social media

The nature of social media means that your organisation needs to ensure it is updated and regularly monitored by someone in your team, ideally multiple people. Conversations do not only happen within standard office hours, in fact, often the reverse. Managing various company social media profiles can be time-consuming, and the resources needed to execute this element of your digital marketing strategy effectively should not be underestimated. Some festivals ask volunteers to do this, and this can be a really effective way of engaging audiences from subcultures you don't know very well yourself. But we would recommend caution in handing over your main communication tools – you need to supervise what is being said in your name.

There are a number of social media management software tools you can use to manage your feeds, including Buffer, Tweetdeck, Sprout Social and Hootsuite. The services range in price – some have free versions – but this depends on the package required, and factors in how many profiles you are managing, and how many users need access.

Scheduling and timing

Researching what times your target audience is most active online will give a good idea of optimal post times to ensure your content is seen. Most social media management tools allow you to schedule content for posting in the future. This means you can prepare your posts in advance, select which accounts you want them to go out on, and the software will post it at a time you decide. You can also repeat posts for different times and see which pick up most the engagement.

There are things to keep in mind when doing this, however. Remember that if you pre-schedule content you will need to change the post if there has been any difference in information, such as a change of time, venue, or lineup. Also, it is worth being aware of what else is happening online and judging if your content is appropriate. For example, in the event of a tragedy such as a terrorist attack, consider if your cheery or humorous tweet is the correct tone – if not, reschedule it for another time.

Another consideration when scheduling content is maintaining an authentic voice. Overuse of scheduled content or repeated messages, rather than conversations and new ideas, will look robotic rather than conversational.

Social media advertising

In a noisy digital world, it can be difficult to cut through the hundreds of messages your audiences will see on a daily basis. Depending on the algorithms used by the platform, the feeds of your audience might be altered in different ways – for instance, their feed might not display in chronological order, or they might be tailored so that they see content from accounts they engage with regularly first.

For example, it is now well-documented that brands are experiencing difficulty in getting significant engagement with their organic Facebook posts and are having to spend more on promoted content to ensure visibility in their audience's feeds.

A post by social media management tool, Hootsuite, states:

"On Facebook, organic reach has been on decline for some time. The world's largest social media platform is opting to give users more content from friends and family in their newsfeeds. At the same time, it's showing less from publishers and pages. "You'll see less public content like posts from businesses, brands, and media," Mark Zuckerberg said at the start of 2018, "and the public content you see more will be held to the same standard - it should encourage meaningful interactions between people" (Hootsuite, 2018).

To boost the reach of social media messages, you can opt to utilise paid advertising. Organic content is where you post from your chosen social media platform in the usual way, with no charge from the provider. Paid content is social media advertising, where you pay a fee to have your content displayed in people's feeds. This often appears as 'promoted' or 'sponsored' content.

Major social networks all have options for paid media, such as Facebook and Twitter Ads, allowing you to target users based on a wide range of factors such as geographical location, age, marital status and interests which makes it a powerful marketing tool. Costs can vary according to the potential reach of the advert, the size of the audiences you are targeting and what objectives you set for the advertising campaign but can start at reasonable prices with easy-to-control daily budgets.

Designing an effective advert will include strong visuals, aligned with your branding, as well as powerful messaging and a clear call to action (as discussed earlier in this chapter).

Email marketing

Email marketing is a widely used strategy for arts and cultural organisations and can be a useful tool for communicating with your audiences. These can take a number of forms, including an 'e-shot', which is a marketing email to a defined list of people to promote a particular event. It is often very visual, using graphics to catch the reader's attention. Another style is an 'e-news-letter', which is more of a roundup of different messages and range of news items, images and links.

Email marketing has a number of benefits. It can reach many people at once, including those who are less active on social media, and you have more space to communicate your message than on social media. Effective email marketing will result in users taking the desired action (call to action) such as making a group booking or sharing an event on social media.

There are challenges to email marketing. You need to build a mailing list, with appropriate data protection and handling measures (see Chapter 9), which is time-consuming. Once you have a list of recipients, you need to ensure a significant percentage of them read the communication and take action as a result. You will be competing with many other marketing emails, therefore getting a good return on investment with email marketing can be challenging. Monitoring the number of opens and clicks, through your analytics, will provide insight into what is working, and what isn't.

There are a number of email marketing providers. Larger companies often opt to run their email marketing through a CRM (customer relationship management) system such as Salesforce, Hubspot, Mailchimp or Raiser's Edge, which is aimed at not-for-profit companies to support fundraising strategy. For email marketing alone, there are providers such as Mailchimp who offer both free and paid-for services.

A good marketing email will be well-designed and easy to read, using elements of your visual brand, and strong imagery, and be concise. Be very clear about the message the email is communicating. The subject line is crucial and can determine whether the email is read or instantly deleted. Try to create some interest and intrigue, and don't be afraid to be a bit playful – you can even use emojis – if appropriate to your audience.

Digital public relations and communications

The online sphere has had a significant impact on public relations (PR), making it much easier to share messages, connect directly with the public, connect with journalists and media, and monitor coverage. Press releases and key announcements with accompanying images should be released on your website, via email to your targeted list of recipients and through social media.

Writing media releases

Press releases are designed to provide timely information to the press about your festival, with the aim of getting media coverage – online, print or broadcast. Effective press releases will:

♦ **Give clear information**. The release should be written in plain English, and give an outline of the key messages in the first paragraph – when, where, who and why. Good spelling and grammar is a must. You need to be able to quickly communicate your story as journalists and news desks are increasingly stretched. Your headline should concisely get your point across. For example, 'Internationally-renowned jazz artist to headline summer festival'.

♦ **Be targeted and relevant**. If you are aiming for local or regional coverage, highlight the local angle – is the festival making use of a new venue? Are any of the artists from the area?

If you are targeting specialist or trade press, research what the publication usually covers and craft the story accordingly. If your festival is multi-artform but you have a significant theatre strand, for example, make sure you tailor and highlight that aspect of the lineup for a theatre-based blog or website.

If you are approaching national media, you need to make sure you have something unique and newsworthy. For example, are any of your artists creating groundbreaking work with international influence? Can you offer an exclusive artist interview? If so, make that clear from the email subject line.

♦ **Ensure a contact is given for follow-ups**. Make sure you have contact details (phone, email) for your press or marketing lead where they can be contacted quickly and easily. Be prepared: media requests often happen outside of normal office hours.

Developing a target list

You will need to decide where you will send your press releases. Many PR and communications professionals will have a list of contacts, but this may be something you need to develop. Start by researching where you want coverage, and looking up contact details online and on publication websites. Most journalists are now active and contactable on Twitter. Larger companies with significant budget will often use media management services such as Gorkana, Vuelio or Cision.

Developing media partnerships

Getting press coverage can be challenging, especially for new and emerging festivals. A commonly-used tactic is to develop media partnerships. These can help give credibility to your festival amongst your target audience and guarantee coverage. For example, Leicester's *Handmade Festival* partners with *Upset* and *Dork* magazines, which places them in front of young rock, indie and alternative music fans. Heavy metal festival *Download* has a stage sponsored by Kerrang! Radio. The key to successful partnerships is ensuring they are mutually relevant to the audience and beneficial to all partners.

Crisis communications

Protecting the reputation of your festival is, of course, a top priority. No company is immune from bad press or negative social media comments, and these scenarios need to be managed carefully. The digital world has increased the speed at which word can spread – and often, social media is where the crisis has originated – so having a plan of action is essential.

Online audiences expect transparency and authenticity. If something has gone badly wrong, more often than not the best approach is to deal with things head on. Attempts to hide information often backfire – a phenomenon known as the Streisand effect, so named after the American actress and singer Barbra Streisand who sought to suppress photos of her Malibu villa only to increase public attention on it.

Your plan of action should outline who is responsible for executing the crisis communications, and who should give interviews or statements, if applicable, and be adaptable depending on the scale of the crisis. For instance, a short statement on social media might be an appropriate response to minor online criticism, whereas a more serious situation, such as public safety, would warrant more extensive communications.

Monitoring coverage

You can use a number of tools to monitor press coverage. For example, Google Alerts allows you to set up an email alert for when your selected keywords or phrases are mentioned online. You could set one up for the name of your festival, to see where it has appeared online, as well as for related subjects such as 'UK art festivals' to discover which journalists and publications are covering them, for example.

Social Mention is a search engine that allows you to search phrases across social media and blogs. It will give you insights such as 'reach', 'passion' and 'sentiment'— how positively or negatively your festival is being discussed.

Measuring success

As with any marketing activity, you will need to evaluate its effectiveness. Digital technology makes it much easier to do this, with a great number of online tools which can demonstrate how successful the different elements of your digital marketing strategy have been.

Website

Google Analytics allows you to track activity on your site, such as how many visits it received during a set period, how many of these were unique visitors, where they are located, how they discovered your website (e.g. through a search engine, or social media) and what device they were using.

There are similar analytics tools, such as Hitwise, which glean information such as what sites users visited directly before and after they visited yours, to see what related searches they make. This can give clues as to who your competition might be, or indeed which brands or press you might want to consider working with.

Identify the most useful data for your campaign and consider how you can use it. For example, if you know where website visitors are located, you might want to target advertising to areas you are not currently reaching.

Social media

You can measure your social media performance through various tools. Each platform has its own analytics tools, for example, Facebook Insights and Twitter Analytics, which give key metrics such as the total number of impressions (how many feeds your post appeared in) and which posts received the most engagement (e.g. shares, retweets, mentions and likes).

Social media management software tools also have inbuilt analytics systems and allow you to generate reports that detail your social media performance over a specific period. This information is particularly useful in determining social content strategy, as you can see what types of post are engaging to your audience and when. You might discover that your Facebook posts, for instance, perform better when you have video content, or your Instagram posts get more likes on weekends.

Email

Your email marketing or CRM system will provide analytics which will help you understand how well your emails are performing. Key metrics include: opens (how many people opened the email), clicks (how many clicked through on your links), and conversions (how many people performed the desired action when clicking a link, i.e. purchasing a ticket). It will also show whether your list of subscribers is growing or not, and email bounce rate (how many were not delivered).

Running a digital campaign: a step-by-step guide

01 Market and audience research

Who are you targeting?
What are their needs and interests?
What types of media do they consume?

02 Aims and objectives

Identify what you aim to achieve with the campaign.
Set SMART (Specific, Measurable, Achievable, Relevant, Time-bound) objectives.

03 Messaging

Define your message - what are you communicating to your target audience?
Produce relevant content - straplines, marketing copy, press releases and social media posts.

04 Channels

Identify the mix of channels you will use based on audience research. For example, social media, website, print collateral and email communications.
Tailor your strategy for each channel.

05 Budget, timeline and team

Set a budget for the campaign.
Agree a timeline of when it will start and end, and identify key points of campaign activity.
Agree roles and responsibilities within the team.

06 Campaign execution

Deliver the campaign according to your plan, adapting and responding as you need.

07 Evaluation

Evaluate the success of the campaign - did you meet your overall aims and objectives?
Which elements of the campaign were successful, and which were not - why?

Figure 11.2: Digital campaign diagram

A digital campaign is a set period of concentrated and targeted marketing communications activity. Often multi-channel in nature, campaigns seek to maximise influence across defined audience groups to highlight a specific event or product.

Creativity is central to delivering a successful campaign. You need to be distinctive and catch your audience's imagination through your concept. Personalisation and user-generated content are powerful tools. A good example is Coca-Cola's 'Share a Coke' 2013/14 campaign, which encouraged people to purchase bottles with their name on. The focus on the individual made the content incredibly shareable, as people fought to find their name and share pictures with their social networks using the hashtag – blending physical product with the online sphere.

Planning a campaign needs thorough consideration and planning, and the timing should align with key points of your festival timeline – around your lineup announcement or in the run-up to the event, for instance.

Increasing the festival lifecycle

One of the most significant changes the arrival of digital technology has wrought has been over the extending of the lifecycle of the single event. Traditionally the post-event period has been for evaluation, thank-you's and clear up/wrap. Now the post-event period can mold into the pre-event period as relationships are continued with existing audiences and new audiences are engaged almost immediately the formal festival has ended. The use of social media as discussed means a constant conversation can continue throughout the year and posting of the developing programme, artists and events can generate mounting expectations and excitement. This is not only true for audiences, but all stakeholders can now be continually re-engaged and re-energised. As it is cheaper to maintain and foster all relationships on an on-going basis than to have to start again and rebuild anew every year, digital technology has altered the timeline of festivals, and has enabled continuous engagement.

Programming digital artworks

The Department for Digital, Culture, Media and Sport paper, *Culture is Digital*, states: "The UK's future will be built at the nexus of our artistic and cultural creativity and our technical brilliance" (2017: 4). It goes on to say:

"Digital experiences are transforming how audiences engage with culture and are driving new forms of cultural participation and practice. As technology advances, so do the behaviours of audiences, especially younger audiences. We are no longer passive receivers of culture; increasingly we expect instant access to all forms of digital content, to interact and give rapid feedback. Audiences are creating, adapting and manipulating, as well as appreciating art and culture" (ibid: 9).

It also states that:

> "Technology allows cultural experiences to be more accessible than ever; whether viewing collections online, experiencing immersive theatre or purchasing e-tickets for productions. We can look at a painting, read a novel, discover the heritage on our doorstep, or listen to music at a moment's notice, on multiple platforms and wherever we are in the world. Cultural organisations are beginning to harness the potential of digital technology to engage audiences through new formats and mediums and by diversifying their distribution channels.... In using new technology, there is the potential to reach out to new as well as existing audiences, including those who may have been previously disengaged or uninterested, and provide a hook for audiences to experience culture in new or 'deeper' ways" (op. cit.)

Artists across mediums are increasingly incorporating digital technology and thinking into the production of their work. Collaborations between artists and technologists are pushing boundaries, creating new content and allowing for greater levels of audience interaction and engagement. There are a number of prominent artists who focus on the production of digital and new media artworks.

For example, UK artists Blast Theory produce politically-driven interactive art that exists both physically and virtually, using various technologies from mobile phones, to video streaming and gaming platforms. The work is toured to exhibitions and festivals all over the world. The indie band Arcade Fire have produced interactive music videos, including 2011's *The Wilderness Downtown*, which saw the band collaborate with Google Chrome to build a music video using HTML5 and the Google Maps platform which allows users to enter their hometown address and view a personalised experience.

There are a number of festivals exploring online programming, bringing a virtual element to festival attendance, where audiences can experience artworks without being present, through websites, apps, live streaming and audio. In fact, some festivals are entirely 'attended' online, such as *#ScotLitFest*, Scotland's virtual literary festival. The festival uses social media, video and online chat to deliver its programme of events across the world.

Technology can be built into programme design (as noted in Chapter 2) to enhance the audience experience and cultural engagement. Often the aim is to produce heightened 'sensory' experiences through a combination of things such as digital projections, virtual reality headsets and music. These experiential aspects of digital technology have been explored by Arcadia Spectacular, as discussed in the case study.

Industry example: Arcadia Spectacular

Arcadia Spectacular designs experiential shows and spaces for festivals. Directors Pip Rush and Bertie Cole first came together in 2008 to design and produce an area in the south east corner of the *Glastonbury* Festival site. Described by Cole as "a spire built out of scrap", The Afterburner was designed as a beacon to draw people to the sound system within it. Utilising a post-apocalyptic themed setting complete with flaming trees it was envisaged as a chill out space but became one of the most interesting and celebrated areas of that year's *Glastonbury*.

Moving beyond *Glastonbury* the Arcadia team have designed and produced successful events around the globe. For their 10th Anniversary Festival in Queen Elizabeth Olympic Park in London they produced the *Metamorphosis* show using a wide range of technical equipment and engineering. The focal point of the show included a fifty-ton flame spewing mechanical spider made out of repurposed military technology (Arcadia, 2018). There were around 200 lighting fixtures connected by 8 kilometers of cable on the spider alone (TPI, 2018). However, the show also incorporated elements of theatre, circus, sculpture, pyrotechnics, traditional song, dance and 'electrical wizardry' (Lords of Lightning, 2018).

Figure 11.3: Arcadia Dreamtime Spider

Cyrus Bozorgmehr (Head of Communications) says that Arcadia designs innovative event technology made of recycled hardware as a way of exploring the relationship between technology and human intent: "*Metamorphosis* was about change, transformation, it made total sense on that stage because that's a symbol of transformation, it's all recycled materials".

The technology Arcadia deploys has a significant 'wow factor', for Arcadia technology is only one of the many tools available when they design spaces and experiences that will trigger a range of senses for the participants. As Bertie Cole says, "essentially we are creating an environment or a space in which people can really let themselves go. It's a sensory environment where you walk into it, literally and you can really, really let go in there. The design and the space and the effects and the music and the performance and the sculpture and all of these different elements that we bring together in these environments are all really carefully crafted and bonded together. It's alchemy really, you bring them together and you create an experience that's much greater than the sum of its parts. One of the biggest additions to that is the crowd themselves, they are also a huge part of it".

Unusually for electronic dance music festival producers, Arcadia invest a significant amount of design resources into developing a narrative for their shows. Prior to their involvement in the *Metamorphosis* show, members of the Whadjuk Noongar (an indigenous community from Western Australia) had performed The Yallor Keeninyara, a traditional song and dance designed to ask "the Dreamtime spider of Garrup to weave a web of unity" (Arcadia, 2018: 4). Originally incorporated into a performance in Perth, Australia in November 2016 this collaboration between Arcadia and the Whadjuk Noongar came about because Arcadia were scheduled to produce a show on Kings Park, land that was historically ancestral land of the Whadjuk Noongar. "Spider's dreaming is in Kings Park, in the middle of the city. We actually performed it on the oldest of ceremonial grounds where our people used to sing this song traditionally" (Barry McGuire, Keeper of Song for the Whadjuk Noongar, 2018).

This collaboration became significant in the development of the Arcadia 10th Anniversary Festival. Arcadia invited the Whadjuk Noongar to London in order to reprise their performance on land that was culturally significant to the people of London. Bertie Cole was quick to confirm the importance of incorporating external influences into the event design process; "Massively important. I think we see ourselves as a huge collaborator really and Pip and I can't build and create and have the input into this thing at the rate that is needed to deal with the size of the expectation that is required with us now so collaborating with different people is a massive part of it".

The range of influences Arcadia incorporate into the design process provides them with a rich and varied palette. What they do with it is to design shows and festivals that are the antithesis of what they felt was wrong with contemporary festival design. "They were really linear, there was a lot of corporate presence at them and it was all based on the headliners and the big music. It was all based on these big stages that just followed the same formula every time. It was kind of dull, it was a bit like watching TV on a big scale. We set about trying to create that sort of in the round campfire magic on a massive scale," says Cole.

As an organisation Arcadia is constantly striving to be at the cutting edge of technological innovation. However, they are also aware that technology alone will not deliver the immersive sensory experiences that they seek to design. The collaboration between Arcadia and the Whadjuk Noongar provided Arcadia with "a profound understanding of the roots and universality of the traditional festival experience" (op. cit.). The narrative that developed was informed by the synergies that both collaborators identified in each other's work.

Bertie Cole, Cyrus Bozorgmehr, and Barry McGuire talking with Kevin Chambers

The potential for festivals to incorporate digital as part of their programme is limitless, and undoubtedly there is a perceivable growth in hybrid festivals or having hybridity as an aspect of the festival. However, as with any festival experience – digital or not – the audience experience is key. To effectively present digital work, there are a number of important considerations. Things can, and do, go wrong.

♦ **Technical infrastructure.** It is important that your festival venue can accommodate digital work. Your operations team will need to ensure they understand the requirements of the piece; from additional power supply, strong internet connectivity and audiovisual set up right down to considering how it might be affected by the weather.

♦ **Setting audience expectations.** Let audiences know very clearly how they can engage, in advance if that is possible, or suitable (you may not want to give the game away!). Will they need to download an app - if so, is there adequate WiFi provision so they do not have to use their own data package? What equipment will they need, i.e. a smartphone, headphones, etc? Will the work require any prior technical experience or knowledge? Is a festival volunteer or steward on hand to help with troubleshooting?

♦ **Surrounding environment.** If the piece involves sound, will they be able to hear it within a busy festival environment? If public WiFi is available, will it be able to handle the increased traffic of many users at once? Will accessing it involve a lengthy sign-up process that might put people off?

♦ **Online work.** Does the website or app need to be accessed on a particular browser, or will the user need to download additional software, or enable pop-ups? Do you want users to upload their own content? If the work is to be viewed online, is this clear in your marketing materials? Are websites listed in your festival programme? Is it clear from your social media messages?

Adopting a digital culture

Digital culture has a unique, but fluid and changeable, set of principles. In *Digital Cultures*, Doueihi argues:

"The digital environment is first and foremost a culture of rapid change and adaptability: it is a cultural phenomenon driven by social adaptations of technological innovations and thus it calls for a dual inquiry into its inner mechanisms and structures. This dual perspective will need to be both descriptive and analytic, both technical and cultural (2011: xvi)."

As discussed earlier, the digital revolution is not just a technological one. It is a cultural paradigm shift, and it has influenced society in myriad ways beyond the devices and software we use. It is easy for festival managers, producers, marketers and programmers to get caught up in using the latest technology, over what works best for the intended audience. The key is to adopt a digital culture over preoccupation with the technology itself; it is about the depth of experience that technology facilitates.

Whilst audiences are looking for digital engagement and demand in this area is increasing, unless your event is specifically about technology – for example, a fair or a trade show – then the technology itself should not be the focus. Requiring the latest high-tech gadgets and using complicated technical jargon can make an event feel very exclusive and can be alienating to some audience groups. Also, not all digital work is 'high-tech'; much of it uses quite simple and widely available technologies such as SMS (text messaging) or a cameraphone.

Having a digital focus, or incorporating digital technology into your festival's programming, shouldn't need to centre the technology. Rather, consider what it can do to further the aims of your festival and increase value for audiences. Is it adding value to your event, or causing a distraction?

As you adopt digital culture and thinking to your festival, consider the following principles: access, collaboration and inclusion. The web as we know it was founded on egalitarian ideals that still exist today as we see liberation movements, community action and cutting-edge innovation driven forward using digital platforms. However, it is easy to consider digital as a utopia and a great leveler, where anyone with an internet connection can prosper. But the same hierarchies that exist in our society exist online. Governments, corporations and media conglomerates still exert control in these spaces. The digital space is, therefore, not a neutral one.

> "One must keep in mind that new technologies will always empower some while disempowering others. Technology is merely a tool that can be used for many purposes depending on who is using it, why, where, and when" (Lindgren, 2013: 15).

Access is a fundamental core of digital culture: to the internet, to devices, to information. And as access to the internet grows, especially in the UK as we discussed earlier, consider what access might look like to different groups. Who has access and who does not? Who might you be excluding if you centre specific technologies and platforms over others? Or through your design, branding and usability, or the language used in your marketing and communications? As festival managers, we need to move away from a sense of digital elitism and assumptions, and put focus on meaningful engagement and collaboration with communities to understand what audiences want from cultural events in order to create truly inclusive environments.

Exploring digital culture through festivals

There are now a number of festivals, which focus specifically on digital art and culture. For example, *Frequency Festival of Digital Culture* in Lincoln, *Brighton Digital Festival* and Manchester's *Future Everything*. These festivals present and explore digitally-produced and influenced work from artists all over the world, and present global issues. They tend to be politically and socially aware in nature, examining society in a digital world, and the culture shift we are witnessing.

For example, *Frequency Festival* in Lincoln celebrates the potential of digital innovation and embraces current societal debates:

> "*Frequency Festival of Digital Culture* is a biennial festival hosted in the city of Lincoln, providing a platform to celebrate the pioneering spirit of digital innovation and culture through exhibition, creative collision and debate" (http://frequency.org.uk/about/)

In its manifesto, *Brighton Digital Festival* directly addresses themes of digital inequality and distribution of power:

> "Digital privilege and power is unequally spread across our city. We risk inequality and injustice being perpetuated into a future in which technical access and know how become ever more important (2017: 3).

> The voices of all people need to be heard in order to inform the creation of a collective future that is better for all" (Ibid.).

Summary

The digital world has provided a cultural shift for festivals globally. The increased opportunity for fast, responsive and tailored marketing communications as well as in-depth, collaborative audience engagement is undoubtedly beneficial for festival managers. The rapid pace of change means that managers need to constantly adapt in order to stay relevant to a diverse and, arguably, more demanding audience.

We have looked at the elements that form a digital strategy, such as website, social media, email, as well as PR and comms. We have considered how these elements relate to your marketing and audience development plan, and how they interact with traditional forms of marketing. We have also discussed how to include digital in your festival programming, and what 'digital culture' means for your festival, especially in terms of access and inclusion, and not putting too much focus on technology itself, but as a tool to be harnessed.

Festivals that understand and adopt digital ways of thinking will have a real advantage as cultural events become more digitally-influenced in marketing, programming and operations. Those who can take this understanding and use it to innovate will be the leading festivals of the future.

References

Arcadia (2018) 10th Anniversary Festival. [Programme for a festival held at Queen Elizabeth Park, 5th May 2018]. Bristol: Arcadia Spectacular.

Brighton Digital Festival (2017) http://brightondigitalfestival.co.uk/wp-content/uploads/2017/06/brighton_digital_festival_Manifesto_2017.pdf

Castells, M. (1996) *The Rise of The Network Society*. Oxford: Blackwell.

Castells, M. (1997) *The Power of Identity*. Oxford: Blackwell.

Castells, M. (1998) *End of Millennium*. Oxford: Blackwell.

Chaffey, D., and Ellis-Chadwick, F. (2015) *Digital Marketing: Strategy, Implementation and Practice*. London: Pearson.

Department for Digital, Culture, Media and Sport (DCMS) (2017) Culture is Digital https://www.gov.uk/government/publications/culture-is-digital

Dahl, S. (2015) *Social Media Marketing*. London: Sage.

Doueihi, M. (2011) *Digital Cultures*. Harvard: Harvard University Press.

Frequency Festival of Digital Culture (2018) http://frequency.org.uk/about/

Fry, H. (2018) *Hello World: How to be Human in the Age of the Machine*. New York: Doubleday.

Hootsuite (2018) Organic Reach Declining. https://blog.hootsuite.com/organic-reach-declining/ (Accessed 25 August 2015).

Legal Ombudsman (2013) The Business Case for Good Complaints Handling. http://www.legalombudsman.org.uk/downloads/documents/research/Business-Case-for-Good-Complaints-Handling-Final-for-publication-20-11-13.pdf. (Accessed 29 August 2018)

Lessig, L. (2005) *Free Culture: The nature and future of creativity*. London: Penguin Books.

Lindgren, S. (2013) *New Noise: A cultural sociology of digital disruption*. New York: Peter Lang Publishing.

Lords of Lightning (2018) *Creative Genius Meets Electrical Wizadry*. http://www.lordsoflightning.co.uk/about [Accessed 20th July 2018].

Martin, V. and Cazarré, L. (2016) *Technology and Events: How to create engaging events*. Oxford: Goodfellow.

McCluhan, M. and Lapham, L. (1994, 1964) *Understanding Media - The Extensions of Man* Cambridge Mass: MIT Press.

Ofcom, (2018) *Communications Market Report 2017*. https://www.ofcom.org.uk/research-and-data/multi-sector-research/cmr/cmr-2017

Sprout Social (2016) https://sproutsocial.com/insights/data/q2-2016/ accessed 25 August 2018

Total Production International (TPI) (2018) *NRG Takes on Arcadia*. https://www.tpimagazine.com/nrg-takes-on-arcadia-spectacular/ [Accessed 22nd July 2018].

World Wide Web Consortium (2018) https://www.w3.org/standards/webdesign/accessibility (Accessed 23 August 2018)

Wyzowl (2018) The State of Video Marketing, https://blog.hubspot.com/marketing/state-of-video-marketing-new-data (Accessed 23 August 2018).

Author index

S Subject index

Printed in the United States
By Bookmasters